Models of Political Economy

Political economy – a discipline that has grown massively in terms of its popularity and importance in recent years – applies the language and techniques of economic theory to political phenomena.

Models of Political Economy provides students with a rigorous introduction to the basic methodology of political economics, utilizing the notion of economic man to explore and evaluate models of rational decision making in various environments.

In depth attention is given to key areas such as:

- Game theory and social choice;
- Public policy decision making;
- Principal theories of justice and mechanism design.

Models of Political Economy will prove an invaluable introduction to a burgeoning field within economics and political science.

Hannu Nurmi is Academy Professor at the Academy of Finland and Professor of Political Science at the University of Turku, Finland.

Models of Political Economy

Hannu Nurmi

Routledge
Taylor & Francis Group

LONDON AND NEW YORK

First published 2006
by Routledge
2 Park Square, Milton Park,
Abingdon, Oxon OX14 4RN

Simultaneously published in the USA and Canada
by Routledge
270 Madison Ave, New York, NY 10016

*Routledge is an imprint of the Taylor & Francis Group, an Informa
Business*

Transferred to Digital Printing 2006

Typeset in Times New Roman by
Keyword Group Ltd

British Library Cataloguing in Publication Data
A catalogue record for this book is available
from the British Library

Library of Congress Cataloging in Publication Data
A catalog record for this book has been requested

ISBN 10:0–415–32705–9(hbk)
ISBN 10:0–415–32706–7(pbk)
ISBN 10:0–203–35855–4(ebk)

ISBN 13:978–0–415–32705–3(hbk)
ISBN 13:978–0–415–32706–0(pbk)
ISBN 13:978–0–203–35855–4(ebk)

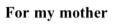

For my mother

Contents

List of Figures

List of Tables

Preface

Models come in many variations. Some are used for describing an object, process, system or other entity in a simplified way. What simplification means is at least partly up to the persons or groups for whom the models are presented. Other types of models are more mathematical in nature. Sometimes they are used as calculation devices, e.g. in determining how a one-percentage point increase in inflation influences the level of unemployment. One could make a distinction between models for thinking and models for solution. The former are relatively loose constructs useful in analyzing, explaining or predicting what is happening. The latter, in turn, are often policy-making instruments. Political economy as the study of phenomena, structures and processes of interaction between politics and economics makes use of both types of model. The models for solution are typically advanced versions of models for thinking and, therefore, in this introductory text we shall concentrate on the simpler class of models. In other words, we shall focus on models that are mainly used in describing and analyzing interactions of individuals, institutions and organizations.

This book is intended for the first text on modeling of political economy. I have tried to keep the technical details of models pretty much in the background, putting the emphasis on a relatively broad overview of various modeling approaches and their basic principles. In terms of mathematical background required for successful independent study of this text, no more than high school mathematics is assumed. In section 8.7 we make use of the first derivative of a continuous function, but even there the argument should be accessible without knowledge of calculus.

The text is intended to be used as material in a one-semester course on political economy. Since this text is an introduction to models, it would fit nicely together with another, more substance-oriented introduction to political economy.

During the relatively long period of time in which this book was written I have incurred numerous intellectual debts. It is a pleasure to acknowledge these debts now and express my sincere gratitude to the following persons and institutions. My colleagues Hannu Salonen and Matti Wiberg of University of Turku read the manuscript and made me aware of several errors in an earlier version. A similar role was played by Tommi Meskanen, who not only checked the more technical parts of the text but also devised the algorithms for computations reported in section 6.4. My research associates Juha Helin, Elina Kestilä and Maria Suojanen have carefully read the manuscript and suggested several improvements. Some parts of the manuscript were also commented upon by Antti Pajala. I am also grateful to Rob Langham and Terry Clague of Routledge for encouragement and support. The work on this project was made possible by my former and present employer, University of Turku and Academy of Finland, respectively.

Hannu Nurmi
Turku, June 2005

1 Introduction

This book deals with the tools needed for understanding political, social and economic life. Our main subject, political economy, gained – according to a widely held view – the status of a distinct area of study in the 18th and 19th centuries, in other words, well before the modern disciplinary classification was introduced. The early practitioners of political economy were moral philosophers rather than economists or political scientists. The devolution of economics, sociology and political science from the master science, philosophy, was still many decades away at the time when Adam Smith and David Hume outlined their ideas of political economy. In his classic treatise of 1776, the former defined political economy as follows (Smith [1776] 1961):

> Political economy, considered as a branch of the science of a statesman or legislator, proposes two distinct objects: first to provide a plentiful revenue or subsistence for the people, or more properly to enable them to provide such a revenue or subsistence for themselves: and secondly, to supply the state or commonwealth with a revenue sufficient for the public services. It proposes to enrich both the people and the sovereign.

Some 70 years later, James Mill ([1844] 1995) resorted to a familiar analogy:

> Political Economy is to the State what domestic economy is to the family. ...[Political economy] has two grand objects, the Consumption of the Community, and that Supply upon which the consumption depends.

Smith's definition is phrased in a manner familiar from the early modern political science literature. The main task of scientific activity was to be of assistance for rulers (see Skinner 1978). The origins of the modern political science can be traced to the mirror-of-princes texts of the 15th and 16th centuries. These aimed at counseling princes in their search for virtue and greatness. In Smith's view the task of political economy is to assist the rulers in providing well-being to their subjects and in securing the necessary means for running what would today be called the public sector. In Mill's definition, what distinguishes political economy from household economy are the actors, not the activities. Both economies depend on the satisfaction of consumption and supply needs.

The classic views basically amount to extending the principles of running a successful household to a new domain, namely to the affairs of the state. Political economy was seen as an essential aspect of statecraft. The provision for consumption and the requisite supply assume a view of the operation and organization of the actors involved. Despite the strong emphasis on statecraft, the authors of the classical period did not envisage much of a role for the state or statesmen in the running of the economy. Left alone by the state, private economic agents (consumers, producers, merchants, etc.), while pursuing their own interests, were supposed to bring about outcomes that are collectively optimal. Thus, the markets were assumed to regulate themselves with beneficial outcomes for both the state and the people. In fact, the classic authors all but did away with the 'political' in political economy.

This approach was strongly opposed by Marx who questioned the evolutionary mechanism underlying the classical view. While Smith had argued that markets emerge as a result of the welfare maximization pursuit of the actors and can be viewed as facilitating this pursuit, Marx questioned the 'arrow of causality' of the theory, namely that the individual interests bring about the economic organization known as markets (see Marx [1939] 1973). In Marx's view it was rather the economic organization with its production relationships that determined the individual interests. The production relationships, in their turn, were based on the development of the productive forces. The Marxist analysis entailed a considerable enlargement of the scope of political economy. Most importantly, the class structure of the society was to be seen as part and parcel of political economy.

The neoclassical view of political economy agrees with the classic one in treating the economy as an analytically separable subsystem of the society, but introduces new philosophical and technical elements. To wit, the foundations of economic behavior were sought in the utilitarianism and marginal calculus was invented to explain the workings of the economies (see Caporaso and Levine 1992: 79–99). With the assignment of utilities to outcomes and to actions producing them, the domain of political economy widened from the classical one to cover basically all human action.

Over the span of some 200 years, the concept of political economy has thus acquired several distinct meanings. Most definitions, however, share the idea of an interaction of two conceptually distinct societal subsystems – the political subsystem and the economic one. It would thus seem possible to use this idea as the focal point in outlining the proper domain of the concept. Unfortunately, the concept of politics is equally multi-faceted. In various times and places, politics has denoted the art of government, power, public affairs, authoritative allocation of scarce resources and conflict management (see e.g. Heywood 1997: 4–12).

Also the concept of economy takes on several meanings. This is the case not only in everyday parlance but also in the texts of the prominent authorities of political economy. In the classic political economy writings of Smith stressing the separation of the economy from politics, the former seems to pertain to markets and the behavior of actors in market transactions. But there is also another meaning attached to the concept of economy in Smith's (and also in Marx's) view. In this meaning, economy consists of particular types of activities, namely those related to production of goods and services (Caporaso and Levine 1992: 24). Production and exchange are thus the basic characteristics of an economy. There is, however, a third more general connotation of 'economic'. This relates to the reasoning underlying economic activities. It is their deliberative and calculating nature that makes them economic (Caporaso and Levine 1992: 21–24). What makes a deliberation economic is the importance given to costs and benefits as well as the suitability of means to ends. Economy in this sense can obviously be extended far beyond production and exchange.

Even though the concept of economics is less disputed, it seems – given the wide disagreement over the meaning of politics – difficult to delineate the domain of political economy as an intersection of two reasonably well-defined subsystems. A more promising approach might be to concentrate on what kinds of activities are involved in political economy. Caporaso and Levine (1992) see the common core of various views on political economy in systems of want satisfaction. This certainly includes the classic and neoclassic views. Also the Marxian concept would seem to fall within the realm of this abstract characterization. On the other hand, systems of want satisfaction as such may include ones that we would not like to count as parts of political economy. For example, a family may establish a 'system' for allowing smokers to indulge in their habit in a designated room to minimize the inconvenience for non-smokers without depriving the smokers of their short-term pleasure. While this system is undoubtedly related to want satisfaction, it does not belong to political economy in the intuitive sense of the term. The reason for this conclusion is that the system in question is not public in the sense that matters political are thought to be. So, while the notion of want satisfaction captures an essential aspect of political economy, it is too wide to provide a definition of it.

In this book we adopt a characterization of political economy that rests largely on one of the concepts of economics mentioned above, namely one emphasizing the reasoning underlying the activity. We shall define political economy as the application of means–ends reasoning to behavior in the public realm. In other words, we see the defining feature of political economy in the calculus that economic and political actors resort to in political and economic life. Understood in this sense, the concept of political economy includes that of public choice (Mueller 2003: 1). The latter is commonly defined as the application of economic reasoning to non-market settings, in general, and to politics, in particular. Thus, political economy is essentially wider than public choice in applying similar reasoning to economy as well as to politics. Our particular focus renders the distinction between public choice and political economy inconsequential since what we shall be dealing with is the type of reasoning that has been called economic. Whether it is being applied to politics or economy is of secondary importance in our analysis.

Extending the idea of economic reasoning to non-market settings is tempting mainly because the principles of this reasoning can be expressed in a concise way. The specification of those principles and their analysis has been the primary contribution of the rational choice theory. At the outset this theory was mainly preoccupied with setting up the principles of behavior in fairly stable environments. So, for example, in classic political economy the profit maximization in markets was viewed as an important instance of rational behavior. At the same time the properties of the markets as an institution were discussed by Smith and his followers. The political economy of today is interested not only in the principles of market behavior but in analogous principles in other spheres of human life. However, along with the behavior principles, the properties of the institutions are very much focused upon also. This focus is a natural consequence of the observation that principles of rationality may differ in different institutional environments. A given type of behavior may result in desired outcomes in certain institutional settings, but may fail to do so in others. Consequently, if one's interest is in securing certain types of outcomes, both the prevailing institutions and the behavior principles they are likely to be accompanied with should be taken into account. In fact, in terms of the likelihood of achieving certain types of outcomes, it becomes possible to talk about rational institutions in the means–ends sense. Thus, the principles of rationality can, under some circumstances, be extended to institutions as well as to behavior principles.

Our discussion will proceed as follows. In the next chapter we introduce some basic concepts of philosophy of science with the aim of specifying how the current research in political economy relates to the most common goals of scientific inquiry. Although political economy as a field can be viewed as *sui generis*, the research into it may well be characterized using the standard vocabulary of philosophy of science. The next chapter introduces the basic agent of the political economy, economic man or *homo œconomicus*. This idealized agent is fundamental to political economy which in its neoclassical version approaches its research object from the point of view of choice under various types of constraints. Choices, in turn, are seen as the results of calculus or deliberation or, more generally, decision making. Thus, the chapter on *homo œconomicus* will dwell on the principles of decision making. This discussion is based on an assumption of a passive environment which, of course, runs counter to the intuitive view of the decision settings in political economy. Therefore, the next chapter introduces other deliberating agents and outlines the basic ingredients of the theory of games, one of the primary tools of modern political economy.

Group decision theory can be viewed as an extension of game theory to the setting where members of a group make collective decisions, for example on the provision of collective goods. However, this theory has emerged largely independently of game theory and forms a link between market behavior and the design of institutions. These two subjects will be introduced and analyzed in separate chapters. The chapters on evaluation of public policies and theories of justice are basically applications of game and group choice theory to political economy. However, the former uses results from other fields as well, notably from multiple criterion decision theory and the theory of aggregation. The theories of justice, in turn, introduce new concepts, namely those related to fairness, into the theory of political economy. While most of the game and decision theoretic literature emphasizes efficiency, it is obvious that considerations pertaining to justice also enter the design and evaluation of institutions in political economy.

The crucial concept of this text is that of decision. Political economy consists of structures, events, developments and patterns in which human decisions play a central role. Therefore, a text on the models of political economy must devote primary attention to analyzing the basic ingredients of decision making. We shall begin by focusing first on decisions in stable and non-reactive environments to become familiar with the basic vocabulary as well as with the essential performance criteria. The first model is thus one with one active agent, the decision maker, aiming at specified goals resorting to the choices available to him/her (hereinafter, her). We then proceed to strategic environments by introducing other agents with similar or different goals and choice options. In group choice settings the new element is the institutional framework within which the choices are made. With strategic actors acting under specified institutional constraints we have the basic tools for modeling political economy. Extending these to cover settings where institutions also undergo change (evolution) or can be deliberately designed to achieve certain ends is the subject of the last chapters of this text.

1.1 Suggested reading

In addition to the Caporaso and Levine (1992) text referred to above there are several treatises that aim to cover the entire field of political economy. Hillman (2003) and Mueller (2003) are excellent – and extensive – overviews of the relevant literature. Both authors have also made important contributions to the research in the field of political economy. Dahl and Lindblom (1976) as well as Lindblom (1977) are often regarded as a modern classic in political economy. Freeman (1989) provides a systematic comparison of several politico-economic systems and a concise exposition of the main theoretical approaches. A useful introductory text is Przeworski (2003). For advanced readers, Austen-Smith and Banks (1999, 2005) as well as Persson and Tabellini (2000) are excellent texts, the former with an emphasis on political theory and the latter on determinants of economic policy. There are two major periodicals specializing in political economy: *Journal of Political Economy* and *European Journal of Political Economy*, but several others, e.g. *Social Choice and Welfare*, *Public Choice*, *Homo Oeconomicus* and *Economics of Governance*, also regularly publish articles in this field.

2   What are we aiming at?

Research in political economy is motivated by a wide variety of reasons. Some authors aim at making policy recommendations, others point to successes and/or failures in economic policy. Some works aim at making sense of what happened in the past, while others strive for predicting the future. Some writers derive their research problems from scholarly literature, others from everyday political and economic events. On closer inspection, these and many other motivations can be reduced to a fairly small number of basic goals of scientific inquiry: explanation, prediction, causal attribution and theory building. These have been extensively dealt with in philosophy of science. In this chapter our focus is on what this field of research tells us about these basic goals of scientific work. Admittedly there may be other, more personal goals involved in scholarly work; for example, authors may aim at fostering their academic careers and/or at impressing their colleagues. These motivations belong to the field of sociology and psychology of science which is beyond the scope of the present work.[1]

2.1   Explaining political economy

In political economy, as in many other fields of research, the interests of scholars and laymen often differ. Yet there are also problems that both of these parties deem important. These are typically related to major politico-economic events, such as major policy statements, unexpected changes in developmental trends or emergence of new institutions. Thus, few would doubt either the scholarly or lay importance of President Roosevelt's announcement on 8 December 1941 which amounted to the United States joining the Second World War against Germany and Japan. Similarly, the economic policy announcements of Alan Greenspan and Jean-Claude Trichet concerning the monetary policy of Federal Reserve and European Central Bank, respectively, are of obvious interest for both researchers and citizens as are, albeit for different reasons, the decisions of the main actors (primarily the chief executive officer and the chief financial officer) in the course of events that led to one of the largest corporate downfalls in history, the bankruptcy of Enron Corporation in December of 2001 (see e.g. Bryce 2002).

Also the European Council decision made in Laeken, Belgium in mid-December of 2001 to commence the framing of a constitution for the European Union by setting up a convention was a decision of both academic and practical importance. In 2004 the convention published its proposal for the constitutional treaty of Europe. It outlines the basic rights of the citizens of the European Union, the legal competency of the Union, its basic institutions and their working principles, the financing of the Union and many other more specific regulations. The ratification process began in the member countries in 2005. Some countries decided to subject the treaty proposal to a referendum. In early summer of 2005, the proposal was rejected in two referenda: one in France and one in the Netherlands.

With regard to the decisions and events just described it is natural to ask why they were made or why they took place. Answers to these questions are normally called explanations of the respective decisions or events. Thus, when a historian points to the air force attack on Pearl Harbor in December 1941 and the ensuing policy planning discussions in the United States government which, a day later, culminated in the declaration of war against Japan, what she aims to provide is an explanation of the event. Similarly, the accounts reporting the debates in boardrooms of Federal Reserve and European Central Bank are intended as explanations for the decisions announced by the respective chairmen. In a similar vein, the explanation of what caused the nosedive of Enron's stock market value in 2001 is sought in the decisions made by its leadership.

At first sight, the explanations of the same events and decisions may vary from one audience to another. What is a good explanation for a normal 5-year-old child may not convince an adult with university degree and vice versa. There seems to be an inherently *subjective* element involved in explanations. This is a proper subject for psychology or sociology of science. What philosophy of science, especially its analytic tradition, has attempted to do is to provide *objective* general criteria for valid explanations. Of particular importance is Carl Hempel's (1965) program which aims at setting up general requirements to be fulfilled by any account, presented in any field of inquiry, in order to be considered scientific explanation.

Carl Hempel (1905–1997) was one of the leading representatives of the analytic tradition in the philosophy of science. A student of the great names of the famous Vienna Circle – Carnap, Schlick and Waisman – he received his doctorate in Berlin. In 1930s he emigrated first to Belgium and later to the US where he taught at Yale, Princeton and Berkeley. His main works are related to concept formation, confirmation theory and the nature of scientific explanation (Murzi 2001).

The basic idea in Hempel's view is that explanations are arguments. Arguments, in turn, are statement sequences arranged so that some statements – called conclusions or, in the present contexts, *explananda* (in singular, *explanandum*) – can be derived from others – called premises or *explanantia* (in singular, *explanans*). Of particular importance is deductive derivation. In his earliest models of explanation Hempel insisted that *explananda* be derivable from *explanantia* as in a deductive argument (Hempel and Oppenheim 1948). Deductive arguments are characterized by the property that once their premises are true, their conclusions must also be true. Thus, in a valid explanation the thing to be explained must be linked to statements that are (i) true, and (ii) must logically entail what is to be explained. The essential feature is that, given the information contained in the premises, the event to be explained was to be expected (Hempel 1965: 367–368). In later accounts, Hempel retreats somewhat from the strict deducibility requirement, but not from the desideratum that, given *explanantia*, the *explananda* are to be expected.[2]

In scientific explanation as seen by Hempel, the statements that explain a fact or phenomenon contain universal laws, i.e. statements that maintain some necessary connection between certain types of facts or phenomena. Paramount examples of these statements are laws of nature which connect, for example, volume, pressure and temperature of gases. To explain phenomena amounts to showing that they are in fact instances of a general law that covers these types of phenomena. For this reason Hempel's view is often called the *covering law* account of explanation.

When applying Hempel's idea to human sciences, the first problem we encounter is that, at least intuitively, much – indeed, most – of our behavior is not subject to law-like regularities. This is, of course, not to say that there are no laws of behavior, but, at least, our present day knowledge does not include them to the extent that one could argue that many – let alone most – social science explanations were based on them.[3] Yet, explanations abound in the social sciences, but rather than law-like universal statements they typically invoke more restricted invariances or tendencies which may include exceptions. So, the increase in investment is often explained by the decrease in the interest rates, even though some investors may – for various reasons – decrease their investments. Similarly, a person's higher than average income may be explained by her university degree, although not all persons with degrees make higher than average earnings.

Now, Hempel would undoubtedly argue that the two examples are not genuine explanations, but at best explanation sketches insofar as they do not contain proper laws among their premises. There is no law stating that whenever interest rates are decreased, there will be an increase in investment, or that whoever acquires a university degree will necessarily earn more than she would have done without it. Rather than natural laws we are dealing here with regularities that allow for exceptions, often a large number of them. Nevertheless, many explanations in political economy are precisely of this type. They conform to two basic Hempelian requirements, namely that the explanatory premises are held to be true and that, given the facts stated in those premises, the *explanandum* was to be expected. But they are not deductive arguments showing that, given the premises, it was necessary that the *explanandum* took place. Thereby, the ordinary explanations in political economy do not satisfy the *symmetry of explanation and prediction*, a hallmark of Hempel's basic explanation model.

Making the event to be explained highly likely is, however, not always enough, in the absence of natural laws. A well-known example is the account that purports to explain a person's recovery from the common cold in a period of a week by stating that she consumed daily amounts of vitamin C, and that there is a regularity which states that anyone taking vitamin C regularly will overcome the common cold within a week (Salmon 1971: 33). The problem with this account is that even if the premises of the purported explanation were true, they are essentially irrelevant given the fact that most people recover from a cold within a week regardless of their vitamin consumption. So, even true premises that make the *explanandum* highly likely may not amount to an acceptable explanation. The regularities included in the explanatory premises have to be relevant to the occurrence of the event explained.

But what do we mean by relevance in the context of explanation? The basic reason for rejecting the just-mentioned explanation is that it points to a mechanism that has nothing to do with the event to be explained. Consuming vitamin C has no effect on recovery from a cold within a week of its inception. The irrelevance is due to the independence of the fact to be explained and the proposed factors: the recovery would ensue even without the vitamin consumption. This independence, in turn, rests on what we currently hold as true mechanisms of human physiology.

In a similar vein, when explaining the fact that the United States declared a war against Japan, we look for acts, factors and phenomena that are true, make the declaration likely and are relevant for the occurrence of the *explanandum*. Since the latter is a symbolic event, the search for explanatory premises calls for an analysis of perceptions, anticipations, goals and choice opportunities of relevant actors rather than finding a relevant set of natural laws from which an objective state of affairs can be deduced. For within the framework of our knowledge the relevant mechanism resulting in the fact to be explained consists of these types of considerations. The accounts of the war declaration and other examples presented in the beginning of this section differ from the Hempelian one in allowing for mechanisms that are not law-like in the sense of natural laws.

To explain something is, thus, to demonstrate that this something was to be expected, given knowledge of the premises. So, at first sight the only thing that distinguishes explanation from prediction is that in the former the phenomenon we are interested in has already occurred, while in the latter it has not. But we can predict things without really understanding how they come about. For example, on the basis of everyday observations without any knowledge of the celestial mechanics we may predict that night is followed by day. Yet, it would be difficult to call this an explanation of any particular break of dawn since it gives us no answer to the question of why the sun rises. The description of our solar system provides such an answer, showing once again that in a genuinely scientific explanation predictive accuracy needs to be accompanied with relevant regularities.

2.2   Building theories

In the analytic tradition of philosophy of science, explanations are related to theories through laws. Laws play a crucial role in explanations and they are the building blocks of scientific theories. More precisely, theories are hierarchically organized systems of laws. Each law is positioned on a certain level of abstraction which means that it is on the very highest level or derivable from more abstract laws. In either case it allows for less abstract laws and other statements to be derived from itself. To give an example, we might have a general theory of human behavior. From this we should be able to derive the theory of political behavior and economic behavior as specifications of the general theory in restricted environments.

This example is very close to the notion of theory one encounters in political economy. Its highest level consists of the principles of rational choice behavior. From these one then proceeds towards empirical observations via various environmental specifications. Thus, we have the theory of choice under certainty, risk and uncertainty. Postulating a strategic multi-actor environment leads to the theory of games. Various further specifications yield the theory of mechanism design, bargaining and electoral institutions. Most of these will be dealt with in the following chapters. Before going into the details of these and other theories, let us relate them to the basic concept apparatus of philosophy of science.

It is obvious that the theory of choice behavior differs in several important respects from the concept of theory encountered in advanced natural sciences, e.g. in elementary particle physics, mechanics or organic chemistry. Firstly, instead of natural laws determining the behavior of the objects of study, the theory of choice consists of principles of behavior which the objects (human individuals) may choose not to obey. The awareness of the objects of study of the principles that determine their behavior is a consideration that is absent in natural sciences. Thus, the principles are necessarily of a contingent nature. Secondly, the theory of choice is clearly incomplete in the technical sense of the term. *Completeness of a theory* means that all statements known to be true of the domain of reality that the theory speaks of are derivable from it. An extensive body of evidence suggests that this is not the case in the theory of choice. In many contexts the choice behavior derivable from the theory blatantly contradicts empirical observations. Thus at best the theory is applicable in restricted rather than universal domains.

As Giere (1979: 63) points out, if anything is the goal of scientific activity, scientific theory is. It not only contains a set of established laws, but can also be used in pushing the frontier of knowledge further. Theories together with empirical specifications suggest new hypotheses for empirical work. For example, from decision theory one can derive a number of predictions, i.e. statements describing choice behavior in specified contexts. Confronting these predictions with empirical findings on the choice behavior of real world actors, one is able to evaluate the theory itself. In fact, the *hypothetico-deductive method*

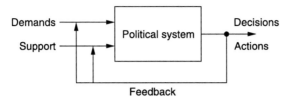

Figure 2.1 Easton's political system view.

consists of systematically confronting the predictions of a theory with empirical material.

Theories have thus a double role in scholarly work: they present the achieved results (laws) in condensed form and, with the aid of empirical observations, allow for the evaluation of our knowledge. As a caveat, one should add that this view of theories does not cover all usages of the term. Very often 'theory' means no more than a concept apparatus used in describing reality. For example, the diagrammatic description of political systems devised by David Easton (1965: 112) does not contain laws organized in hierarchical fashion, but merely a frame-work for categorizing observations (Figure 2.1). Yet, this framework is often called a systems theory. This is quite legitimate, but confuses two important aspects of scientific work, namely the evaluation of statements or statement systems on the one hand, and using concepts in describing reality on the other. To keep these two aspects separate it would be advisable to employ another concept for constructs that are mainly descriptive rather than explanatory or pre-dictive tools. An obvious candidate for such a concept is that of a model which, in fact, is used by Easton in outlining Figure 2.1.

2.3   Models

The concept of a model takes on many different meanings in everyday and scien-tific parlance. Thus we may encounter miniature models of buildings and vessels, mathematical models of natural or social processes, role models and model theory, to name just a few prominent usages. Achinstein (1968: 209–225) suggests a threefold classification: (i) representational models, (ii) theoretical models, and (iii) imaginary models. In the first class we find true, distorted and analog models. The unifying characteristic is that the models represent an object. A representational model is a man-made construct that represents something which is not necessarily man-made. It is primarily a tool enabling the analysis or experimentation of the entity of which it is a model. The use of these types of models in political economy is very restricted. Perhaps the best examples are gaming models of, say, international trade, where persons represent countries and the idea is to learn something about the interaction between countries with varying natural resources, etc. These models are primarily teaching tools.

Theoretical models in Achinstein's terminology refer to constructs that characterize the object of study in theoretical terms. Examples from physics include the corpuscular model of light which states that light is basically a set of moving particles, and Bohr's model of atom which makes specific assumptions regarding the position and movements of nucleus and electrons (Achinstein 1968: 212). The defining features of this model concept is that rather than representing its object it states some assumptions regarding the object. Thus, the above two examples claim something about the research object, namely that light is basically particle movement and that electrons relate to nuclei in a specific manner. The property that distinguishes theoretical models from theories proper is that they do not purport to describe all aspects of the research object but are intended as convenient simplifications useful for explaining or predicting certain phenomena or structures. When a person says she has a theory about something, that usually means that she is convinced that the theory is true. In contrast, if a person has a model of something, that does not make the same truth claim. Indeed, one could argue that by speaking of a model rather than a theory, the person *ipso facto* believes that the description given in the model is not literally true, but a useful approximation.

Theoretical models include mathematical, statistical and computational ones. These abstract certain features of the research object and express their relationships in formal expressions. The usefulness of these models stems from their amenability to formal manipulations. The models encountered in modern political economy are predominantly of this type, i.e. theoretical, simplified descriptions of objects of study. However, there are also models of Achinstein's third type, namely imaginary models. These are distinguished from theoretical and representational ones by not involving any commitment to the truth of the description. Indeed, to the contrary, imaginary models make assumptions regarding the study objects that are known to be false. The assumptions and, consequently, the models themselves are tools of thought experiments. These models are also common tools of political economy.

The main features of models in political economy:

- they are simplified descriptions of a part of reality
- they state explicitly a set of assumptions regarding the composition and working mechanism of the object under study
- they are constructed with manipulability in mind
- the same study object may be modeled in several different ways depending on the use of the model (prediction, explanation or simulating past behavior)

Models are basic tools of political economy and, indeed, of many other fields of inquiry. Amenability to analysis and experimentation is their fundamental property. In fact, much work in political economy is focused on the study of models rather than the part of the world they are models of. Models are refined, elaborated, extended and solved. In these works the borderline between theory and model is often blurred. Sometimes the concept of theory is used in a wide, overarching sense as, for example, in the concept of game theory which basically covers the theoretical study of game models. In other contexts the model concept is wider than that of a theory. For example, one can speak of solution theory of two-person game models meaning the derivation of predictions from models describing interaction between two persons. The wide variation in the usage of the terms theory and model should be kept in mind when studying the texts of political economy. In the following we use these terms in loose conformity with the existing literature. Proposing some kind of terminological orthodoxy would not be helpful in outlining the basic ideas.

2.4 Interpreting acts

The concepts of theory, model and explanation have been dealt with in philosophy of science mostly from the perspective of natural sciences. Many central concepts and ideas of social sciences are eschewed in those discussions. Of particular significance is the interpretation of facts or phenomena. There may be phenomena and processes that are difficult to interpret in natural sciences in the sense that certain measurements may give rise to different views of what is happening, but in social sciences these types of interpretation problems are essentially aggravated by the fact that the objects of study (individuals, groups) are also interpreting what is happening in their environment. Moreover, the interpretation can, without any changes in the objective features, modify the observable behavior of those objects. For example, ways of conducting negotiations may vary in different cultures· what is considered proper in one culture (e.g. going straight to business), may be looked upon as impolite or offensive by representatives of other cultures. Thus, provided that law-like regularities would constitute the core of theories and explanations also in social sciences, the interpretation of facts, acts, utterances, etc., poses a problem not encountered in other sciences.

Consider again the example of explaining the declaration of war by the United States in December 1941. If we were dealing with a natural event we would be looking for laws or other regularities that connect the events of declaration of war with some events of a type that occurred preceding the declaration. A possible candidate for such a regularity would be one stating that whenever individuals deem themselves threatened, they undertake actions to remove the threat. The United States or, more specifically, its top leaders, felt threatened as a consequence of the air attack on Pearl Harbor and thus resorted to measures to remove the threat by issuing the declaration of war.

To take another example mentioned above, consider the decision of the leaders of the European Union to set up a convention to frame a constitution for the Union. One could again look for a regularity that connects events of the type represented by the decision to events of the type preceding the decision in time.

Such a regularity might be one that says that whenever faced with growing uncertainty, individuals undertake to reduce the uncertainty by measures deemed appropriate. In this case, the uncertainty consists of the forthcoming enlargement of the European Union and the accompanying dramatic increase in decision-making complexity.

Neither of the above-mentioned regularities would count as a natural law. Yet, the explanations suggest a principle of action followed by individuals in settings involving threat. But in human affairs, threat itself may be a matter of interpretation. The bombardment of one's fleet, as happened in Pearl Harbor, is pretty obviously an unequivocal threat, but decision complexity is certainly a matter that may be looked upon by different individuals in a different manner. Some may see it as a threat, others an opportunity, and still others deem it as an additional cost offset by other considerations. The crux is that in human decision-making we shall often be dealing with situations perceived in different ways by individuals in identical positions. Thus, natural laws are unlikely to be found in these settings. Even in cases where event types may seem to be regularly or causally connected to other event types involving human decisions, there is bound to be a 'teleological ring' between the event types, to use von Wright's (1971: 85) term. Thus, even though one may observe that oppressed people regularly rebel and occasionally manage to overthrow their oppressors, this regularity (which is by no means without exceptions) is mediated by a phase of perception and deliberation on the part of the oppressed which may or may not lead to an uprising. Similar teleological rings, of course, permeate economic regularities, e.g. ones that connect interest rate changes to investment behavior or labor costs to capital movements.

2.5 Normative and factual models

The models we shall mainly be dealing with are built on behavior principles. These are to economic and social theory what natural laws are to theories in physics or chemistry. In contradistinction to the laws of natural sciences, the principles can often be given two types of interpretations, factual and normative. By factual principle of behavior we mean regularity of observed behavior, e.g. that people tend to raise their hand in an auditorium to attract the attention of the speaker. The normative principle, in contrast, pertains to behavior one thinks ought to guide behavior, e.g. that in a bus full of people young persons ought to relinquish their seats to old ones.

Systems of factual and normative principles can be – and often are – called theories or models. Often the principles themselves or the intended field of their application reveals whether one is dealing with factual or normative system of principles. But there are systems in which the dividing line is particularly thin. Many models of political economy are in this category. There are certainly models that are easily classifiable as factual ones, e.g. many macro-economic models linking employment, interest rates, exchange balance, etc. But the models based on individual behavior are sometimes difficult to classify.

The reason for this is the notion of rationality that forms the basis of the behavior principles in these models. Rationality is certainly a desirable property of a pattern of behavior in many – if not all – circumstances. But it is also natural to think that individuals act in a rational manner in matters related to political economy. After all, as was pointed out above one of the definitions of political economy is to see it as an economic approach to political choices. This, in turn, amounts to postulating rational behavior on the part of the individuals. Thus, it would seem that to the extent that events in political economy do not coincide with those predicted by our theories, the discrepancies can be explained by the failure of the actors to behave according to the dictates of normative rationality.

This is, however, too simplified a view. The concept of rationality, normative or factual, is open to a wide variety of different interpretations. In other words, even though one may envision simple settings where nearly all reasonable people might agree on what is the rational way to proceed, there are circumstances of just a modicum of complexity where the dictates of rationality imply several non-equivalent ways of behavior. We shall discuss these in the next chapter.

Another central concept of political economy, namely optimality, lends itself to normative and factual interpretations as well. Of course, achieving optimal outcomes is by definition the best one can do, but optimal behavior by each member of a group of individuals may lead to outcomes that are worse than other outcomes for all group members. Thus, optimality on one (individual) level may contradict optimality on another (group) level.

The third central concept is justice. It is at first sight a purely normative concept, something inherently desirable. As John Rawls (1971) puts it: justice is a fundamental value of all well-organized societies. This means that shortcomings in justice cannot be compensated with other aspects of the society, such as an increase in the standard of living, defence capability or excellence of educational institutions. But along with normative content, justice also has a factual content which refers to people's perception of justice in the prevailing institutions.

John Rawls (1921–2002) is considered to be one of the most important political philosophers of our time. In his main work *A Theory of Justice* (1971), he builds a theory of how the principles of justice can be viewed as a result of a voluntary social contract between self-regarding actors acting in a situation which precedes the emergence of a state. The theory is to be seen as an alternative to utilitarianism. Rawls was the foremost modern representative of the social contract tradition. His other main works are *Political Liberalism* (1993), *The Law of Peoples* (1999) and *Justice as Fairness* (2001).

Normative political economy deals with concepts such as rationality, justice and optimality, specifies their exact meaning and studies the compatibility or incompatibility of various meanings as well as the relationships between these and various other normative concepts. Factual political economy builds models that attempt to describe the real world in a simplified manner that allows for detailed analysis of some aspects of real economies and polities. One typically looks for solutions of models, i.e. some kind of stable outcomes or equilibria which constitute the theoretical predictions of models. These then operate as tests of the validity of models. However, more typical are uses of models in the evaluation of politico-economic institutions. By building models out of planned institutions, one may conduct experiments on them and estimate the effects of various outer impulses or shocks on the behavior of the institutions. One may also vary the structure of the model to see the effects of the variation on various aspects of the institution.

2.6   Suggested reading

The philosophy of science is a vast field. Basic concepts discussed above are dealt with in an accessible style in Achinstein (1968), Giere (1979) and von Wright (1971). The issue of whether the social sciences require a specific mode of accounting for events, structures and – above all – acts has given rise to an extensive debate over the past decades. Much of this debate turns on themes discussed about a hundred years ago by Dilthey (1914–1927). In the 1960s the methodological controversies reappeared in the works of Habermas (1972, 1988), Apel (1967) and other representatives of the so-called Frankfurt school. The philosophical theory of human action is discussed in Davidson (1980) and the theory of speech acts elaborated in Searle (1980, 1996 and 2002).

3   *Homo œconomicus*

The basic constituent in models of political economy is the economic man, *homo œconomicus*. The economic man is a theoretically simplified model of the individual. At first approximation it can be viewed as the residue remaining when all non-economic aspects are removed from real world individuals. In particular, in this model the individual is supposed to be rational in the sense of calculating the consequences of her behavior under prevailing and anticipated circumstances. As all models, the economic man is a simplification. Without simplification we could not describe, let alone analyze, political economy. Yet, the model of economic agent is often deemed inadequate and misleading. Indeed, it is one of the most debated constructs in modern social and political theory. It is, therefore, important to outline it in some detail. In models of political economy the economic man appears in the form of an assumption. It is therefore appropriate to discuss the role of assumptions and their types in the study of political economy.

3.1   The role of assumptions in theory

In his collection of methodological essays, Milton Friedman (1953) provides the following provocative characterization of the role and nature of assumptions in economic theory:

> Truly important and significant hypotheses will be found to have assumptions that are widely inaccurate descriptive representations of reality, and, in general, the more significant the theory, the more unrealistic the assumptions (in this sense).

This statement has become known as the F-twist.[4] In its time it gave rise to a hot scientific and philosophical debate (Musgrave 1981; Nagel 1979; Tietzel 1981). The main source of provocation was the alleged inverse relationship between significance and realism. Indeed, it would be nearly absurd to maintain that one could construct significant theories just by making sure that one's assumptions are unrealistic. This is, however, not what Friedman is arguing. Rather, he says that one of the hallmarks of significant theory is that its assumptions are unrealistic.

No direct causal attribution is thereby made; at least not of the sort that would imply that unrealism guarantees significance. Even so, many challenges have been presented to Friedman's view (see e.g. Nurmi 1983a for an overview).

Examples of 'F-twisted' assumptions:

- Individual firms behave as if they were seeking rationally to maximize their expected returns.
- Political parties operate as if they were maximizing their short-term electoral support.
- Voters vote for parties advocating policies that maximize the voter's short-term income.
- There is no government, i.e. the entire economy consists of private firms and consumers.
- Officials in bureaucracies behave as if they were maximizing the budget of their bureaus (Niskanen 1971).

Alan Musgrave (1981) argues that Friedman's view overlooks the fact that many types of assumptions can be found in scientific theories. Each type has a specific role in those constructs. More devastating for the F-twist is, however, Musgrave's conclusion: it is incorrect for each assumption type.

Let us briefly assess the validity of the conclusion and list the three assumption types.

- *Negligibility assumptions*. These state that some factors which could be expected to have an effect on the phenomenon under investigation actually do not have any effect at all or at most an effect that is undetectable. For example, the color of a falling object is typically assumed to have no effect on its acceleration. Or, the mechanism used in casting ballots in elections is assumed to have only a negligible effect on the election results.
- *Domain assumptions*. These specify the domain of application of a theory. The theory of ideal gases is assumed to apply only to very specific types of gases.
- *Heuristic assumptions*. These are done in order to simplify the manipulation of theories, e.g. by assuming certain parameter values in mathematical formulae in order to make the derivation of solutions possible.

To argue that the F-twist holds for negligibility assumptions is tantamount to saying that in significant theories the assumptions regarding factors or variables that can be overlooked in the analysis are more unrealistic than similar assumptions in less significant theories. Under the not too implausible view that unrealistic assumptions are descriptively false, the F-twist seems hardly applicable to this assumption type, for if a negligibility assumption is untrue, this obviously means that the factors or variables omitted should not, after all, be omitted. Under the stated assumptions the theory does not 'work'. This does not as such imply that theories with more false negligibility assumptions would be any more significant than theories where such assumptions are fewer. What can be inferred, though, is that the former are 'simpler' than the latter.

Milton Friedman (born 1921) is known as the pioneer and leading representative of the monetarist school of macroeconomics. Convinced of the superior efficiency of free markets in all economic circumstances, he has also advocated their adoption in the developing countries. Known as a leading proponent of the supply-side economics his main works are *A Monetary History of the United States* (with Anna Schwartz) (1963), *Essays in Positive Economics* (1953) and the best-seller *Free to Choose* (with Rose Friedman) (1980). In 1976 he became the Nobel Memorial Laureate in economics.

In the case of domain assumptions, the conclusion is similar for one obvious reason: by adding descriptively false assumptions one can restrict the validity of the theory, not make it more significant. It is possible that a negligibility assumption which turns out to be false under the domain of intended application is turned into a domain one. Suppose that one's theory of economic behavior would include as a negligibility assumption that government activity has no effect on national economy. Once it turns out that the assumption is descriptively false, one may turn the assumption into a domain one by stating that the theory is to be applied only under systems where government's activity has a very small effect on the operation of the economy.

In the case of heuristic assumptions the F-twist seems a more tenable position. To use Friedman's own example, consider the hypothesis 'under a wide range of circumstances individual firms behave as if they were seeking rationally to maximize their expected returns'. The part of the hypothesis starting with 'as if' seems to be a heuristic assumption and the entire hypothesis can be translated into the following counterfactual statement: 'if the firms were seeking rationally to maximize their expected returns, then their behavior under a wide range of circumstances would resemble the observations.' The two statements seem to have an identical meaning. Yet the latter looks very much like a heuristic assumption. Whatever else Friedman may want to convey with his 'as if' clause, he obviously does not say that the firms are seeking rationally to maximize their expected returns. Rather he seems to suggest that they may have a wide variety of other goals, but their behavior resembles closely one that would ensue from expected return maximization. Moreover, he argues that looking at the observations from the 'as if' angle helps us in predicting behavior.

Now, the unrealism of assumptions seems in this case more defensible than in other types of assumptions. The heuristic assumptions are invoked by virtue of their usefulness in predictions. This does not, however, justify the F-twist in so far as it postulates an inverse relationship between unrealism and significance. What can be argued, though, is that there is no direct reason to reject the F-twist when applied to heuristic assumptions, while such reasons exist *vis-à-vis* negligibility and domain assumptions.

The above assumption types are not clear cut. As we just pointed out, assumptions may 'migrate' from one type to another. Indeed, whether an assumption is a negligibility, domain or heuristic assumption may be seen as a matter of interpretation of models. Thus, for example, Friedman's example above may be looked upon as a domain assumption stating that the theory applies only to firms that maximize their expected returns as a matter of operative principle. Similarly, it can be viewed as a negligibility assumption that suggests that all other aspects except return maximization can be neglected in modeling firms. Finally, and perhaps most plausibly, it can be seen as a heuristic assumption useful in predicting behavior in heretofore unexplored settings.

This kind of ambiguity in the interpretation of assumptions pertains to the economic man as well. It can be viewed as a negligibility assumption stating that all other aspects except pursuit of utility maximization can be ignored in building models of political economy. On the other hand, it can also be argued that the economic man is a domain assumption, i.e. applicable only in contexts where individual utility maximization is the dominant behavioral principle. Indeed, the standard defense of a theory that contradicts observations is that its domain assumptions are not valid in the context of the study. However, the most important interpretation of the economic man is that of a heuristic assumption with instrumental value in deriving predictions, accounting for observed phenomena, experimenting with policy alternatives and designing politico-economic institutions. It is typically not intended as a counterfactual statement; that is, in the models of political economy the economic man is not an assumption known to be false. Rather it is a simplification believed to be true of a reasonably wide class of agents and/or behaviors. Its assumed heuristic value is in enabling the model-builder to account for a large set of observations – the larger, the better.

3.2   Aspects of rationality

The economic man is not a universally shared set of assumptions, but a fairly wide consensus exists on one of the properties of the model, namely rationality. Rationality and the theory built around it can be viewed from two angles: normative and descriptive. Under the former interpretation rationality relates to how one ought to behave, while the latter view pertains to how one does behave. Elster (1986: 2) argues that the normative view allows us to explain behavior by showing that it was rational and that the person in question had goals and beliefs that made it appropriate for her to behave in the way she did. We can then say that the behavior took place because the person thought it was rational. The success of the behavior in achieving some goals is not adequate for its explanation unless one can show that the person had both the goals and beliefs that connected her activity to those goals.

Jon Elster (born 1940) is a Norwegian-born social philosopher, political scientist
and economic historian. His work focuses on fundamental concepts of social sciences, such as rationality and justice. He has also written a number of works on
methodology of historiography and political psychology. Some of his best-known
books are *Ulysses and the Sirens* (1979), *Making Sense of Marx* (1985), *Local
Justice* (1992), *Alchemies of the Mind* (1999) and *Ulysses Unbound* (2000).

The descriptive view of rationality, on the other hand, is less directly applicable
in explanations. However, if we assume that a person is rational, this guides us
to investigate her goals and beliefs in accounting for her behavior (Harsanyi
1986: 83). Thus, the descriptive view of rationality also has a role to play in the
explanation of behavior. Postulating rationality implies that one should focus on
means–ends relationships and beliefs underlying observed behavior.

John C. Harsanyi (1920–2000) was one of the most influential game theorists of
the 20th century. Apart from his important contributions to the solution theory of
games, he wrote extensively on welfare economics and moral philosophy. Harsanyi
subscribed to a version of utilitarian thinking in moral philosophy. His main works
are *Essays on Ethics, Social Behaviour and Scientific Explanation* (1976), *Rational
Behaviour and Bargaining Equilibrium in Games and Social Situations* (1977),
Papers in Game Theory (1982) and *A General Theory of Equilibrium Selection in
Games* (with Reinhard Selten) (1988). Harsanyi won the Nobel Memorial Prize in
economics in 1994.

What then is rational behavior? Two types of definitions can be found in
the literature. Thin rationality means that actors possess consistent preference
rankings and make their choices according to those rankings. Thick rationality,
in turn, augments the thin one by adding requirements that pertain to the nature
of goals pursued (see Herne and Setälä 2004 for an overview). In other words,
a person is rational in the thick sense if, in addition to fulfilling the requirements of
thin rationality, her behavior is directed towards reasonable goals, her means are
reasonable with respect to the ends she is pursuing, and her expectations regarding
her environment are reasonable. Thus, thick rationality essentially extends the
notion of rationality by imposing conditions upon goals and beliefs.

In empirical research rationality can form the basis of two distinct methods,
namely the method of revealed preference and that of posited preference (Riker
and Ordeshook 1973: 14–15). In the former, one infers the preferences or goals
by observing people's behavior, thereby assuming that the observed behavior
is rational. The question asked is thus basically the following: given that the
individuals made the observed choices under the circumstances which were also
observed, which goals are such that the pursuit of them would make the choices
rational? A full answer to the question would require us to dwell on the belief

systems of the individuals. A typical setting for such questions is one where some unexpected type of behavior emerges. A trivial example would be a scene where one sees a group of people suddenly running on a street, but also unexpected buying and selling behavior in the stock market belongs to the same class of situations where the method of revealed preference is often instinctively used.

The method of posited preference calls for a somewhat different setting. To wit, one may be interested in finding out what kinds of effect a new piece of legislation might bring about. For example, would an increase in minimum wage reduce the plight of the working poor or to the contrary put more of them out of work? The introduction of new legislation is always based on some goals and thought experiments on how reasonable people would act on the new setting created by the proposed legislation. Postulating rationality on the part of the actors often gives a useful benchmark for assessing the effects of new legislation.

The goal most often discussed in defining rationality is that of increasing, indeed typically maximizing, one's welfare. MacDonald (2003: 552) defines rationality in terms of three components: purposive action, consistent preferences and utility maximization. As we shall see later on, the last two components are intimately related: without consistent preferences, utility maximization does not make sense. In the absence of information about more specific goals of human activity, the welfare maximization is often assumed to be the goal that all individuals are striving for. A theoretically more useful concept is, however, that of utility maximization. The latter is more useful because it is more general. While individual welfare maximization is associated with egoism, utility maximization allows for a wide variety of different social changes – including changes that increase other persons' welfare – that the actor might derive utility from. This point is significant since one of the most frequently voiced objections against rational choice theory is its alleged basis on egoistic behavior. As we shall see, this is a misconception. What the theory is based upon is goal-directed behavior with respect to consistent preferences. The reason behind arranging alternatives in a given order of preference is not significant, i.e. it may be egoism, altruism or some other principle.

3.3   Making choices under certainty

Rational choice theory is based on the concept of decision. What makes individuals or groups rational is that they make rational decisions. Rational decisions, in turn, are those that result in the achievement of the goals of the decision maker (DM, for brevity). Without goals, there is no way of distinguishing rational and non-rational decisions. Both goals and decisions may be hidden or private information accessible only to the DM. Thus, a person may decide to apply for a position in an organization, but may not reveal her decision until the very last moment of the application period. Similarly, a general may order part of her troops to prepare an attack to the enemy positions in A even though her goal is to capture a different position in B.[5] So, the goals are not always observable from the acts and the latter are not always simultaneous with the decisions. Yet, to outline the basic constituents of decision making, we shall begin with a setting where both goals and decisions are observable.

Consider a committee which consists of a chairperson and two members. The committee makes its decisions using the majority rule so that any proposal which is supported by at least two persons is adopted. Otherwise the proposal is rejected. Suppose that the committee is to decide whether a given project receives funding. Each member can either support or oppose the funding or abstain. The voting takes place so that the members indicate their stand first whereupon the chair gives her opinion. The latter thus casts her vote in full knowledge of the others' votes. Assume that the two members express opposite opinions about the project: one favors funding, the other rejection. It is therefore the chair's vote that determines the outcome: if she votes for funding, the project is funded, otherwise it is not. This is the setting of a decision under certainty. What kind of behavior could be regarded as rational under these circumstances?

Obviously, the chair has three options at her disposal: to vote for funding, to vote for rejection or to abstain. Without information about her goals it is impossible to tell which of these actions is rational. Assume that the chair would like to see the project funded. Should this be the case, the rational thing for her to do is to vote for funding since this guarantees funding. If she, in turn, would not like to fund the project, then she has one way to achieve this: to vote for rejection. Should she be indifferent between funding and not funding, abstaining would obviously be the best choice for her as it would lead to non-decision (since neither of the basic options receives at least two votes). In a situation involving two outcomes, the information regarding the preference of the DM over the outcomes gives us a way to distinguish rational behavior: it is the choice of that decision alternative which leads to the preferred outcome.

Let us assume that, instead of being the chairperson in a group, the DM is given the exclusive power to determine the order in which a set of project proposals is to receive funding. She does not know the overall budget constraint, i.e. the total amount of funds available, but she knows that the projects will be funded in the order she proposes until the available budget is exhausted. Since the DM has the sole authority to determine the outcome, we need not make any assumptions regarding the behavior of others. On the other hand, what is needed for defining rational behavior is the DM's preference order with respect to the projects. More specifically, the DM has to be able to compare any pair of projects in terms of preference, that is, for any projects x and y, the DM is required to have an opinion according to which either x is preferred to y, or y is preferred to x. In technical terms, the DM's preference has to be *complete*. Sometimes this requirement is called *connectedness*. Why is this requirement called for? Suppose that it were not satisfied, i.e. for some pair of projects the DM could not say which one is at least as preferable as the other. This would then mean that of these two projects, the DM could not fund one since she does not know if it is at least as preferable as the other. Nor could she abstain since this would mean that one project is as preferable as the other. So, none of the three action alternatives could be justified with reference to an underlying preference of the DM.

Another requirement on the DM's preferences is logical consistency or, in technical terms, *transitivity*. This states that whenever a project, say project 1, is considered at least as preferable as another project, say 2, and the latter at least as preferable as a third project 3, then it has to be the case that project 1 is at least as preferable as project 3. For example, if a voter in the U.S. presidential elections of 2000 preferred Nader to Gore and Gore to Bush, then transitivity requires that she preferred Nader to Bush. If the preferences do not satisfy transitivity, it is impossible to form a preference order or ranking, i.e. a sequence of candidates so that each candidate is located in only one position in the ranking. Together with completeness, transitivity guarantees that such a sequence of priority exists and each candidate is positioned in one and only one place in it.

If the requirements of completeness and transitivity are imposed on the DM's preferences we can justify or 'rationalize' actions by referring to preference relations: an action is rational just in case it leads to the preferred outcome. This is the basic idea of what is called *thin rationality* (Elster 1983). Rational are actions that are consistent with preferences which, in turn, are complete and transitive. It is worth emphasizing that the principle or rationale underlying the preference ranking has thus far played no role at all. In other words, the definition of thin rationality is not based on any specific principle which is used in forming the preference. In particular, the preferences may or may not be egoistic or altruistic, local or global.

Connectedness and transitivity of preferences enable us to construct a sequence of alternatives from best to worst, possibly including ties. In any event, each alternative is positioned in one and only one position in the sequence. We may thus consider rational an action that chooses the alternative which is best in the sequence. The same reasoning can be extended to any subset of alternatives. In the case that several alternatives are tied for the best position, the choice of any one of them may be deemed rational.

The requirements needed for the construction of a preference ranking of alternatives are quite mild. Yet, it is not difficult to envision a situation where an intuitively perfectly reasonable person may find it impossible to meet them. Consider again the presidential candidates Bush, Gore and Nader. Suppose that a voter would rank Nader higher than Gore because she likes the environmental policies of the former to those of the latter. Suppose, moreover, that the same voter prefers Gore to Bush because of the employment and incomes policy considerations, i.e. she thinks that Gore's policies would have brought about more jobs and more even income distribution than those of Bush. By transitivity we would now infer that the person in question prefers Nader to Bush. It is, however, quite possible that the voter has the opposite preference. She might, for example, have thought that Bush's policies on crime prevention are preferable to Nader's. If these three considerations or criteria – environment, employment and crime prevention policy – are deemed the sole determinants of the voter's preference in the way described, then the voter's preference relation over the three candidates becomes cyclic: Nader is preferred to Gore, Gore to Bush and Bush to Nader. In fact, a cyclic preference could also result by assuming that the voter considers

Table 3.1 Cyclic individual preference relation

Environment	Employment	Crime prevention
Nader	Gore	Bush
Gore	Bush	Nader
Bush	Nader	Gore

each of these three criteria equally important and that her preference ranking is that shown in Table 3.1.

Nader is better than Gore on two criteria out of three. Similarly, Gore is preferred to Bush on two criteria. The same holds for Bush with respect to Nader. There is nothing unreasonable in this type of preference relation. Yet, because of its intransitivity it makes it impossible to say which choice of candidate would be rational from the voter's point of view. If the voter chooses Nader, it can be pointed out that Bush is preferable on two criteria out of three. If she chooses Bush, the same argument can be built in favor of Gore, etc.

Very often the preferences are not visible. Rather, their role is to provide a rationale for making choices. If only one candidate can be voted upon, the voter may break the tie between all three candidates by emphasizing one criterion at the cost of the others, invoking further criteria or by some random mechanism (e.g. rolling a dice). The last device suggests that the voter is indifferent between all three alternatives. The other two stratagems amount to transforming the cyclic preference relation into a transitive one. Thus, the starting assumption of decision theory gets at least a partial justification from the observation that cyclic individual preferences are not visible in practical choice situations.

Now, given the complete and transitive preference relation, what, then, would be the rational thing to do? Under certainty, the DM's choice determines the outcome. Thus, given that a candidate, say Nader, is ranked first in the voter's preference order, she should obviously vote for Nader and thereby get him elected. Voting otherwise would make the voter's preference ranking highly questionable.

When we are certain about the results of our actions, the specification of what a rational actor would do is, thus, straightforward: she chooses whichever action leads to the best outcome according to her ranking. Naturally, things become more complicated when the results of actions are not fully known at the time of decision. This, of course, is typically the case in elections where no voter alone decides the outcome. For example, in the U.S. presidential elections of 2000 many Nader supporters ended up voting for their second-ranked alternative instead of their favorite in an attempt to undermine their worst-ranked candidate's chances of being elected.

3.4   Choices under risk

Suppose that the DM knows that her action leads to one of several outcomes, but does not know which one. She has a preference ranking over the outcomes so that she is not indifferent between them. To see the difference between this setting and the one discussed above, consider an example. You have just finished writing your first novel and the time has now arrived to look for ways of making it accessible to the reading public. This being your first one, you have not got around to contacting publishers before finishing the book. Being a literary person you have read many novels of similar genre to yours and have – upon talking to representatives of publishers – learned that there are three major publishers in the field you are working on: companies A, B and C.

Company A is the most prestigious. Its distribution and marketing network is very wide, its books are on exhibit in every major book fair in the world and most of its novels are reviewed in important literary magazines. Company A's main drawback is that it is very selective. It publishes in relative terms far fewer manuscripts received than its competitors. Company B, in turn, accepts a clearly higher percentage of manuscripts than A, but – perhaps partly because of this – tends to enjoy lower prestige. It also spends less on marketing books and its international visibility is more modest. Company C, finally, publishes nearly all manuscripts it receives, but requires the authors to play a role in marketing the books.

Having carefully collected the statistics provided by the publishers, you summarize the data in Table 3.2.

The value assigned to the companies reflects your assessment of the mental (fame, honor, esteem) and material (royalty and other payments) benefit that would accrue to you if the company in question would publish your book. Approaching company A with your manuscript would, thus, give a large benefit should it accept the text in its publication program. The probability of this happening is, however, very small. Company B's value to you would be less, but probability of success higher than in A's case. Company C would give you a small benefit, but almost certainly.

The above setting appears in various disguises in many everyday decision situations. The most trivial settings notwithstanding we are often faced with choices which may lead to many different outcomes each distinguishable by the benefit ensuing from them as well as by the likelihood that the outcome is reached. For example, individual career choices often boil down to varying income prospects as well as possibilities of reaching them once the career choice has been made. Situations in which the best outcomes also have the best success probability are intuitively obvious, i.e. we do not typically spend much time on them. The difficult ones have at least some similarity to the one summarized in Table 3.2.

Table 3.2 Publishers' data summary

Company	A	B	C
Value	Large	Medium	Small
Likelihood	Almost hopeless	Reasonably good	Excellent

What distinguishes this situation from that discussed in the preceding section is that we now have to compare choices in terms of two – rather than one – criteria: value and success likelihood. Unfortunately, the data in Table 3.2 are not sufficient to guide us in the choice of the best alternative. Or, to phrase it somewhat differently, reasonable people might end up with different choices, given the data of the table. A person opting for company A might argue that she chose A despite the slim chances of success since she regarded the value of success so much that even a small likelihood of achieving it makes it superior to the other alternatives. Besides, she might feel lucky. Another person could choose C and justify her choice by thinking that things just have the tendency of turning against her and that the main thing is to get the work published. A third person could opt for company B because it guarantees a reasonable probability of success and a modicum of media exposure.

The difficulty of judging the rationality of decisions in Table 3.2-type situations stems from the vast variation in the possible content of the expressions 'large', 'medium' and 'small' when applied to values and 'almost hopeless', 'reasonably good' and 'excellent' when these denote probability values. Let us assume that instead of these verbal expression we have numerical values that can be added and multiplied. We may assume that the author looking for a publisher is exclusively preoccupied with the income she is entitled to if her book is accepted by the companies. For simplicity we assume that each company pays out the entire value of the contract in a single lump sum upon accepting the manuscript. Company A would offer her a contract assuring her the sum of $x(A)$ if her work would be accepted. Similarly contracts with companies B and C would give her $x(B)$ and $x(C)$, respectively. We assume that $x(A) > x(B) > x(C)$ which is consistent with Table 3.2. The success probabilities, in turn, are p_A, p_B and p_C, respectively, indicating the likelihood that each company makes a contract with the author. In accordance with the table we can assume that $p_C > p_B > p_A$. Table 3.2, now takes the form of Table 3.3.

Since each company has the option of rejecting the manuscript, we need to assign a value to the outcome of the manuscript being rejected as well. Let us assume that the value of this outcome is zero regardless of which company rejects it.

If the author decides to approach company A with her manuscript, she faces two possible outcomes: the manuscript is accepted or it is rejected. The value of the former outcome is $x(A)$ and that of the latter is 0. The work is accepted with probability p_A and rejected with probability $1 - p_A$. The latter probability

Table 3.3 Publishers' quantitative data

Company	A	B	C
Value	$x(A)$	$x(B)$	$x(C)$
Probability	p_A	p_B	p_C

follows from the fact that, given the choice of company A, there are only two mutually exclusive outcomes: acceptance and rejection. The probability of the latter is the same as the probability of the former not occurring, $1 - p_A$. The expected value of choosing company A, denoted by $EV(A)$, is thus: $EV(A) = p_A \times x(A) + (1 - p_A) \times 0 = p_A x(A)$. Similarly, the expected values $EV(B)$ and $EV(C)$ of submitting the manuscript to company B or C yield: $EV(B) = p_B x(B)$ and $EV(C) = p_C x(C)$, respectively.

The expected value is the weighted average of the values associated with all the possible outcomes ensuing from a choice. The weights, in turn, are the probabilities of the corresponding outcomes materializing, given that the choice has been made. Suppose that for a given choice all outcomes are equally likely. In our example, this means that for some company the probability of acceptance and rejection are equal, i.e. both 1/2. Then the expected value of submitting one's manuscript to this company is the average of values associated with acceptance and that of rejection (which we assumed to be zero).

To take another example closer to everyday life in many urban areas of the world, consider a passenger embarking on an inner-city bus or tram ride. The tickets costing 2 euros can be purchased from machines located near the bus stops. Passengers riding without validated tickets face the inspection charge of 100 euro if caught by inspectors. Now, a passenger has found out that the probability of an inspector riding on any given bus or tram is p. Consequently, the probability that there is no inspector on a given ride is $1 - p$. The passenger may either purchase a ticket or enter the bus without one. The choice of buying has two possible outcomes: the passenger travels the desired distance with or without facing an inspector. Either way, she pays two euros. The choice of riding without a ticket may also have two outcomes: the passenger is confronted with an inspector and is caught or she does not encounter an inspector on her ride.

Using the vocabulary of decision theory, we may say that there are two states of nature which, together with the DM's choice, determine the outcome: the state in which an inspector is riding on the bus, and the state in which there is no inspector on the ride.[6] Combining these states with the choices gives us Table 3.4.

Suppose that the bus company has decided to randomly assign inspectors to buses so that on average one passenger in every 100 is inspected. The expected value of buying a ticket is not dependent on the inspection probability since $EV(buy) = p \times (-2) + (1 - p) \times (-2) = -2$, no matter what the value of p. The expected value of the don't buy option,

Table 3.4 Passenger's values

State of nature	Choice	
	Buy a ticket	Don't buy
No inspector	−2	0
Inspector	−2	−100

in contrast, varies with the value of p. When $p = 1/100$, its expected value
$EV(don't\ buy) = 1/100 \times (-100) + 99/100 \times 0 = -1$.

The expected value of not buying a ticket, thus, exceeds that of buying one.
But what is the expected value? More specifically, how does this value compare
with the value accruing to the DM under certainty? Obviously, it is different in
the sense that it has nothing to do with what happens to the passenger without
a valid ticket when she embarks on a bus ride on a given day at a given time.
Depending on whether an inspector happens to ride on the same bus, she may
lose 100 euros or nothing at all. Neither one of these coincides with the expected
value. For a passenger with a valid ticket it really tells what she is bound to
benefit in monetary terms once entering the bus.

The nature of expected value hinges on the notion of probability and has
been the subject of an extensive philosophical debate (Carnap 1962; Edwards
et al. 1963; Reichenbach 1949; Salmon 1967). According to the most common
(frequency) view of probability, the expected value is the average of the value that
the DM would get if the decision situation were repeated an indefinite number of
times, given that she would make the same choice on every occasion. Thus, -1
is the average value that the passenger would get per ride if she would embark
on every journey without a ticket. The average is the sum of a sequence of zeros
and -100s divided by the number of rides.

Similarly, in the publishing example, the expected values of choosing each
publishing house represent theoretical average benefits for an author submitting
her manuscript to the company indefinitely many times. Clearly, the expected
value is a highly theoretical concept. Yet, it can be linked to rationality in the
same manner as choice under certainty. That is, it can be shown that under
fairly plausible assumptions concerning preferences, the behavior that strives at
maximizing the expected values of choices can be seen as rational in pretty much
the same way as choosing the highest valued alternative can be seen as rational
under certainty. This point will be elaborated shortly.

Suppose now that using expected utilities as guidelines for action is rational.
It follows then in our bus passenger example that a rational passenger never
purchases a ticket since if she did, she would lose 2 euros on every ride with
the average benefit obviously equal to -2. She doubles her average benefit in
monetary terms by not buying a ticket. Obviously, the bus company needs to
reconsider its inspection fee policy.[7] Alternatively, the company might consider
placing more inspectors on the buses so as to decrease the expected benefit from
riding without a ticket.

3.5   Choices under uncertainty

The above bus rider calculus is based on the assumption that the passengers know
the probability of encountering an inspector upon stepping onto the bus. Moreover, we have assumed implicitly that this probability is the same as that with
which the bus company assigns inspectors to its buses. Both of these assumptions
may be challenged as unrealistic: the passenger may be in an unfamiliar town

and thus unaware of the inspection policies, or the bus company may change its policy at irregular intervals. Intuitively, it would seem more reasonable to assume that instead of an objective probability, the passenger has a more or less precise hunch or guess of what is going to happen to her when embarking upon the bus ride with or without a ticket. She knows that if caught without a ticket, she will be fined. She also knows that if she is not caught, she will get a free ride.

Here, being inspected or not being inspected are two mutually exclusive conditioning events which, together with her choice, determine the outcome and the benefit for the passenger. The conditioning events or states of nature are not known to the passenger to the extent that she could assign objective probabilities to them. Thus, she is not able to compute the expected benefit accruing to her from the acts of buying or failing to buy a ticket. This setting characterizes decision making under uncertainty: one has a pretty good idea of what happens if various conditioning events occur, but has only a vague estimate of the likelihood of those events. Clearly, the calculus of expected benefits is not applicable here, at least not in the form outlined in the preceding section.

Yet, there are settings involving uncertainty where there are rather obvious ways of telling good decisions from bad ones. Consider the following simple coin picking game situation (Table 3.5) (Hamburger 1979: 17). There are four coins on the table and two players take turns in picking them up. On each turn, the player has to pick up either one or two coins. The player who gets the last coin wins and collects all the coins that were originally on the table.

Suppose you are the player who has the first turn. Should you pick one or two coins? Obviously, you should pick one since regardless of what your opponent does, that guarantees that you still have either one or two coins left when it is time for your second turn. Moreover, it guarantees that you can win the game on your second turn. So, on your first turn picking one coin is a good decision, while picking two coins is a bad one. It is bad since it opens the door to victory to your opponent. Table 3.5 illustrates this.

The outcomes in Table 3.5 are based on the assumption that each player is rational in the most straightforward sense: given two outcomes, one of which is her victory and the other her defeat, the player chooses the former. Thus, for example, if you choose one coin and your opponent also chooses one, you are faced, on your second turn, with the choice between winning (i.e. picking two coins) or losing (picking one coin, whereupon your opponent takes the remaining coin and wins).

Table 3.5 Coin picking game

	Your choice	
Opponent's choice	Choose one coin	Choose two coins
Opponent chooses one coin	You win	You win
Opponent chooses two coins	You win	The opponent wins

In the example of Table 3.5 your choice of one coin at the outset is the best one in the sense that no matter what your opponent does, it guarantees victory, while choosing two coins is very likely to result in your defeat. Choice theory uses the concept of *dominance* to characterize this type of choice situation. An option (choice, strategy, action, etc.) is said to *weakly dominate* another option if choosing the former in all circumstances results in outcomes that are at least as good as – and under some circumstances strictly better than – those resulting from the latter. The circumstances in Table 3.5 refer to the opponent's choices or states of nature.

The option 'pick one coin' clearly dominates the option 'pick two coins' for you since under both choices of the opponent it leads to at least as good an outcome as the latter option and under one choice of the opponent, namely 'pick two coins', it results in a strictly better outcome for you.

It may happen that an option leads to strictly better outcomes than its competitor under all circumstances. In this case it is said that the former *strongly dominates* the latter. As an example, suppose that you are offered a ticket in two simple lotteries, A and B. Both consist of a single throw of dice. If the throw results in the side with six dots showing up, you win 10 euros in lottery A. Otherwise you win just 1 euro. In lottery B you win 20 euros if the side six shows up. All other outcomes give you 2 euros. Surely lottery B strongly dominates lottery A since no matter which outcome emerges, your payoff is strictly larger in B than in A.

Situations involving weakly dominated options are encountered in many everyday choice situations. Often these are ignored since the choices made are considered so obvious that not much attention is paid to them. For example, when in Britain each individual car driver is well advised to drive on the left-hand side since this choice dominates (at least weakly) the option of driving on the right. Similarly, when taking a test the students often submit papers to the instructors even though they are uncertain about the acceptability of their essays. The act of submitting is seen as weakly dominating the act of not submitting.

An interesting class of situations emerges in the evaluation of activities or institutions with many performance criteria. For example, in evaluating institutions of higher education, several aspects of performance are usually invoked in the overall assessments: the quality and quantity of research conducted, the quality and quantity of teaching and training, the external impact of the institution on its environment, etc. Often the criteria are discussed, modified and elaborated by the representatives of the institutions under scrutiny. In these discussions, the introduction of criteria that favor their institutions can readily be seen as a weakly dominating option *vis-à-vis* settling for those already existing. Similar settings arise in many evaluations of public-sector activities, but are not restricted to these. Also those private-sector institutions and activities that are intuitively multi-dimensional (profitability, quality of service, environmental soundness, etc.) are subject to similar strategic considerations by participants.

The point of these examples is to show that there are situations in which the knowledge of the states of nature – be it certain or probabilistic – is not essential for making choices that can be justified as rational in the sense that they exclude dominated options. However, in many cases, and certainly in the most interesting ones, there are no options that dominate all the others. Some options are best under some circumstances, while other options result in best outcomes under others. In these kinds of settings various *decision principles* come into play (see e.g. Giere 1979: 337). Most of these reflect not so much rationality but attitude towards risk.

Thus, for example, a person might adopt the principle that focuses on the very worst outcome ensuing from any option under all conceivable circumstances and chooses that option that gives her the largest benefit under the worst scenario. This principle is often called the *maximin principle* or *play-it-safe rule* since it maximizes the minimum payoff for each option. It can be viewed as a version of the expected utility maximization principle in the sense that for each option it assigns the probability of unity to one state of nature, namely the one which together with the option in question brings about the minimum payoff.

Rather than rationality, the play-it-safe rule exhibits pessimism on the part of the DM. A mirror image of this rule is the *maximax principle* or *gambler's rule* which focuses attention to the largest payoff that may ensue from each option and chooses that option for which this payoff is the largest. In other words, this rule looks for the option that is associated with the largest possible benefit. Obviously, the rule is based on extreme optimism. As for maximin, this rule can also be seen as an expected utility maximization assuming that for each option one state of nature – namely the one that together with the option leads to the best possible outcome – gets a probability weight of unity.

Between maximin and maximax rules various variations can be envisaged. To wit, the rationalist rule which assigns each state of nature an identical probability and chooses the option which maximizes the expected utility under this probabilistic assumption. While maximin and maximax rules assume, for each option, that one state of nature will materialize with certainty, the rationalist rule regards every state of nature equally probable. Obviously, these probability value assignments are mere guesswork since, by definition, under uncertainty one does not know the probability distribution of the states of nature.

Another rule that can also be seen as a mediating position between maximin and maximax is Hurwicz's rule (Hurwicz 1951; Milnor 1954). It is based on computing for each option the weighted average of the utility of the best outcome and the worst outcome. The weights assigned to these utilities reflect the DM's degree of optimism: the larger the weight assigned to the best outcome, the higher the degree of optimism. The weights vary from 0 to 1. With the former value Hurwicz's rule boils down to maximin, with the latter to maximax rule.

Suppose that in the above riding example, the passenger has no idea of the probability of encountering an inspector on the bus. All she knows is that the ticket costs 2 euros and that if she is caught without a valid ticket, she will pay 100 euros. Obviously, the maximin rule dictates buying a ticket since the minimal payoff associated with it is −2 euros, while not buying a ticket may bring about the −100 euros in payoff. The maximax rule, in contrast, calls for not buying since the best that can happen for a rider is that the ride is free, i.e. the payoff is 0. The buy option, on the other hand, would bring about the payoff −2 in any event. The rationalist rule would give both states of nature – one in which the inspector is encountered and one in which there is no inspector on the bus – the probability of 1/2, whereupon the expected payoffs of 'don't buy' and 'buy' are −50 and −2, respectively. Hence, the rationalist rule would recommend buying. Hurwicz's rule, finally, would also recommend buying whenever the passenger's degree of optimism is less than 49/50.

The above rules make very limited use of the fact that there are often many states of nature which together with the option chosen determine the outcomes. The above example does not reveal this since there are only two states of nature in it. The number of states can, however, be increased by assuming that instead of policy of constant fines for free riding, the bus company allows the inspectors to determine – within some reasonable limits – the amount to be paid by the free-riders caught. Despite the added states of nature the calculations still focus on at most two of these states. Maximin looks at the worst case scenario, maximax the best case one and Hurwicz's (1951) rule computes the weighted average of these. Only the rationalist rule uses information associated with all states of nature combined with options. Its probability assignment is, however, often somewhat questionable: all states are given an equal probability.

If one has some hunches or intuitions that can be expressed as probabilities of various states occurring, one could easily avoid the problematic equiprobability assumption of rationalist rule. Thus, one can use the intuitive or subjective probabilities as if they were objective. Thereby the decision making under uncertainty can be transformed into that under risk. Instead of expected utility maximization, one could then aim at maximizing subjective expected utilities of options. The computation of the best option is in all respects identical with the expected utility maximization under risk.

3.6   Axioms of rational behavior

All the principles of choice under uncertainty have some justification which makes them plausible under some decision settings. The maximin rule amounts to guaranteeing a reasonable *security level* in making decisions. Consider a person trying to catch a bus which is about to leave the stop on the opposite side of a very busy road. Even if missing the bus would mean being some 10 minutes late in arriving at an important meeting, many people would choose to cross the street at traffic lights rather than hurrying to the other side of the road in the midst of the traffic. The former type of behavior can be viewed as maximizing the minimum benefit since the option of running across the street regardless of the traffic may end up with a disaster (serious bodily injury or even death), while crossing at the traffic lights will at worst result in being late in the meeting. In general, if the worst possible outcomes are bad enough, it makes intuitive sense to try to avoid them.

The maximax rule, on the other hand, can be justified in circumstances where the options differ mainly in terms of the best outcomes that are associated with them. The rationalist rule, in turn, may be motivated by stating that since there is no information suggesting that any of the states of nature would be more or less likely to occur than the others, it makes sense to regard them equally probable.

Some of the principles discussed above have, however, somewhat firmer than intuitive foundation. Indeed, some arguably embody rationality in the sense of satisfying axioms of rational behavior under well-defined classes of circumstances. These principles all belong to the set of *utility maximization rules* (see Harsanyi 1977: 22–47). In other words, the utility maximization under certainty, risk and uncertainty can all be viewed as rational choice principles. Rationality is here understood in the 'thin' sense, that is, behavior is rational if it is in accordance with the preferences of the actor under scrutiny. This means that an actor makes a rational choice if she chooses A rather than B whenever she prefers A to B. If she is indifferent between A and B, she is equally likely to choose each of them.

To see how this view of rationality relates to utility maximization, consider a person faced with the choice between A and B and ask what conditions would her preferences need to satisfy in order for us to be able to judge whether her behavior is rational or not. Obviously, the person has to be able to establish a preference relation between A and B. In other words, she has to be able to say whether A is preferred to B, denoted by $A \succ B$, or B is preferred to A, denoted $B \succ A$, or she is indifferent between A and B, denoted $A \sim B$. In technical terms we must assume that her preference relation over options A and B is complete (or connected). Were none of the above three possibilities to hold, we would not be able to say that whatever she chooses is in accordance with her preferences.

Another requirement we must impose on the preference relation is *asymmetry* of the strict preference. That is, if A is preferred to B, then B must not be preferred to A. On the other hand, the indifference should satisfy *symmetry*: if the DM is indifferent between A and B, then she surely must be that between B and A.

Suppose now that the above conditions are satisfied in the choice situation involving A and B. Then it is possible to assign real numbers to A and B so that, when choosing between these two, the DM acting in accordance with her preferences acts as if she were maximizing the numerical values. For example, if she prefers A to B, we can assign A the value of 100 and B the value of 10 whereupon the DM – if picking A in accordance to her preference – *eo ipso* maximizes the value assigned to the alternatives. Similarly, if she prefers B to A, we assign B a larger numerical value than to A, guaranteeing thus that the behavior that reflects preferences maximizes the numerical value.

The remaining possibility is that the DM is indifferent between A and B. Then it would seem natural to state that a rational person chooses A and B with equal probability of 1/2 if she is indifferent between the two. By assigning both A and B an identical numerical value, we notice that a DM who chooses A and B with equal probability does in fact maximize the numerical value which happens to be identical for both options because of the underlying indifference.

The numerical values assigned are commonly called *utility* values. Formally, utility is seen as a function defined over outcomes or alternatives. Hence in the two alternative settings the DM appears to be maximizing her utility function by selecting the alternative she prefers to the other or by choosing both options with the same probability if she is indifferent between them.

What we have sketched above is a synoptic proof of a *representation theorem*. What we have seen is that preference relations can be represented by numerical (utility) values in a way that preserves the fundamental features of the relation, i.e. that one of the alternatives is preferred to the other or that they are indifferent.

Two alternative cases are, however, hardly general enough for modeling real-life decisions. More often than not, the set of available options is much larger. In general we are dealing with a set A of alternatives. It turns out that we can extend the representation theorem to these more general settings by imposing two relatively mild additional conditions on preferences. The first is transitivity of weak preference relations. This amounts to the following requirement. Suppose we take three alternatives a_i, a_j, a_k of A so that $a_i \succeq a_j$ and $a_j \succeq a_k$. Here $\succeq$ denotes the relation 'at least as preferable as' or 'is better than or equal to' or 'is no less preferable than'. Transitivity now requires that $a_i \succeq a_k$. In other words, if alternative i is at least as preferable as alternative j and if the latter is at least as preferable as alternative k, then also i must be at least as preferable as k. For example, if you feel that beer is no less preferable than milk and you also feel that milk is no less preferable than water, then transitivity requires that you also feel that beer is no less preferable than water.

The other condition pertains to two types of subsets of alternatives: the inferior sets and superior sets (Harsanyi 1977: 30).[8] These are defined for each alternative, say, a_i. $I(a_i)$ denotes the former and refers to those alternatives that are either less preferable than a_i or indifferent with it. The superior set $S(a_i)$, in turn, consists of those alternatives which are at least as preferable as a_i according to the DM's preference relation. The condition called *continuity* states that for any a_i both $I(a_i)$ and $S(a_i)$ are closed sets. Closed sets are sets that contain all their boundary points. The requirement that $I(a_i)$ is closed amounts to saying that whenever there is a sequence of options $a_1, a_2, \ldots$ that converges (i.e. becomes increasingly similar) to option a_0 so that for each option a_j in the sequence $a_i \succeq a_j$, then also $a_i \succeq a_0$. What continuity says in essence is that small changes in properties of options are not accompanied with large changes in the attractiveness of options. In other words, if a sequence of options becomes arbitrarily similar – albeit not identical – with a given option a_0 and all options in the sequence are either in the inferior or superior set of a_i, then a_0 is also in the same set (either $I(a_i)$ or $S(a_i)$) as the options in the sequence.

Completeness, transitivity and continuity are the only requirements that a DM's preference relation needs to satisfy to fall within the realm of utility maximization.[9] When dealing with situations involving certainty we can, thus, state that rational behavior is nothing but utility maximization if the DM's preferences are complete, transitive and continuous. In other words, if these assumptions regarding preferences are satisfied, then whenever the DM chooses in accordance with her preferences, she acts as if she were maximizing her utility. To see why this is so it is useful to first notice that completeness and transitivity of preferences imply that one can form a list of options representing the DM's preferences so that each option appears only once in the list with the most preferred alternatives in the beginning and the least preferred at the end of the list. Completeness guarantees that all options can be seen as either on the left, on the right or on the same position as any given alternative. Transitivity, in turn, guarantees that each option can only appear in one position in the list. Once this list has been constructed, it is possible to assign numbers to positions on the list so that larger numbers are given to the more preferred alternatives. Alternatives in the same position are assigned the same number. So, when acting in accordance with her preferences the DM in fact maximizes her utility. The principle whereby she makes her choices is in technical terminology called *utility rationalizable* (Aleskerov and Monjardet 2002: 30). In other words, her choices can be justified with reference to the underlying utility function.

The representation of the individual preference relation is, thus, solved. However, the number assigned can be chosen in many ways since the only requirement imposed is that more preferred alternatives are associated with a larger number than are less preferred ones. It is clear that the familiar mathematical operations on numbers, such as addition, multiplication or division, do not make sense when applied to numbers representing preference relations. More precisely, the results of those operations on numbers do not have a counterpart in the preference relations. This brings us to the other aspect pertaining to measuring preferences: the *uniqueness* of the resulting number assignment. The above axioms guarantee that any function of assigning numbers to options that preserve the ordinal properties of the options, i.e. keeps the listing of options the same as the listing of the assigned numbers, is an equally good way of representing preferences. Accordingly, the function is often called the *ordinal utility function*.

To represent *options under risk* or *risky prospects*, we need new axioms, some of which are reminiscent of the corresponding axioms under certainty. Before dwelling on the axioms, let us consider a utility function that is defined for risky prospects. In other words, the function assigns utilities to options (choices, acts, policies), each consisting of a probability distribution over a set of certain outcomes. That is, a risky prospect consists of a list of outcomes and a list of probabilities with which these outcomes occur. The utility function, then, indicates the utility of each such prospect. To illustrate, in the preceding section we discussed the option of embarking on a bus ride with a valid ticket. The other option was traveling on the bus without a ticket. The outcomes that may ensue in this example are (i) that at some point during the bus ride the passenger encounters an inspector, and (ii) she will not encounter an inspector during her ride. Suppose that the bus company has decided to randomly assign inspectors to buses so that overall the probability of encountering an inspector is 0.1. Traveling on a bus without a valid ticket can now be considered a risky prospect with two outcomes: either encountering an inspector without a ticket or not encountering one without a ticket with probabilities of 0.1 and 0.9, respectively. Similarly, the option of riding with a valid ticket is a risky prospect with outcomes: seeing an inspector and showing her one's ticket or not seeing an inspector but having the ticket.

The outcome probabilities are the same in both cases, but the benefit differs. Assume now, as we did in the case of certainty, that the DM is capable of forming a complete and transitive preference relation over the outcomes. In our example it should not be difficult. The worst outcome is clearly that in which the passenger without a ticket has to face the inspector. The ordering between the three remaining outcomes is more debatable. From a purely monetary point of view, the outcome associated with not encountering an inspector while carrying a valid ticket is worse than not meeting her when not having a ticket. After all, the only objective difference between these two outcomes seems to be that in the former one has lost two euros in purchasing the ticket. Similarly obvious seems to be the ranking between the two outcomes associated with the state of nature where an inspector is riding on the bus: it is (much) better to buy a ticket than not to buy one. The only non-trivial comparison involves the outcome associated with buying a ticket: is it better that the inspector shows up or not? In purely monetary terms these are equivalent: one loses 2 euros in both states of nature.

Assuming that the DM has constructed a complete and transitive preference relation over the outcomes is tantamount to assuming that she is able to work out a preference order over both the trivial and non-trivial comparisons. We denote the outcomes by letter pairs (B, NI), (B, I), (NB, NI), (NB, I) where B and NB denote the act of buying and not buying, respectively, while I and NI refer to the presence or absence of the inspector. As was pointed out in the context of certainty, the complete and transitive preferences can be represented by utilities. This means that we can assign utilities to the outcomes in a natural way, i.e. so that the utilities represent the preferences. We denote the utilities as $u(B, NI)$, $u(B, I)$, $u(NB, NI)$ and $u(NB, I)$. Now, each outcome is associated with a fixed monetary loss for the DM. For example, (B, I) and (B, NI) involve the loss of 2 euros, while (NB, I) and (NB, NI) amount to losses of -100 and 0 euros, respectively. It is tempting to equate these values with utilities, but it is well-known that typically utilities are not linear functions of monetary amounts [10] Hence, we shall resort to the more general notation in which we simply refer to the utility ensuing from a given monetary amount. This may vary from person to person.

The risky prospect associated with not buying a ticket upon entering the bus can be written as $[(NB, I), p; (NB, NI), 1-p)]$, where p is the probability that there is an inspector on the bus and $1-p$ is the probability of there not being one. Similarly, the risky prospect of buying a ticket can be expressed as $[(B, I), p; (B, NI), 1-p]$. In this notation one thus lists all the possible outcomes with their occurrence probabilities so that each outcome–probability pair is separated from others with a semicolon.

Let us now define a utility function with the *expected utility* (EU, for brevity) property. Given outcomes $O_1, \ldots, O_m$ with probabilities $p_1, \ldots, p_m$ and utility values $u(O_1), \ldots, u(O_m)$, the utility function u has the EU property if the risky prospect $[(O_1, p_1; \ldots; O_m, p_m)]$ is given the following utility:

$$u(O_1, p_1; \ldots; O_m, p_m) = p_1 u(O_1) + \cdots + p_m u(O_m) \tag{3.1}$$

In other words, the utility function has the EU property if it associates the utility of any risky prospect with the weighted average of the utilities of the outcomes, any of which may ensue under the prospect. Moreover, the weights are equal to the occurrence probabilities of those outcomes. So, for example, if a person gets 5 euros if a given toss of a fair coin results in heads facing up and 0 euros otherwise and if her utility function has the EU property, then she assigns the act of throwing the coin the utility:

$$u(heads, 0.5; tails, 0.5) = 0.5 \times u(5) + 0.5 \times u(0) = 0.5 \times u(5)$$

The EU property singles out a unique way of attaching utility values to risky prospects. In a way, it represents a consistent way of handling options which involve probability elements. It is, however, by no means obvious that utility functions with an EU property would be more common in practice than other types of utility functions. In fact, as will be seen in the next chapter, empirical evidence tends to suggest that under some circumstances it is quite common to deviate from the dictates of EU utility maximization. Yet, it turns out that any DM who is rational in this sense and whose preferences satisfy a few intuitively plausible conditions, axioms, does in fact have a utility function that represents her preferences and, moreover, has the EU property. The DM thus acts as if she were maximizing her expected utility.[11]

The first axiom postulates completeness and transitivity of the preference relation over risky prospects. In other words, it requires that the DM be able to order all risky prospects so that each prospect occupies one and only one position in the order. This axiom is thus an extension of the completeness and transitivity condition to risky prospects. The second axiom is an analogous extension of the continuity requirement. It says that both the inferior and superior sets are also closed in the case of risky prospects.[12] The third axiom is called *monotonicity in prizes*. It is also known as the *independence axiom*.[13] It states that if $A \succ B$ and $p > 0$, then $(A, p; C, 1 - p) \succ (B, p; C, 1 - p)$. If the latter strict inequality is replaced with a non-strict one, the condition is known as Savage's (1954) *sure thing principle*. Both versions capture an intuitively plausible requirement: if the probability of winning is the same in two lotteries, one should prefer the lottery where the amount won is larger.

The representation theorem concerning rational choice under risk establishes the conditions for the existence of utility function with the EU property that represents the DM's preference relation. It states that whenever the above three axioms are satisfied, the behavior of a DM that acts in accordance with her preferences can be represented as a maximization of an EU function. It states nothing about how common utility functions with the EU property are. All it says is that whenever those three axioms about the preference relation are fulfilled, there exists a utility function with the EU property that represents the relation and, to the extent the DM acts according to her preferences, her behavior can be seen as EU maximization.

When compared with decision making under certainty, the risk modality in fact introduces only one new axiom, the first two are already present in the axiomatization of the decision making under certainty. It should be observed, though, that these two axioms are now extended to the domain of risky prospects. Forming a preference order over certain outcomes is in many cases much less demanding than doing the same for risky prospects (lotteries). In return to adding a new axiom – monotonicity in prizes – we, however, get a considerably more specific utility function than in the case of certainty. To wit, the three axioms together guarantee the existence of a utility function with the EU property. Thus, not only do we get to know the order of the options in terms of utility but we also learn how the DM evaluates risky options in terms of the certain outcomes that constitute – with given probabilities – the prospects.

As in the case of certainty, also under risk the representation theorem is accompanied with a theorem that shows the uniqueness of the method of assigning utility values to risky prospects. The theorem says that the utility assignment is unique up to affine transformations. In other words, all utility functions that result from a given function, when its values are multiplied by a constant and another (possibly the same) constant is added to the products, is also a utility function. This means that if u is a utility function that satisfies the three axioms of the representation theorem, then v is also an equally valid utility function if

$$v(x) = k \times u(x) + b \tag{3.2}$$

where k and b are constants with k > 0. Here x denotes an option under consideration. Thus, there are infinitely many utility functions representing the same preference relation over risky prospects even though the relation satisfies all three axioms. However, once the zero point and unit of the utility scale are fixed, this infinity reduces to unity, i.e. when zero point and unit are fixed only one utility function remains that represents the DM's preferences.

In the most general setting, namely that of uncertainty, an analogous axiomatization exists (see Harsanyi 1977: 41–47, for proofs; see also Anscombe and Aumann 1963). A complicating factor is the absence of objective probabilities. Instead, the representation theorem establishes the conditions for the existence of a utility function with the *subjective expected utility (SEU) property*. We are now dealing with uncertain prospects, that is, unknown probability distributions over certain outcomes. It is helpful to think of these prospects as outcome scenarios where the materialization of each outcome is conditioned by some events and the probability of these events is unknown. For example, an uncertain prospect might be one in which one wins 10 euros if team A wins an ice-hockey match, but loses 1 euro if the game ends in a tie or team B wins. As in certainty and risk modalities, we try to determine which conditions on preferences over uncertain prospects have to be fulfilled to guarantee the existence of a utility function that represents those preferences and has, moreover, the SEU property.

Robert J. Aumann (born 1930) is one of the most influential game theorists of modern times. His contributions extend to many areas of game theory: solution concepts, classifications of games, repeated games, market games. Several age cohorts of leading game theorists have been trained under his supervision. Aumann's most important book-length works are *Values of Non-Atomic Games* (with Lloyd Shapley) (1974), *Lectures on Game Theory* (1989), *Repeated Games with Incomplete Information* (with Michael Maschler) (1995) and *Collected Papers* (2000). In 2005 he became a Nobel Memorial Prize winner in economics.

The first axiom requires that the DM has a complete and transitive preference relation over uncertain prospects. That is, for any pair of such prospects, she is able to say which one is at least as preferable as the other. Furthermore, this preference relation has to be transitive. The second axiom requires that the DM's utility function over risky prospects has the EU property. This is to say that the axioms pertaining to the risk modality have to be fulfilled. The third axiom is called the monotonicity in prizes for uncertain prospects or sure thing principle for uncertain prospects (Harsanyi 1977: 44). It states that whenever two prospects have identical conditioning events (such as victory, loss or tie) and the former results in at least as preferable payoffs as the latter under each contingency, then the former prospect is preferred to the latter.

The representation theorem establishes that the satisfaction of the above three axioms by a DM's preference relation is equivalent to an observer being able to represent her preferences by a utility function that assigns uncertain prospects utility values according to the SEU principle. This principle gives each prospect the utility value which is a weighted average of the utilities possibly associated with the prospect using as weights the subjective probabilities of the conditioning events. Hence, a DM who acts according to her preferences and whose preferences satisfy those axioms is *ipso facto* an SEU maximizer, that is, is in fact maximizing her expected utility using as probability weights her subjective judgments of the probability of the conditioning events.

As in the case of certainty and risk, the principle of assigning utility values to uncertain prospects is not unique; there are literally an infinite number of equally justifiable utility assignments. However, as in the case of risk, once the zero point and the unit of utility is fixed, there is only one way of attaching utilities that satisfies the three axioms. Hence, the utilities under risk and uncertainty are called *cardinal utilities* in contradistinction to ordinal ones. Cardinal scale measurements are distinguishable from ordinal ones in guaranteeing one property that remains invariant regardless of the way in which utilities are assigned. To wit, the ratio of differences between measurements is the same regardless of which cardinal measurement is used. To see this, consider two cardinal utility functions; u and v defined by equation (3.2). Let us now assign utilities to four options x, y, z and w using v and measure the ratio of the utility difference between the first two to the utility difference of the latter two options.

$$\frac{v(x) - v(y)}{v(z) - v(w)} = \frac{k \times (u(x) + b) - k \times (u(y) + b)}{k \times (u(z) + b) - k \times (u(w) + b)} = \frac{u(x) - u(y)}{u(z) - u(w)}$$

Thus, it turns out that the ratio of utility differences does not change when one cardinal measure is replaced with another. This is the defining property of cardinal scale measurement.

We have now outlined the basic model of rational decision maker, *homo œconomicus*. The crucial – and sole – defining feature is the action in accordance with preferences. This and some fairly mild assumptions regarding preferences ensure that rationality is tantamount to utility maximization. Thus, the question of how large a portion of human action is based on utility maximization turns on the extent to which those assumptions regarding preferences characterize our opinions. So, the question of whether utility maximization is the guiding principle of human action does not require an *a priori* answer, but depends on empirical evidence. It is, after all, an empirical question to determine to what extent people's preferences can be expressed in terms of preference relations having certain formal properties (completeness, transitivity).

Despite their intuitive plausibility the axioms of rational behavior have been challenged since empirical evidence seems to suggest that reasonable people often deviate from the dictates of the EU or SEU maximization. In the next chapter we shall turn to some of these challenges.

3.7 Suggested reading

Two volumes written nearly half a century ago make still very pleasant and informative reading as introductions to decision theory: Luce and Raiffa (1957) and Chernoff and Moses (1959). Axiomatic characterizations are also discussed in Harsanyi (1977). The concept of thin rationality is introduced in Elster (1983). Informative assessments of rational choice explanations are given by Dowding (1995) and Blais (2000). The former focuses on coalition formation and the latter on the act of voting. The distinction between decision theory and decision analysis is pursued in Raiffa (1994). Useful overviews are French and Xie (1994) as well as Schoemaker and Russo (1994). All three last mentioned articles are included in Ríos (1994).

4 Economic man under attack

As we have seen, rational behavior can, under a few relatively undemanding conditions, be seen as utility maximization. That is, people who act in accordance with their preferences and whose preferences can be represented by complete and transitive preference relations act as if they were maximizing the value of their utility function. It is sometimes argued that very often people just do not aim at maximizing their own utilities. Rather, they aim at guaranteeing the best possible outcomes for their families, children, pets etc. So – the argument goes – the model of economic man is doomed to fail for the simple reason that it applies to a very restricted set of circumstances, namely to the transactions of economic actors. This argument, which appears in various camouflages in the literature, is based on a misunderstanding of thin rationality by extending an example of what a person might want to maximize, profit or wealth, to the entire spectrum of human behavior. Utility is not necessarily measured in monetary terms. Person 1's preference over outcomes or the acts leading to them might well be conditional upon person 2's expressed or anticipated happiness or pleasure under those outcomes. Consequently, the argument of person 1's utility function might be a variable or set of variables that have very little or nothing to do with person 1's income or welfare level in various outcomes.

The criticism of the rational choice theory that equates rationality with egoism is, thus, based on a misunderstanding. Essentially more serious critique against the theory originates from studies that purport to show that reasonable people tend to deviate from the predictions of the theory in a systematic fashion. In other words, under certain types of environments one can expect that deviations from EU or SEU maximization are frequently encountered. Moreover, not only are the deviations rather commonplace, but they seem to make sense, intuitively speaking.

4.1 Classic paradoxes

The first serious criticism against the expected utility theory was presented much prior to the axiomatization of the theory itself. The decision setting called the *St. Petersburg paradox* was discussed by Daniel Bernoulli in 1738 (see Bernoulli 1954 and Bernoulli 1968 for English translations).[14] Suppose that a person, call him Peter, tosses a coin until heads face up. He promises to pay another person, Paul, 1 ducat if heads show on the first throw, 2 ducats if heads show on the second, 4 ducats if heads show on the third, etc.[15] The problem is to determine Paul's rational payoff expectation or alternatively the amount he should be willing to pay to participate in the coin tossing game. The expected payoff is:

$$E(\text{payoff}) = \frac{1}{2} \times 1 + \frac{1}{4} \times 2 + \frac{1}{8} \times 4 + \cdots = \frac{1}{2} + \frac{1}{2} + \frac{1}{2} + \cdots$$

Obviously, the expected payoff is infinite. Thus, Paul should be willing to pay any amount of money he can get his hands on to participate. Yet, regardless of the rate at which the ducat is converted into the currencies of our time, very few of us would be willing to pay even the weekly salary for the opportunity to take Paul's place. Does this demonstrate that we are irrational? No, says Daniel Bernoulli, since our expected utility is not the same as the expected payoff. Rather, 'the utility resulting from any small increase in wealth will be inversely proportionate to the quantity of goods previously possessed' (Bernoulli 1968: 17). In his argument, Bernoulli resorts to logarithmic utility function so that

$$u(x) = \log(x)$$

Here, however, x includes the wealth already in the possession of the decision maker, i.e. Paul. Supposing that Paul is in the possession of 50,000 ducats, his expected utility of participating in Peter's game is:

$$u(50{,}000 + y) = \frac{1}{2} \times u(50{,}000 + 1) + \frac{1}{4} \times u(50{,}000 + 2) + \frac{1}{8}$$
$$\times u(50{,}000 + 4) + \cdots$$
$$= \frac{1}{2} \log(50{,}001) + \frac{1}{4} \log(50{,}002) + \frac{1}{8} \log(50{,}004) + \cdots$$

Even though the payoff sum increases without a limit, the sum of weighted logarithms approaches a finite limit. Solving for y yields the value of roughly 9 ducats (Machina 1987: 123). In other words, the price Paul should be willing to pay for participation is at most 9 ducats.

The crux in resolving the St. Petersburg paradox is the introduction of the concept of utility and the *principle of decreasing marginal returns*: the higher the existing utility level, the smaller the utility increase that accompanies a fixed payoff increase. This principle can be seen to underlie, for example, progressive income taxation: the loss of a given amount of income causes a smaller utility loss at higher income levels than at smaller ones. Stated in a somewhat different fashion: utility is typically not linear in money. If one is very poor, the value of an additional euro is relatively large, but decreases with the increase of the amount of wealth. The curve depicting utility as a function of income is thus normally concave upwards.

Of more recent origin is the paradox that bears the name of the French Nobel laureate Maurice Allais (1953). In its standard version, the paradox appears in a choice situation where one is invited to first choose one of two risky prospects and thereafter to make another choice between two other risky prospects. By defining the prospects in a suitable way, Allais was able to observe choice behavior which is not compatible with the EU maximizing view. Consider first prospects r_1 and r_2 defined as:

$$r_1 = (1,000,000, 1.0)$$

$$r_2 = (5,000,000, 0.10; 1,000,000, 0.89; 0, 0.01)$$

The former prospect gives the payoff of one million euro (the currency can be chosen freely) with a probability of one, while the latter gives a five times larger payoff with a probability of 0.1, the payoff of one million with a probability of 0.89 and the zero payoff with a probability of 0.01.

Consider another pair of risky[16] prospects: r_3 and r_4.

$$r_3 = (5,000,000, 0.10; 0, 0.90)$$

$$r_4 = (1,000,000, 0.11; 0, 0.89)$$

These are both genuine (that is, non-trivial) risky prospects. Now the paradox Allais observed consists of the empirical finding that when asked to choose between r_1 and r_2 there was a tendency among his experimental subjects to choose the former and when faced with the choice between r_3 and r_4 they also tended to end up with the former. Yet, this choice behavior can be shown to be inconsistent with EU maximization. To see this, let us compute the expected utilities of the four risky prospects. If the decision maker is an EU maximizer, her choice behavior should reflect this.

$$EU(r_1) = 1 \times u(1,000,000)$$

$$EU(r_2) = 0.10 \times u(5,000,000) + 0.89 \times u(1,000,000) + 0.01 \times u(0)$$

$$EU(r_3) = 0.10 \times u(5,000,000) + 0.90 \times u(0)$$

$$EU(r_4) = 0.11 \times u(1,000,000) + 0.89 \times u(0)$$

Now, if one prefers r_1 to r_2 and is an EU maximizer, this means that

$$u(1,000,000) > 0.10 \times u(5,000,000) + 0.89 \times u(1,000,000) + 0.01 \times u(0)$$

Solving for $u(1,000,000)$ yields:

$$u(1,000,000) > \frac{0.10 \times u(5,000,000) + 0.01 \times u(0)}{0.11} \qquad (4.3)$$

If, on the other hand, r_3 is preferred to r_4, as we assumed, we get:

$$0.10 \times u(5,000,000) + 0.90 \times u(0) > 0.11 \times u(1,000,000) + 0.89 \times u(0)$$

and thus

$$u(1,000,000) < \frac{0.10 \times u(5,000,000) + 0.01 \times u(0)}{0.11} \qquad (4.4)$$

Inequality (4.1) says exactly the opposite of what (4.2) asserts. This means that our assumption regarding EU maximization cannot hold for a decision maker whose preferences we have considered.

The crux of the paradox is not the empirical frequency of its occurrence, but the fact that the choice behavior that gives rise to it is intuitively plausible.[17] There is nothing strange in choosing r_1 rather than r_2 and r_3 rather than r_4. What makes r_1 attractive *vis-à-vis* r_2 is that it guarantees a sizable payoff with certainty, whereas r_2 may lead to a zero payoff, albeit with a very small probability. In the latter pair, on the other hand, the most likely outcome under both prospects is that the payoff is zero. Moreover, the probability difference of winning something is nearly non-existent. Thus, it makes sense to choose the option that gives a much larger payoff.

Maurice Allais (born 1911) is a French economist who in the 1940s published two works which provided the main motivation for the Nobel Committee to nominate him the Nobel Memorial Laureate in economics in 1988. The works are *A la recherche dune discipline économique, première partie: L'économique pure* (1943) and *Économie et intérêt* (1947). The former deals *i.a.* with the optimality properties of market equilibria extending and formalizing the earlier results of Adam Smith, Léon Walras and Vilfredo Pareto. The latter focuses on capital accumulation and transaction cost-induced demand for money (Vane and Mulhearn 2005: 168). The experiments on choice behavior under uncertainty were conducted after the publication of these major works.

There is yet another decision making paradox that can be called classic, namely *Ellsberg's paradox*. As Allais' paradox also this one constitutes a violation of EU maximization. Its setting, however, differs from Allais' in focusing on uncertain rather than risky prospects. Consider a jar containing altogether 90 balls, 30 of which are red. The remaining 60 consist of white and blue balls in an unknown proportion. You are asked to choose an uncertain prospect from a pair of prospects

Table 4.1 Ellberg's paradox

	Color (and number) of balls		
	Red	White or blue (60)	
Options	(30)	White	Blue
1	$100	$0	$0
2	$0	$0	$100
3	$100	$100	$0
4	$0	$100	$100

and thereafter pick a ball from the jar at random. Its color together with your choice of prospect determines your payoff. Then the procedure is repeated with another pair of uncertain prospects, i.e. you make your choice of prospect and pick a ball again.[18] The first pair of prospects consists of 1 and 2, the other consisting of prospects 3 and 4. Prospect 1 gives you $100 if the ball you pick happens to be red, otherwise you get nothing. Prospect 2 gives you $100 if the ball is blue, but nothing otherwise.

Prospect 3 gives you $100 if the ball is either red or white. If it is blue this prospect gives you nothing. Prospect 4 finally results in payoff $100 if the ball is either white or blue. Otherwise the prospect gives you nothing. The payoffs related to prospects are summarized in Table 4.1.

Daniel Ellsberg (born 1931), American scholar and political activist, is best-known among the general public for his role in the Watergate scandal that led to the resignation of President Richard M. Nixon in the early 1970s. Ellsberg wrote his PhD thesis on risk, ambiguity and decision making in the early 1960s (published as a book in 2001). He then worked in the RAND Corporation as a strategic analyst focusing mainly on nuclear war issues and decisions in crisis situations. His work on the war in Vietnam brought him to the Defense and State Departments of the US government. He contributed to a secret study on the background of and the reasons for the Vietnam war. This study, later known as *The Pentagon Papers*, led to a substantial erosion of the support of the Vietnam war. Recently, Ellsberg has strongly protested the US invasion of Iraq.

In his experiments, Ellsberg (1961) found that many people would choose 1 over 2, but 4 over 3. This choice behavior is inconsistent with EU maximization. To see this, let the probability of blue balls be q. Since we know that the probability of a red ball being drawn is 1/3, the probability of a white ball is $2/3 - q$. Let us assume that the utility of 0 payoff equals 0. Now, for an EU maximizer the preference of option 1 over option 2 entails:

$$1/3 \times u(\$100) + 2/3 \times u(\$0) > 1/3 \times u(\$0) + (2/3 - q) \times u(\$0) + q \times u(\$100)$$

or

$$1/3 \times u(\$100) > q \times u(\$100) \tag{4.5}$$

On the other hand, the preference of option 4 over option 3 yields:

$$2/3 \times u(\$100) + 1/3 \times u(\$0) > 1/3 \times u(\$100) + (2/3 - q) \times u(\$100)$$
$$+ q \times u(\$0),$$

whereupon we get:

$$q \times u(\$100) > 1/3 \times u(\$100)$$

which contradicts the inequality of equation (4.5).

Allais' and Ellsberg's paradoxes show that intuitively reasonable behavior may result in choices that do not maximize the expected utility of the decision maker. This then means that at least one of the axioms discussed in the preceding sections has been violated. A common culprit or suspect has been the monotonicity in prizes or sure-thing principle. There is also experimental evidence that points to difficulty in forming transitive preference relation over risky prospects. Consider the following list of risky prospects:

1. ($5.00, 7/24; $0, 17/24)
2. ($4.75, 8/24; $0, 16/24)
3. ($4.50, 9/24; $0, 15/24)
4. ($4.25, 10/24; $0, 14/24)
5. ($4.00, 11/24; $0, 13/24)

The expected values of payoffs increase from top to bottom (from value $1.46 to $1.83). Tversky (1969) found in his experiments that a sizable subgroup of his experimental subjects exhibited behavior whereby in adjacent pairwise choices, they preferred the prospect with the higher maximum value (and smaller expected payoff), but in the comparison between the extreme prospects preferred the one with the higher probability of winning (and higher expected value). As an example, one could single out behavior preferring the first prospect to the second one, the second to the third one, the third to the fourth one, the fourth to the fifth one and, yet, the fifth prospect to the first. These subjects thus exhibited intransitive preference relations.

Yet, the behavior is by no means intuitively irrational. The fact that the consecutive comparisons end up with the higher prospect of being preferred to the lower one can be explained by the minuscule difference in probabilities in contrast to easily distinguishable payoff differences. However, when the prospects are further apart, the probability differences also enter the calculus. Thus, the fifth prospect offers a probability of nearly 50% of winning something, while the first option contains less than one-thirds of the probability for a non-zero payoff.

One should not, however, lose sight of an important consequence of preference intransitivity, namely that a person with intransitive preferences can be financially exploited almost *ad libitum*. Suppose that Mr Smith is offered a ticket to one of the following sports events: (1) Liverpool vs. Manchester United football game, (2) New York Islanders vs. Calgary Flames ice hockey game or (3) Real Madrid vs. Barcelona football game. Smith likes (1) more than (2) and (2) more than (3), but when faced with the choice between (1) and (3), he prefers (3). He might consider football typically more boring than ice hockey (which explains his preference of (2) to (3)), but he anticipates that the atmosphere at Liverpool's home ground is likely to be intense enough to turn his preference of games around. On the other hand, he finds Spanish football much more to his liking than English football. Hence, given a choice between the two football matches he chooses (3). Clearly, Smith's preference relation is intransitive.

Suppose now that Mr Jones has a ticket to each of these three events. He gives Smith one of them, say (1). Smith is obviously pleased, but knowing that Jones also has tickets to the other events, offers to give Jones the ticket back and give him $x if Jones gives him a ticket to (3). After all, he prefers (3) to (1). Jones accepts the offer. While counting his money he reminds Smith that he also has a ticket to (2) which he is willing to impart if Smith pays him something and gives back his ticket to (3). Smith accepts the offer, receives a ticket to (2) and gives Jones $y plus the ticket to (3). Jones now has $x + y and tickets to (1) and (3). Smith realizes that he prefers (1) to (2) and thus offers to give Jones his ticket to (2) back sweetened with a small amount, say $z, in cash if Jones gives him a ticket to (1). We have now reached the situation we started from, namely Jones giving Smith a ticket to (1). There is a crucial difference, though: Jones has become $x + y + z richer on the way. The process may be continued as long as Smith has any money left to offer. This process is called the *money pump*. It shows that no matter how intuitively plausible an intransitive preference relation may be in some circumstances, following it in one's choice behavior is a receipt of economic disaster.

Not just transitivity but also the completeness of preference relation may come into question. A well-known case where completeness seems to fail is the *preference reversal phenomenon* (Lichtenstein and Slovic 1971). The phenomenon occurs when a person says that she prefers option A to option B, but at the same time indicates that she is prepared to pay more for B than for A. The phenomenon is paradoxical to the extent that very often willingness to pay is used as an indicator – indeed the sole indicator – of preference.

Figure 4.1 represents two lotteries, the left and right circle. Each lottery involves a random throw of a dart. In the left lottery the payoff is $0 if the dart hits the vertical line shown in the figure. Otherwise the payoff is $4 in the left lottery. The lottery on the right, in turn, gives $16 if the dart lands on the smaller area of the circle. Otherwise, there is a zero payoff.

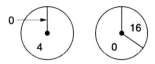

Figure 4.1 The preference reversal experiment.

Experimental evidence seems to suggest that when asked which of the two lotteries the experimental subjects prefer, a sizable portion of them indicate preference for the left lottery. However, when asked how much the same subjects would be willing to pay for participating in each lottery, the right lottery seems to be given a higher price (see also Grether and Plott 1979). Obviously the willingness to pay cannot always be used as a synonym for preference. An open question still, more than 30 years after the initial observations of preference reversal, is to what extent economic and political phenomena are vulnerable to it. Yet, some attempts to account for them have been made. We shall discuss one such attempt shortly.

Charles R. Plott (born 1938), an American economist and political scientists, is one of the pioneers of laboratory experimentation of choice behavior, markets and other socio-economic mechanisms. Plott has also made important contributions to axiomatic social choice theory and to the study of regulatory and de-regulation policies. He has established a leading center of experimental economics at California Institute of Technology in Pasadena. Some of his most important works are collected in *Collected Papers on the Experimental Foundations of Economics and Political Science*, vols 1–3 (2001). Another important text is *The Allocation of Scarce Resources* (with David Grether and Mark Isaac) (1989).

4.2 The prospect theory

The significance of the preceding puzzling findings is in their systematic nature. In other words, the observations cannot be accounted for by referring to random variation in human behavior patterns. Rather the occurrences seem to have some invariant characteristics. Yet, the findings referred to above are by no means universal. Indeed, in most cases it is only a minority of experimental subjects that exhibits the behavior that is inconsistent with the EU theory. With this caveat in mind, we now briefly review some of the literature that has evolved in the decision making field in an effort to account for the findings.

Prospect theory is based on the idea that the deviations from EU maximization observed in experimental settings are due to differences the experimental subjects perceive in prospects that are associated with identical expected utility values. For example, suppose that a person's utility for money is of the form: $u(x) = x$ where x is a given sum of money. Now it may well be the case that this person sees a clear difference between receiving 50 euro and participating in a lottery that gives her the same amount in expected value, e.g. as a result of the toss of a fair coin. In other words, the person may perceive that $u(50) \neq \frac{1}{2} u(100) + \frac{1}{2} u(0)$.

If she thinks that the left-hand side is greater than the right-hand one, she is *risk averse*. If the converse is true, she is a *risk taker*. Just in case she finds both sides equal, she is risk-neutral. These three possibilities are called *risk postures*.

Kahneman and Tversky (1979) argue that the observed systematic deviations from EU maximization behavior are due to various aspects of prospects that are not taken into account in EU calculus. These aspects are reflected in three effects observable in experiments. The first is called the *certainty effect*. An instance of this effect can be seen in the Allais paradox discussed in the preceding section. In the comparison between r_1 and r_2 the first thing that strikes the observer is that r_1 is, in fact, not risky at all, but guarantees a large payoff with certainty. In the second comparison, namely that between r_3 and r_4, the EU considerations call for the choice of the former under the rather reasonable assumption that the utility of 10% chance of $5,000,000 is greater than the utility of 11% chance of $1,000,000. In the latter pair of prospects both are genuinely risky, while in the former pair one is a certain prospect.

Daniel Kahneman (born 1934) and Amos Tversky (1937–1996) developed the prospect theory which accounts for the deviations of choices from the predictions based on expected utility maximization under risk. Over two decades, these two psychologists singled out several intuition-based principles or heuristics and systematic biases in human decision making. Kahneman has also studied individuals' perceptions of fairness in economic transactions. Tversky's interests extended to the foundations of measurement theory as well. Their main works can be found in two collections: *Judgment under Uncertainty: Heuristics and Biases* (Kahneman *et al.* 1982) and *Choices, Values and Frames* (Kahneman and Tversky, 2000). Kahneman became a Nobel Memorial Laureate in economics in 2002.

One of the principles of prospect theory states that prospects involving certainty get special treatment in decision makers' calculus: their attractiveness exceeds that of risky prospects with the same expected utility. This, however, holds only for utility gains. Another finding or effect found by Kahneman and Tversky is related to losses. It is called the *reflection effect*. It states that the risk posture changes when the payoffs are seen as losses compared to situations where they are seen as gains. Consider for example a person who exhibits risk aversion when confronted with the choice between two options: (1) she can participate in a lottery that gives her 100 euro with a probability of 0.5 and nothing with a probability of 0.5, and (2) she is given 50 euro. Being risk-averse means that she will choose option (2). Suppose now that the same person is presented a choice between (3) and (4) where (3) is the prospect of losing 100 euro with a probability of 0.5 and losing nothing with a probability of 0.5 and (4) means losing 50 euro with certainty. In the Kahneman and Tversky experiments it turned out that a majority of subjects was risk-averse when the options involve gains, but risk-acceptant when they involve losses. In other words, in dealing with losses the subjects tended to choose (3) rather than (4).

The prospect theory contains yet another effect, namely the *isolation effect* or *framing*. This is, in fact, a combination of the two preceding effects. It occurs whenever the choice behavior regarding risky prospects is changed by how the options are presented to the decision maker. The isolation effect is based on the fact that risky options can be presented in several ways. If the way in which the option is presented changes its probability of being chosen by the decision maker, then we have an instance of the effect. Consider, for example, the risky option $r_5 = (100, 0.5; 0, 0.5)$. It can be presented as a two-stage prospect where in the first stage the experimental subject is given 50 euro and in the second stage she participates in the following lottery $r_6 = (50, 0.5; -50, 0.5)$. Or, it can be presented as a three-stage prospect where the subject is given 50 euro in the first stage, another 50 euro in the second stage and in the third stage she participates in the lottery $r_7 = (0, 0.5; -100, 0.5)$.

In one of their experiments, Kahneman and Tversky (1979) confronted half of their experimental subjects with the choice between options (i) and (ii) and the other half with the choice between (iii) and (iv). Option (i) gives each subject first 1000 and then gives her a ticket to a lottery which gives an additional payoff of 1000 with probability 1/2 and nothing with probability 1/2. Option (ii) also gives the subject first 1000, but then gives an additional 500 with certainty. Option (iii) gives the subject first 2000 and then assigns her the lottery with payoffs -1000 and 0, each with probability 1/2. Option (iv) similarly gives the subject first 2000, but withdraws -500 from this with certainty. An overwhelming majority of Kahneman and Tversky's experimental subjects preferred (ii) to (i) and a somewhat smaller majority preferred (iii) to (iv). Yet, it can be seen that (i) is in fact identical with (iii) and (ii) is identical with (iv). Yet, the preference of the majority of subjects seems to reverse depending on the way the options are framed.

The preference for (ii) over (i) is consistent with risk aversion on the positive domain, i.e. when the payoffs are gains rather than losses. The preference for (iii) over (iv), on the other hand, indicates risk acceptance on the negative domain, i.e. with negative payoffs. In the latter choice situation the subjects are already in the possession of the 2000 given to them at the outset. Hence they are making choices which at best result in them being able to hold on to the 2000.

Kahneman and Tversky's prospect theory accounts for the above effects in qualitative terms. Its basic features are embodied in Figure 4.2. The horizontal axis represents positive (gains) and negative (losses) payoffs, while the vertical axis stands for the subjective value assigned to each payoff. The curve

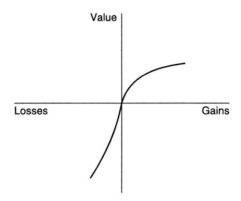

Figure 4.2 Valuation of gains and losses according to prospect theory.

representing prospect valuations according to the prospect theory has the following characteristics:

- it is monotonically non-decreasing in the positive domain,
- it reflects diminishing marginal valuations on the positive domain (i.e. the utility increments corresponding identical payoff increments become smaller when moving from left to right),
- it expresses risk aversion on the positive domain,
- it is steeper in the negative than in the positive domain (i.e. similar pay-off increments are accompanied with much larger utility increments in the negative domain than in the positive one), and
- it reflects risk acceptance in the negative domain.

In essence, the prospect theory implies that the observed deviations from EU maximization are not random but systematic responses to uncertainty. It states that people tend to value certain gains more than risky prospects resulting in identical gains in expected value. Similarly it states that, given a fixed certain loss, we are more willing to risk even higher losses if these are accompanied with real chances of losing nothing. It also says that losses loom larger than gains with identical absolute value.

4.3   Further anomalies

The prospect theory explains some crucial features of behavior patterns under risk. In particular, it accounts for the special 'treatment' that options with certain payoffs enjoy in choice behavior. Similarly, the effects of the framing of options are clearly revealed in this theory. In a way, the prospect theory is an attempt to improve upon EU maximization just as the introduction of utilities helps to understand certain anomalies, such as the St. Petersburg paradox. Prospect theory argues that the utility values of alternatives are relative in an important sense.

That's to say, the utility of an alternative varies with the reference point of the decision maker. If she is looking at an alternative as a gain with respect to her present level of welfare, she is likely to exhibit risk aversion, while she accepts risk if she is dealing with losses. By describing a risky prospect in different ways one is able to move the reference point of the decision maker, thus, making downright contradictory choices intelligible. This is analogous to transforming the EU values of options by taking into account the reference point with respect to which the options are evaluated.

None the less, there is a fundamental similarity between EU maximization and prospect theory, namely in both cases the choice behavior is explained in terms of something that pertains to the options at hand. The options are seen as possessing a property – call it *attractiveness* – that determines the choices. The underlying principle of choice is the same in both theories: the decision makers choose alternatives that are most attractive and the attractiveness is a property of options as such.

There are, however, other choice patterns contradicting EU maximization that cannot be accounted for by the prospect theory. An important class of those patterns consists of behaviors that seem to condition the choices not only on reference points but also on the set of options available. In other words, there are situations in which the choices seem to depend not only on the properties of the options but also on which other options are available. This context-dependence has been observed, for example, in consumer choice experiments (Huber *et al.* 1982; Simonson 1989; Shafir *et al.* 1989, 1990, 2000; Nurmi 1998: 32–37).

Two effects are of particular interest since they suggest that not only pairs of alternatives, but the entire choice context – the entire alternative set, the position of alternatives with respect to 'third' ones – affects the choice behavior. The first one pertains to situations where one of the available alternatives can be seen as a compromise between the others. A three-alternative case is depicted in Figure 4.3. Suppose that alternatives X, Y and Z are described in terms of two properties represented by the horizontal and vertical axis. The alternatives

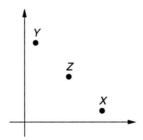

Figure 4.3 Compromise effect.

could be, for example, consumer goods and the axes could represent aesthetic and economic value so that larger coordinate values represent superior values on both dimensions. X is thus the best alternative in aesthetic and Y in economic terms. Suppose now that X is removed and the experimental subject is asked to choose either Y or Z. Once she has made her choice, X is added to the figure and she is asked to choose from the set of all three alternatives in the indicated configuration. There is some evidence that the probability of Z being chosen *vis-à-vis* Y is higher when X is present than when it is absent. This is known as the *compromise effect* for the obvious reason that in the three-alternative configuration Z can be seen as a compromise alternative: better than Y in terms of aesthetic but not economic value, and better than X in economic but not in aesthetic value.

Compromise solutions are quite common in politics, but they appear also in other group choice situations. In selecting a departmental secretary, for example, some academics might emphasize the applicants' language skills, while others might appreciate mainly their text-processing prowess. It is not difficult to envision a setting where three applicants X, Y and Z can be placed in a two-dimensional space as in Figure 4.3, with the horizontal axis representing the level of knowledge of languages and the vertical one the degree of mastery of text-processing techniques. It might well be that Z's chances of being elected are improved *vis-à-vis* Y when X is present from what they would have been had X not applied. The presence of X among applicants might call attention to the linguistic skills dimension and, thus, indirectly to the fact that Z is not the worst applicant on either dimension. Both X and Y are: X on the text-processing skills dimension and Y on the linguistic capability one.

Another effect that pertains to context-dependence of choices is exemplified in Figure 4.4. As Figure 4.3, this figure should also be considered together with another one where one of the alternatives has been removed. In Figure 4.4, alternative X represents a better alternative than Z both in horizontal and vertical dimension. It can, thus, be said to dominate Z. Alternative Y, in contrast, although superior to Z on the vertical dimension is inferior to the latter on the horizontal dimension. Hence, Y does not dominate Z nor does Z dominate Y.

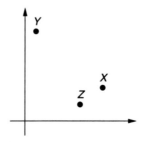

Figure 4.4 Asymmetric domination.

Consider now Figure 4.4 without alternative Z. In this setting one alternative is better than the other on one dimension and worse than the other on the other dimension. The superiority of X or Y depends on the weight assigned to the dimensions: if the vertical dimension is given the primary weight, then Y is better, but if the horizontal dimension is the dominant one, then X is better. With the introduction of Z the situation changes. There is now one contestant alternative, namely Z, that is defeated by one, but only one of the others, namely X. Hence, it could be argued that X is better than Y in virtue of defeating (dominating) something that Y cannot defeat. Indeed, this argumentation would seem to underlie what is known as the *asymmetric domination effect*, i.e. the observation that in situations resembling that of Figure 4.4, individuals' probability of choosing X rather than Y is higher than their probability of choosing X rather than Y in the setting where Z has been removed.

As the compromise effect, that of asymmetric domination also makes sense, intuitively speaking. The notion of one alternative being better than another often has to do with winning some kind of contest. When one alternative dominates another – as X does Z in Figure 4.4 – it can be seen as winning a pairwise contest. If the idea of overall winning is one in which the best alternative is the one that defeats as many others as possible, then it is natural to deem X better than Y since it defeats Z, while Y does not.

What compromise and asymmetric domination effects purport to demonstrate is that there are circumstances under which plausible choices seem to depend on the entire choice situation. Thus, no theory that makes choices contingent on properties of alternatives can account for these choices. If the probability of X being chosen rather than Y is dependent on whether Z is available or not (as in Figure 4.4), then obviously the choice is not determined solely by properties of X and Y. It is worth pointing out that prospect theory is also vulnerable to this type of criticism.

The crucial question, however, is whether the choices that constitute the compromise and asymmetric domination effect pertain to rationality of the choices. That these choices make intuitive sense in some circumstances is not the primary issue. Rather one should ask: is the choice of a 'compromise' alternative always rational? Similarly, is it always rational to pick of two alternatives the one that dominates a third, provided that the other one does not? It seems that the answer to both questions has to be 'no'. Although there are circumstances under which such choices can be defended as reasonable, it simply does not follow that those choices would always be rational. Consider the situation depicted in Figure 4.3 and assume that one of the dimensions, say the vertical one, represents a property that is essential for the success of the chooser, while the other, horizontal, dimension represents a property that is largely irrelevant. To continue the preceding example, suppose that the academic secretary is working in an English-speaking community and will be dealing only with text-processing tasks. Under these circumstances, language skills are largely irrelevant for the task at hand. Thus, choosing Y would seem the only rational choice, regardless of the presence or absence of X. Similarly, in the case of asymmetric domination, if one of the dimensions is largely irrelevant, the fact that one of the alternatives asymmetrically dominates a third one does not make its choice rational. What counts is which alternative is best on the essential dimension.[19]

The context-dependence of choice behavior, therefore, does not seem to challenge the standard maximization concept of rationality. Over the past few decades a considerable literature has emerged on other systematic violations of some of the basic assumptions of probability and decision theory (Kahneman *et al.* 1982; Kahneman and Tversky 2000). The most dramatic ones have been reviewed above. Now, how badly do all these other anomalies shatter the status of *homo œconomicus*? The scholarly community has not reached consensus on this. To the extent that the effects are systematic, they do, of course, call into question the descriptive and predictive value of the standard rationality assumption. The normative importance is, however, a different matter. Even though people systematically violate, say, the transitivity axiom in some risky contexts, the money pump argument still applies, i.e. these people lose money regardless of the outcomes of the conditioning events. Thus, one could argue that systematic violations of rationality are experimental peculiarities that do not survive in the real world. Learning from mistakes would wipe out behaviors that lead to systematic losses. Yet, some effect patterns are relatively frequent. Rather than considering them as unimportant peculiarities, their prevalence calls for the study of the general conditions under which they occur.

Nevertheless, it is fair to conclude with Grether and Plott (1979: 634): 'The fact that preference theory and related theories of optimization are subject to exception does not mean that they should be discarded. No alternative theory currently available appears to be capable of covering the same extremely broad range of phenomena.' Some 25 years later this conclusion still seems correct. All alternatives to the EU and SEU theory seem either more limited in scope or poorer in informative content.

The extensive literature on behavioral economics and experimental study of human decision processes has, however, demonstrated the limits of the standard rationality. Its field of application is the setting where choice is to be made under fixed institutional circumstances from a given set of alternatives. Political economy extends far beyond these types of settings. In particular, the emergence of the institutional settings themselves is often of interest, as are the processes whereby the alternative sets become 'given'. Nobel laureate Vernon L. Smith (2005: 135–150) distinguishes between two types of rationality: constructivist and ecological. The former is in line with the standard view of rationality in emphasizing conscious planning of choices through deliberate use of reason. The latter, in turn, emphasizes emergent outcomes, arrangements and institutions planned by no one and yet surviving and benefiting individuals and communities. The standard *homo œconomicus* clearly belongs to the constructivist type. It can, however, be used in analyzing and evaluating institutions and arrangements.

Vernon L. Smith (born 1927) is a pioneer in experimental economics. His first works in this field were published in the early 1960s. Of particular importance are his results on market institutions, most notably the findings demonstrating that markets seem to result in an equilibrium in a wide variety of experimentally controlled conditions. His results on the role of financial incentives in inducing rational behavior provide the experimental background for the mushrooming of various management incentive schemes in the modern corporate life. Smith's main results are reported in the three volumes of *Research in Experimental Economics* (1979, 1982, 1985). He was awarded the Nobel Memorial Prize in economics in 2002.

4.4   Suggested reading

The observed deviations from the EU principle have provided inspiration to the series of conferences entitled 'Foundations and Applications of Utility and Risk Theories'. The proceedings of these conferences – e.g. Allais and Hagen (1979), Munier (1988) and Munier and Shakun (1988) – contain many important contributions. Critical examinations of and theoretical alternatives to the EU theory have been proposed by several authors: Allais (1979), Binmore (1987) and (1988), Fishburn (1988), Kahneman and Tversky (1979), Machina (1982) and Simon (1972), to name the most prominent ones. More recent alternatives to EU theory are collected in Kahneman and Tversky (2000). The journal *Theory and Decision* is one of the main scholarly outlets in decision theoretical research.

5 Games: descriptions and solutions

Thus far our interest has been on individual decision making in environments characterized by the concept of state. The latter suggests that the environment is in a way passive, but capable of transiting from one state to another unbeknownst to the decision maker. Yet, it is assumed not to anticipate or react to the latter's choices. It is not even assumed to have priorities with regard to its own states or those resulting from the choices of the decision maker. It is, in a word, taken to be a non-strategic entity. Clearly, many settings in political economy do not fit this description. Entrepreneurs cannot assume that entering a new market will go unnoticed by the firms already operating in those markets. Political leaders typically design the campaigns explicitly for the purpose of attracting new supporters from the ranks of other parties. The representatives of the latter are an essential part of those designs. Indeed, almost all purposive action of some interest to political economy takes place in a strategic environment, i.e. one characterized by several goal-directed actors who are aware of the presence of each other and of the fact that the outcomes emerge out of the interactions taking place between them. Game theory provides the most important tools for modeling precisely strategic environments.

5.1 Games, game forms and strategies

To illustrate some basic concepts of game theory, let us consider a slightly modified version of an example discussed by Dutta (1999: 54–55). In 1996 the United Nations was in the process of electing the Secretary General for the period 1997–2001. One of the candidates for the office was Mr Boutros Boutros-Ghali, an Egyptian diplomat, who had already served as the Secretary General from 1992. He was facing two serious contestants, the Norwegian Prime Minister Mrs Gro Harlem Brundtland and a United Nations diplomat, Mr Kofi Annan of Ghana. As things turned out, the most important actors – 'kingmakers' – on the UN scene in this issue were the United States and the coalition of African countries. The US government was rumored to be in favor of a female Secretary and opposed to Boutros-Ghali, while the coalition wanted to continue the latter's term of office. From the media one could infer that the US had the following order of preference over candidates: *Brundtland* ≻ *Annan* ≻ *Boutros-Ghali*.

The African countries, in turn, had the preference: *Boutros-Ghali* ≻ *Annan* ≻ *Brundtland*.

In the election of the Secretary the UN resorts to a procedure that aims at guaranteeing that no voter ends up with her very worst alternative elected. A way to make sure that this will not happen is to give each voter a chance to veto a candidate. Suppose that the US goes first and vetoes one of the candidates. The African coalition may then veto one of the remaining candidates, whereupon the candidate who remains is the winner. Let us denote the choices of the US by A for Annan, B for Boutros-Ghali and H for Harlem Brundtland. For each choice by the US the African coalition can respond in two different ways. Hence, the number of available choices of the coalition is $2^3 = 8$. We denote these by triples of the type (BAB) where the first element B denotes the choice of the coalition if the US has vetoed A, the second element A denotes its choice if the US has vetoed B and the third element B its choice if the US vetoes H. Assume that the players get the utility value 1 if their favorite is elected, value 0 if their second-best alternative is elected and value −1 if their last-ranked candidate wins. We can form Table 5.1.

Table 5.1 UN Secretary General election game

<table>
<tr><td></td><td colspan="8" align="center">Coalition</td></tr>
<tr><td></td><td></td><td>BAA</td><td>BAB</td><td>BHA</td><td>BHB</td><td>HAA</td><td>HAB</td><td>HHA</td><td>HHB</td></tr>
<tr><td></td><td>A</td><td>1, −1</td><td>1, −1</td><td>1, −1</td><td>1, −1</td><td>−1, 1</td><td>−1, 1</td><td>−1, 1</td><td>−1, 1</td></tr>
<tr><td>USA</td><td>B</td><td>1, −1</td><td>1, −1</td><td>0, 0</td><td>0, 0</td><td>1, −1</td><td>1, −1</td><td>0, 0</td><td>0, 0</td></tr>
<tr><td></td><td>H</td><td>−1, 1</td><td>0, 0</td><td>−1, 1</td><td>0, 0</td><td>−1, 1</td><td>0, 0</td><td>−1, 1</td><td>0, 0</td></tr>
</table>

The rows of the matrix represent the choices of the US, while the columns stand for the alternatives open to the African coalition. In game theoretical terminology the rows and columns are called strategies. Sometimes a distinction is made between acts and strategies so that the former denote elementary behavior alternatives, while the latter embody more complex acts: rules of choosing acts under various circumstances (see e.g. Chernoff and Moses 1959). Thus, in the above matrix the US choices are acts, while those of the coalition are strategies since they are conditional on the US choices. In game theory it is, however, quite common not to make any distinction between acts, choices and strategies. In this text these concepts will be used interchangeably.

The entries of Table 5.1 represent all outcomes resulting from the US – or row player in this game – choosing one of its available acts and the African coalition – here the column player – also choosing one of its available strategies. For example, the entry at the intersection of the row *B* and column *BHA* stands for the outcome resulting from the US vetoing *B* and the coalition following the strategy *BHA* which calls for vetoing *H* if the US has vetoed *B*. So, the outcome is *A* since both *B* and *H* have been vetoed. Now, instead of 0, 0 one could write *A* on row *B*'s column *BHA*. This would reveal only the outcome resulting from the choices of players, not the value it carries to the players. If we are interested in the outcomes of choices rather than their value to the players, this would be a perfectly reasonable description of the choice situation. In fact, we would then be dealing with a *game form* rather than a game. A game differs from the game form by adding the information concerning the outcome values. Thus, Table 5.1 defines a two-player game.

The entry 0, 0 at the intersection of row *B* and column *BHA* indicates the value that the outcome *A* has for the players. By convention, the values are separated by a comma with the left digit denoting the value for the row player and the right digit the value for the column player. Table 5.1 gives an exhaustive account of the outcomes of the game in terms of the value that the outcomes are associated with in the players' opinion. This way of describing and defining a two-person game is called the *matrix form*. Sometimes it is also called the *strategic form* since it reveals all possible strategy combinations of players and indicates the resulting outcome values. The latter are often called *payoffs*.

Upon inspecting the entries of Table 5.1 we observe that in each cell the sum of entries equals zero. This feature defines a *zero-sum game*. In these games the players extract payoffs basically from each other: whatever is achieved by one player is lost by the other. The players obviously have a conflict of interest. Similar conflict characterizes all games where the sum of payoffs of each outcome is a constant. These are, accordingly, called *constant-sum games*.

We have now transformed an interaction situation into a form that is amenable to game-theoretic analysis. As in any scholarly activity, the aim is to make the player behavior intelligible *ex post* or predict what will happen *ex ante*. Let us begin with the prediction. Starting from the assumption that the players are rational in the thin sense, we look for strategy choices that lead to the best outcomes for the players. Looking along the rows and columns we observe that each choice of one player can lead to several different outcomes and payoffs. For example, the choice of *A* (i.e. vetoing Annan) by the US can lead to *B* or *H*. In other words, choosing *A* the US may come up with its best or worst outcome. Similarly, choosing *BAA* the African coalition may end up with either Brundtland or Boutros-Ghali, its worst or best candidate depending on whether the US vetoes Annan, Boutros-Ghali (both resulting in Brundtland) or Brundtland. These outcome possibilities express the *strategic uncertainty* facing the players when making their choices.

If there is a strategy that gives a player her best outcome no matter what the choice of the other player, there would be no reason to choose any other strategy. Not only would this strategy guarantee the player her best outcome, but it would also do away with strategic uncertainty. A rational player would almost by definition choose such a strategy. A glance at Table 5.1 reveals, however, that this prescription is not applicable. No row has only 1 entry as the left element in each column. Similarly, no column has only 1 entry as the right element in each row.

So, we have to look closer at the payoffs associated with the strategy choices. Let us consider the strategies in pairs to see if there is a way of telling which in each pair is superior to the other. Let us focus on the US strategies *A* and *B* first. We see that the former leads to a better outcome in two columns, while *B* is better in four other columns. In two columns the outcomes are the same regardless of whether A or B is chosen. Considering now A and H rows, we end up with a similar conclusion: the former leads to a better outcome for the US in four columns, while H is better in two. In two columns, the payoffs for the US are the same. The third pair of the US strategies, B and H, proceeds in the same fashion. Here we see, however, that B is better than H in six columns, while both strategies yield identical outcomes in two columns. Therefore, in the terminology of section 3.5 B weakly dominates H.

Thus, the answer to the question of which strategy would be best for the US is somewhat disappointing: it depends on the choice of the African coalition. What we can say, though, is that H is not the best strategy for the US since there is another strategy (B) that weakly dominates it. Let us now look at Table 5.1 from the viewpoint of the coalition. Now we are able to give a more informative answer. Comparing the two left-most strategies reveals that one of them is unequivocally superior: BAA yields at least as high a payoff as BAB to the coalition no matter which is the choice of the US. Furthermore, there is one choice by the US for which BAA gives not only as high but strictly a higher payoff than BAB. In game-theoretic terminology this means that BAA weakly dominates BAB. But we can do better than say that BAA is to be preferred to BAB by the coalition. To wit, there is a strategy that weakly dominates all the others. This strategy is HHA. It is the *dominant strategy* for the coalition and thus the unambiguously best option. As in decision theory, this prescription follows from pairwise comparison of the alternative strategies in terms of a uniform criterion which determines the pairwise winner. If there is an alternative that wins when compared with any other, then this should be chosen. We shall encounter this intuitive notion of what constitutes the best choice several times later on.

What the dominant strategy prescribes the coalition to do is to veto Brundtland both in the case when the US vetoes Annan and in the case it vetoes Boutros-Ghali, but to veto Annan if the US has vetoed Brundtland. This makes perfect sense, given the preference of the coalition and, in particular, their view of Brundtland as the least-favored candidate. Therefore it is sensible to veto her in all cases except when she has already been vetoed by the US.

Now assume that both players know the information in Table 5.1, i.e. the strategies and payoffs of each other as well as the fact that both know it and that they know that the other player knows, etc. This assumption is called the *common knowledge* assumption in game theory. This implies, in particular, that the US knows that the coalition has a unique strategy that dominates all the others. This, in turn, can be viewed as a very strong prediction that the coalition will choose its dominant strategy HHA. In other words, in pondering upon its choice the US may focus its attention solely on the HHA column. Taking into account the fact that H is weakly dominated by B for the US, we can eliminate the last row in Table 5.1 to end with Table 5.2.

The best response of the US to the dominant strategy of the coalition is clearly B. The end result, then, is that the US vetoes Boutros-Ghali, while the coalition vetoes Brundtland. Thus, Annan is elected.

Table 5.2 Reduced UN Secretary General election game

Coalition

HHA

USA	*A*	−1, 1
	B	0, 0

Games like the one described in Table 5.1 are called *dominance-solvable* since by eliminating dominated strategies we end up with a unique outcome, in this case the choice of Annan. More generally solutions in game theory are to be understood as predictions of what will happen in the game assuming that the players are rational. In some games both players have dominant strategies. The solution is then to be found in the intersection of those strategies. It may also turn out that neither player has a dominant strategy. Various game theoretic solutions have been suggested for those games as well. We shall turn to some of them later, but before that let us focus on another important way of describing games.

5.2   Strategies and extensive form

As pointed out above, the choices of the African coalition differ from those available to the US in being conditional. If they were not, we would have a 3×3 matrix with identical row and column heads A, B and H. We assumed, however, that the process of vetoing is sequential so that the US goes first whereupon the coalition has two remaining options to choose from. Thus, the conditional nature of the coalition choices follows from the way the game is played out in reality. Along with the matrix form there is another way of describing the essential features of the game, namely the *extensive form*. It is particularly useful in games with two players who make their choices sequentially.[20]

In extensive representation the game forms a tree where the branches stand for strategies available to the players represented by nodes. The sequence of moves is from top to bottom. In Figure 5.1 the US makes the first move, i.e. eliminates either A (chooses the left-most branch), B (the middle branch) or H (the right-hand branch). Depending on its choice the African coalition finds itself either in the left, middle or right node. In each of these it is to choose from two options which depend in part on the choice made by the US: in the left node, it can veto either B or H, in the middle one either A or H and in the right node either A or B. Once both players have made their choices we reach one of the outcomes with payoffs indicated at the bottom of the tree.

At the beginning of the tree there is a lot of strategic uncertainty involved in making choices: A can lead to payoffs 1 or −1, B to 1 or 0 and H to −1 or 0 for the US. At the bottom of the tree the uncertainty is completely absent: once

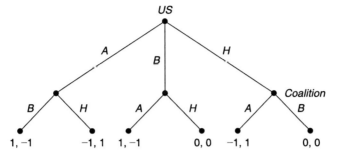

Figure 5.1 UN game in extensive form.

a sequence of moves has been made an outcome is reached and, thus, there is no ambiguity left. To distinguish a rational play from a not rational one, let us consider the two left-most outcomes in Figure 5.1, i.e. $(1, -1)$ and $(-1, 1)$. Which one of these will materialize is determined by the coalition if the US has first chosen A. Since this choice is in fact one between the worst and best possible outcome, it is reasonable to expect that the coalition chooses H and thus the outcome $(-1, 1)$. This is simply another way of phrasing the assumption that the players are rational. By the same token, should the US choose B we can reasonably expect that the coalition chooses H, thus ending up with a $(0, 0)$ payoff instead of $(1, -1)$. Finally, if the strategy of the US is H, we can expect that the coalition chooses A whereupon the payoffs are -1 for the US and 1 for the coalition.

In other words, we know what to expect once the last ones in the sequence of decisions are made by the players. What we do not yet know is which decisions are made before reaching those last decisions, i.e. which branches of the tree have been followed up to that point. Indeed, the assumption of player rationality enables us to reduce the game tree of Figure 5.1 to that shown in Figure 5.2.

This reduction is based solely on the assumption of rationality: since the player at the final decision node can determine which of two outcomes will be the result and since she has a preference relation over the outcomes, the prediction is that

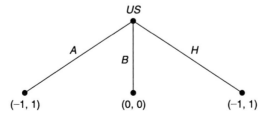

Figure 5.2 Reduced UN game in extensive form.

she will choose the preferred one. Assuming that all the information regarding the extensive form is available to both players and that they both know that the other player knows this, and that the other player knows that they know, etc., the US faces the reduced game tree when making its choice at the outset of the play. What this amounts to is that essentially the US determines which one of the following two payoffs will materialize: $(-1, 1)$ or $(0, 0)$. Obviously, the latter is preferable to the US. Hence we can reduce the game still further so that it amounts to only one outcome, i.e. the election of Annan and thus the payoff 0 to both players.

What we have just resorted to is *Zermelo's algorithm* which is also known as the method of *backward induction* (Zermelo 1913). As just shown, one begins with the last decision nodes in the game tree, that is, the starting point is the last move by the player who is last in the sequence in which the game is played. At this node the player no longer has any strategic uncertainty. Assuming that this particular node is reached – which is not known – the player simply chooses the outcome which gives her the larger payoff. Since there are typically several such last decision nodes, we can thus insert the final outcomes that the player considers best for her into the decision node. Thus, instead of several branches emanating from the node we now have a single payoff indicating what will be the outcome if this node is reached. Let us assume that the last move is the kth (in the UN example $k = 2$). The player making the $(k-1)$th move now knows the outcomes ensuing from her moves since the strategic uncertainty has been removed by assuming that the last moving player is rational. Now we can make precisely the same assumption regarding the player who makes the $(k-1)$th move. In other words, we assume that she chooses the outcome which is best for her. Hence, we can also replace this player's decision node by an outcome, i.e. the one that gives her the highest payoff. Continuing this process, we will eventually reach the starting node of the game tree.

Now we have two predictions for the UN game: the one resulting from discarding dominated strategies in matrix form and the outcome of backward induction. A reasonable question to ask now is: how do they relate to each other? As was pointed out in the preceding section, the dominant strategy for the coalition is *HHA* and against this strategy the dominant option for the US is *B*. Thus, the players following the dominant strategies end up playing *B* and *H*, whereupon Annan emerges as the outcome. Using backward induction we observe that taking into account the coalition's preferences with respect to the final outcomes, the US effectively has to choose either $(-1, 1)$ or $(0, 0)$. The latter is clearly preferable and results from its choice of *B*. Thus, the backward induction outcome is reached when the US chooses *B* and the coalition chooses *H*. Hence, we end up with identical prescriptions for players using dominant strategies and backward induction.

This turns out to be true under very general conditions. Whenever there is a dominant strategy for one of the players, it obviously 'survives' the process of backward induction. So, we end up with the same outcomes using either one of these procedures. Thus far the analysis of games is not far removed from everyday thinking: if a strategy leads to better outcomes than any of its competitors under all circumstances, then it is reasonable to choose it. Similarly, if one's opponent has a strategy that guarantees her the best outcome under any circumstances, it makes sense to assume that she picks that strategy. This is not to say that recognizing dominant strategies would always be easy. Indeed, the repertoire of choices may be very large, e.g. in stock market operations. What can be stated, none the less, is that when there is a unique dominant strategy, it is rational to choose it.

5.3   Solutions

The UN game discussed above is dominance-solvable and thus enables the analyst to make a prediction of what will happen in this game. Alternatively, it gives her a plausible explanation of why the actors behaved the way they did in electing Annan. Not all games, however, are dominance-solvable. Consider the following fictitious competition between two firms entering a new market. Each is able to take over the entire market by resorting to aggressive marketing tactics, negative advertising and cut-throat pricing. However, these methods yield the desired result – market dominance – only if the other firm acquiesces by resorting to normal marketing devices. If both forms engage in aggressive forms of competition, the end result is disastrous for both. If both firms resort to non-aggressive marketing, they essentially split the market. Table 5.3 presents this type of payoff matrix. We can assume, for concreteness, that the entries indicate profits expressed in millions of dollars. Thus, for instance, if one firm resorts to non-aggressive (soft) and the other to aggressive (tough) marketing, the payoff is $1 million for the former and $4 million for the latter. We also assume that aggressive market behavior turns off some consumers so that whenever these behaviors are exhibited the total market diminishes to some extent (here from $6 million to $5 million).

The game of Table 5.3 is one of the best-known two-person non-constant sum games called Chicken. A glance at Table 5.3 reveals that neither player has a dominant strategy. For both, playing soft is better if the other is playing tough, while choosing tough gives a better payoff if the other is playing soft. In a word, the best choice depends on the other player's choice. This is, of course, what one would often expect in game situations. Yet, the dominant strategy argument seems to leave us without a prediction or solution in this situation.

In a classic paper from 1951, John Nash proposed a solution to two person games. Today it is called the *Nash equilibrium*. It is defined as an outcome that

Table 5.3 Duopolistic competition

		Firm 2	
		Soft	*Tough*
Firm 1	*Soft*	3, 3	1, 4
	Tough	4, 1	0, 0

results from strategy choices that are the best responses to each other. In other words, an outcome is a Nash equilibrium if neither player has an incentive to deviate from it, given that the other player's choice is fixed. The solution is intuitively plausible application of the concept of equilibrium state: once reached this state is relatively stable under unilateral (i.e. one player) disturbances.

John F. Nash Jr. (born 1928) is one of the three Nobel Memorial Laureates in economics of the year 1994. Like the other two – Harsanyi and Selten – he is a game theorist, indeed, perhaps the best-known of them all to the general public. This is largely due to Sylvia Nasar's biography *A Beautiful Mind* (1998) and the film based on it. Nash is a mathematician by training. His solution concepts to non-cooperative and bargaining games are classic. They have motivated a large number of younger game theorists to define more refined solutions to various types of games. Nash's central works can be found in *Essays on Game Theory* (1996) and *Essential Nash* (2002), edited by Kuhn and Nasar.

To determine the Nash equilibria in Table 5.3 we start from the outcome 3, 3 which results in both players choosing the soft strategy. This outcome is not a Nash equilibrium since, given the choice of soft by Firm 2, Firm 1 is better off by choosing the tough rather than soft strategy. The same conclusion can be made of Firm 2 when Firm 1's choice of soft strategy is given.[21]

Also the outcome which assigns each firm the payoff of 0 is not a Nash equilibrium. In this case both players prefer any other outcome to this one. Hence, we are left with 1, 4 and 4, 1 as possible candidates for Nash equilibria. It turns out that both of these outcomes are, indeed, equilibria. To see this consider 1, 4. Firm 2 enjoys its highest payoff here and thus, would not benefit from unilateral deviation from this outcome. The same is true of Firm 1 since the only outcome it could achieve by unilateral deviation from 1, 4 is 0, 0, which is even worse for it. Thus, neither firm would benefit from choosing otherwise than it does at 1, 4, provided that the other firm sticks to its strategy choice. The analogous argument shows that also 4, 1 is a Nash equilibrium.

Thus we have two predictions for the Chicken game. They are obviously quite different: one guarantees Firm 1 its highest payoff and Firm 2 its next-to-lowest payoff, while the other switches the roles of the firms. The extensive form of the game Table 5.3 is presented in Figure 5.3.

The dotted line connects two decision nodes representing Firm 2's choice. As the firms are supposed to make their choices without knowing the choice of the other player, we cannot, without distortion, draw the extensive form as if the choices were made in sequence. The dotted line is intended to underline this fact. The nodes connected by the line constitute one *information set*. An information set is thus a set of decision nodes that are indistinguishable to the decision maker. Here Firm 2 does not know whether it is 'located' at the left or right one of the two nodes in the information set.

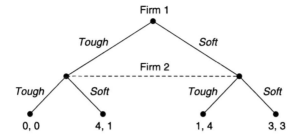

Figure 5.3 Chicken game in extensive form.

Applying Zermelo's algorithm reveals the ambiguity that characterizes Chicken. Since Firm 2 decides whether $0, 0$ or $4, 1$ is the outcome, provided that Firm 1 chooses the tough strategy, it seems likely that by choosing 'tough' Firm 1 ends up with 4. By the same token, the choice of 'soft' by Firm 1 would seem to give it 1. On this basis, then, we can expect Firm 1 to choose 'tough'. But since the moves are simultaneous – or at any rate made under ignorance regarding the other player's choice – Firm 1 does not know whether Firm 2 has already decided upon playing 'tough'. If it has, then the choice of 'tough' by Firm 1 would lead to the disastrous $0, 0$ outcome. It seems, then, that both Nash equilibria survive the elimination process of backward induction.

Nash equilibria seem to provide a solution for games where neither player has a dominant strategy. In fact, it is useful to see the Nash equilibria as generalizations of the dominant strategy equilibria since whenever there is a dominant strategy equilibrium in a game, it is also the unique Nash equilibrium. So, the Nash equilibria essentially extend the intuitive idea of a dominant strategy solution to more general settings.

The generalization is not, however, entirely satisfactory for predictive purposes. As was shown in the Chicken game, there may be more equilibria than one would hope for. Indeed, the situation can in this regard be even worse as shown by Rubinstein's (1982) example (see also Nurmi 1998: 55). Consider that a fixed sum of money, say, $1 million is to be divided among two players. They can make division proposals to each other. In case the proposal satisfies the condition that the entire amount is shared, the players get exactly what is proposed. Otherwise, they get nothing. So, the players, 1 and 2, are to find two numbers q and $1 - q$ with $0 \leq q \leq 1$ so that player 1 gets q million and 2 gets $1 - q$ million. It can be seen that any proposal – i.e. any value of q in the unit interval – is a Nash equilibrium. To wit, if player 1 proposes 3/4 for herself and 1/4 for player 2, this is surely a Nash equilibrium, since once player 1 has specified her own part 3/4, the best player 2 can do is to accept 1/4 since otherwise she will get nothing. Similarly, if player 2 first lays down her demand of 1/4, the best player 1 can do is to accept 3/4. So, when the proposal of (3/4, 1/4) split has been made, it is a Nash equilibrium. The same is true of any proposal $(q, 1 - q)$ where q is a point in the unit interval.

Another problem pertaining to the Nash equilibrium concept is that there are games with no such equilibria in terms of pure strategies, that is, when the strategies considered involve no random, probabilistic or stochastic element. Many situations of pursuit–evasion variety can be seen as constant-sum games without Nash equilibria. Every year millions of dollars are lost by governments around the world because of the fact that firms and individuals do not disclose in their tax forms all sources and amounts of income that should, by law, be reported. Similarly, considerable losses to competitors, governments, consumers and investors are caused by fraudulent practices (misleading reports, collusions, price fixing, etc.) sometimes resorted to by firms in attempts to maximize profits, market shares or political influence. To counteract these types of illegal activities the authorities in market economies have established various control mechanisms. Many of these amount to conducting special audits in firms and other organizations suspected of illegal activities. To illustrate the setting in which there are no Nash equilibria consider a highly stylized game involving the leadership of a firm which could benefit considerably from resorting to illegal accounting practices and the competition authority in charge of executing the legislation in the field. In matrix form the game can be presented as Table 5.4.

Table 5.4 Special auditing game

		Authority	
		Overlook	*Inspect*
Firm	*Play fair*	*a, A*	*c, C*
	Cheat	*b, B*	*d, D*

The strategies available to the firm are cheating or playing according to the competition rules, while the competition authority may either subject the firm to a special audit or look elsewhere. The payoffs are expressed as amounts of utility where the lower-case letters refer to the utilities of the firm and the upper-case ones to those of the authority. Let us assume that cheating is profitable if unnoticed, but costly if spotted. This means that $b > a$ and $c > d$. Let us also assume that inspection costs money, but makes sense if the firm is cheating. In other words, $A > C$, but $D > B$. Under these conditions which characterize *pursuit–evasion games* in general, it can be seen that there are no Nash equilibria if the players can choose only among the two strategies each.[22] Namely, if the (*play fair, overlook*) outcome is looked upon, we see that the firm would be better off by cheating if it knew that the authority looks the other way. So, this cannot be a Nash equilibrium. Neither could the (*cheat, inspect*) outcome be that since the firm is better off by playing fair if it knows that it will be submitted to special audit. Thus, both outcomes along the main diagonal of the payoff matrix are not equilibria because the firm has an incentive to deviate from them, provided that the authority has chosen the strategies leading to those outcomes. Similarly, the off-diagonal outcomes (*b, B*) and (*c, C*) are not equilibria. In these cases it is the authority that has the incentive to deviate from the outcomes, given that the firm has chosen the strategies leading to them. In sum, none of the four outcomes in Table 5.4 is a Nash equilibrium.

An important result of Nash states, however, that all finite two-person games have equilibria if we allow for a generalization of the strategy sets to include the so-called *mixed strategies*. These are strategies dictating the choice of each of the pure strategies with a given probability so that the probabilities assigned sum up to unity. For example, if {*play fair, cheat*} is the set of pure strategies, then $S = (play\ fair, 1/2; cheat, 1/2)$ is a mixed strategy which amounts to playing fair with a probability of 1/2 and cheating with a probability of 1/2. According to Nash's theorem all two-person games where the players have a finite number of pure strategies at their disposal have at least one equilibrium outcome which results either from pure or mixed strategies. To see the meaning of this fundamental result, let us consider a simple special case, namely, one that is obtained from the game of Table 5.4 by assuming that it is zero-sum. We could, for example, think that the game is one of winning or losing and that whatever the authority wins is lost by the firm. The authority wins when the firm predicts its action incorrectly and vice versa. A tie $(0, 0)$ occurs when the firm plays according to rules and the authority does not undertake an audit. The worst outcome (-3) for the firm occurs when it gets caught cheating, while the best (2) for it is to cheat unbeknownst to the authority. If the firm is inspected and found 'clean', its reputation is improved (1), while the authority suffers a loss due to unnecessary work. We thus obtain Table 5.5.

Table 5.5 Zero-sum auditing game

		Authority	
		Overlook	*Inspect*
Firm	*Play fair*	0, 0	1, −1
	Cheat	2, −2	−3, 3

Let us first define the *value of a game* for a player. It is the highest payoff that she can guarantee herself unilaterally, that is, without any favor from the other player. It can be determined by looking at the minimal payoff associated with each strategy and then picking that strategy which gives the largest minimum payoff. In Table 5.5 *play fair* gives the firm at least 0 payoff, while *cheat* has the minimum payoff of −3. The value of the game with just pure strategies taken into account for the firm is then the larger of these two minima, 0. Similarly, the pure strategy value of the game for the authority is −1. These values are associated with the *play fair* and *inspect* strategies.

We now look at the mixed strategies. Suppose that the firm chooses the *play fair* strategy with a probability of 1/3 and cheats with a probability of 2/3. If the authority plays the *overlook* strategy, the expected payoff of the firm is: $1/3 \times 0 + 2/3 \times 2 = 4/3$, while in the case where the authority chooses to inspect the firm's expected payoff is: $1/3 \times 1 + 2/3 \times (-3) = -5/3$. Obviously, this mixed strategy is not an improvement over the pure strategy *play fair*.

The firm may, however, do considerably better in expected payoff terms. A look at the preceding expected payoff calculation shows that the firm does better by assigning a smaller probability to cheating. Consider the value 1/6 to cheating and 5/6 to playing fair. This gives the expected payoff 1/3 regardless of whether the authority plays *inspect* or *overlook*. Hence, the value of the game for the firm also increases to 1/3 when the mixed strategies and expected payoffs are taken into account.

It turns out that the mixed strategy $(5/6, play\ fair; 1/6, cheat)$ is the best the firm can do. This can be seen by modifying the probabilities of pure strategy choices a little and computing the expected payoffs. For example, the mixed strategy $((5/6) + \epsilon, play\ fair; (1/6) - \epsilon, cheat)$ gives the expected payoff $((1/6) - \epsilon) \times 2 = (1/3) - 2\epsilon$ when the authority overlooks, and the payoff $(5/6) + \epsilon + ((1/6) - \epsilon) \times (-3) = (1/3) + 4\epsilon$ when the authority inspects. The former expected payoff is obviously smaller than 1/3 which was shown to result from the firm's resorting to the $(5/6, play\ fair; 1/6, cheat)$ strategy. Thus, increasing the probability of choosing *play fair* does not increase the value of the game for the firm. A similar argument shows that the firm cannot increase the value of the game by decreasing the probability of the *play fair* choice, either. Thus, the value of the game for the firm is, indeed, 1/3 and results from the $(5/6, play\ fair; 1/6, cheat)$ strategy.

Finding Nash equilibria in two-person zero-sum games where each player has two pure strategies (i.e. 2×2 games) proceeds as follows (see e.g. Brams 1975; Hamburger 1979). Firstly, determine whether either player has a dominant strategy. If at least one of them has, then we are done since the best she can do is to choose it, while the other chooses her best response to this choice. This is the Nash equilibrium. Secondly, provided that neither player has a dominant strategy, examine all pure strategy outcomes in order to find out if any of them satisfies the requirement that unilateral deviations do not benefit the deviating player. If such outcomes are found, these are the pure strategy Nash equilibria. Thirdly, to find mixed strategy Nash equilibria, introduce mixed strategies and compute expected payoffs conditional to the other player's pure strategies. To illustrate, consider the general two-person 2×2 zero-sum game of Table 5.6.

Table 5.6 2×2 zero-sum game

| | | Player 2 | |
		Column 1	*Column 2*
Player 1	*Row 1*	$a, -a$	$c, -c$
	Row 2	$b, -b$	$d, -d$

Suppose that a is the highest payoff and that d is the next highest one. In fact, we can make this assumption without jeopardizing the generality of our analysis. To wit, the strategic uncertainty of the players is not changed if one switches the order of rows or columns. Regardless of whether row 1 is above or below row 2 in the matrix, the strategic uncertainty facing player 1 is that by choosing the strategy labeled row 1, she knows that her payoff will be either a or c, depending on player 2's choice. The same applies to columns. Thus, starting from any 2×2 zero-sum game matrix we can – by switching rows and/or columns – end up with the configuration where player 1's highest payoff is in the upper left-hand corner. But can we also reach a configuration where, in addition, player 1's second-highest payoff is in the lower right-hand corner? Not necessarily, but should this not be possible, we already have what we are looking for, namely a Nash equilibrium. To wit, if the second-highest payoff is not in the lower-right corner, it must be either in the lower-left or the upper-right one. Suppose it is in the lower-left corner. In this case we have player 1's highest and second-highest payoffs in the first column. Consequently, player 2's highest and second-highest payoffs must be in column 2. This strategy is, therefore, the dominant choice for player 2 and we find the Nash equilibrium at the intersection of column 2 and player 1's best response to it. If the second-highest payoff of player 1 is in the upper-right corner, then row 1 is the dominant strategy for player 1 and the preceding analysis applies.

So, the only configuration where further analysis is required is the one where a is the highest and d the second-highest payoff. In this configuration player 1 ponders upon mixed strategies that would maximize her expected payoff. She knows that if she chooses row 1 with a very high probability, player 2 will choose column 2 with high probability, since the game is zero-sum. Similarly, the higher the probability that player 1 chooses row 2, the higher the probability that player 2 chooses column 1. Indeed, by making her expected payoff independent of player 2's choice, player 1 guarantees herself the maximum expected payoff. This can be seen by focusing on player 1's expected payoffs for the mixed strategy dictating the choice of row 1 with probability q and row 2 with probability $1 - q$. Given that player 2 chooses column 1, this is $q \times a + (1 - q) \times b$. If player 2 chooses column 2, the expected payoff of player 1 is $q \times c + (1 - q) \times d$. Let us call the former expected payoff (i) and the latter (ii).

Setting these two expected values, that is (i) and (ii), equal to each other and solving for q we get:

$$q = \frac{d - b}{a - b - c + d}$$

Substituting this value for q in (i) or (ii) yields

$$\frac{ad - bc}{a - b - c + d}$$

as the value of the game for player 1. That it is, indeed, the highest value that player 1 can unilaterally guarantee herself can be seen by giving q marginally larger or smaller values and observing that these lead to expected values that make the value of the game smaller for player 1. For example, increasing the value of q marginally (by ϵ), yields a smaller payoff expectation, and hence the value, than (ii). Similarly, decreasing the value of q results in expectation which is smaller than (i).

A similar argument can be built to show that player 2 maximizes her expected payoff by randomizing her choice of column 1 and column 2 using probability values so that the expected values are identical when player 1 chooses row 1 and when she chooses row 2.

By Nash's (1951) theorem we can generalize this procedure to all finite two-person games. In other words, one can find a Nash equilibrium either in pure or mixed strategies. In fact, there are games in which there are both pure and mixed strategy equilibria. The game known as the battle of the sexes is an example. This is shown in Table 5.7. There are several slightly different but game-theoretically equivalent versions of the story, most apparently set in the bygone age of gender stereotypes. A more up-to-date version told by Holler and Illing (2003: 11) goes as follows (see e.g. Osborne (2004: 55–98) for other illustrations). Tina and Oskar have just met and fallen in love. They are planning for an evening out. It turns out that Tina likes football and would very much like to go to the local stadium to see an important match this evening. Oskar, on the other hand, does not much care about football, but would love to see the new Woody Allen film showing the very same night in the local cinema. Both enjoy each other's company to the extent that the worst outcomes for both are ones in which they make different choices. Their planning, however, comes to an abrupt end when Oskar realizes that he has some really urgent business to attend to. So sudden is his departure that afterwards they both realize that they only had time to say that they absolutely need to meet again that same evening. However, the place of meeting was left open. So, where do they go to look for each other: football stadium or cinema?

Table 5.7 The battle of the sexes

		Oskar	
		Stadium	*Cinema*
Tina	*Stadium*	3, 1	0, 0
	Cinema	0, 0	1, 3

There are two pure strategy Nash equilibria in this non-zero-sum game, namely the strategies leading to 3, 1 and 1, 3 outcomes. In addition there is a mixed strategy Nash equilibrium consisting of (1/4, *stadium*; 3/4, *cinema*) for Tina and (3/4, *stadium*; 1/4, *cinema*) for Oskar. This can be seen by observing that once a player, say Tina, has adopted her mixed strategy, the other player, Oskar, cannot benefit by deviating from his mixed strategy. Thus, we have a mixed strategy Nash equilibrium.

5.4 Subgames and trembles

Several equilibria in a game that has four possible outcomes can with some justification be deemed too many for any practical purpose. This observation has led to a search for other solution concepts that would single out the most plausible of the available Nash equilibria and eliminate the intuitively implausible ones. These solutions are aptly called refinements of Nash equilibria. The best-known of them is the *subgame perfect equilibrium* (Selten 1975).[23] This concept aims at solving a specific problem pertaining to some Nash equilibria, namely that they may call for choices that are not rational, given the extensive form representation of the game. In other words, there are Nash equilibria determined on the basis of the matrix-form presentation that make no sense when looked upon from the viewpoint of the corresponding extensive form. Consider Selten's (1978) chain store example presented in matrix form in Table 5.8 and in extensive form in Figure 5.4.

Table 5.8 Chain store and competitor game

		Competitor	
		Enter	*Stay out*
Chain store	*Cooperative*	2, 2	5, 1
	Aggressive	0, 0	5, 1

Table 5.8 describes a situation where a chain store is in a dominant market position in several cities facing, however, potential competition in each of them. The table describes a situation in one city. The competitor ponders upon entering the market or staying out, while the chain store basically has two strategies at its disposal, a cooperative or an aggressive one. The chain store makes its decision after the competitor has made her move, i.e. the moves are made in a sequence.

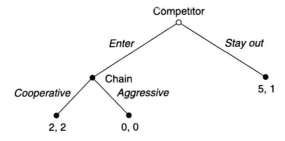

Figure 5.4 Chain store game in extensive form.

Reinhard Selten (born 1930) is a German game theorist and one of the 1994 Nobel Memorial Laureates in economics. His main contributions focus on refining the Nash equilibria. In his work he has emphasized the importance of extensive form games. Selten also belongs to the pioneers of evolutionary game theory. His main works are *Game Theory and Economic Behaviour: Selected Essays* (1999), *Models of Strategic Rationality* (1988) and *A General Theory of Equilibrium Selection in Games* (with John Harsanyi) (1988).

Looking at the matrix-form game, we observe that there are two pure strategy Nash equilibria, i.e. (*cooperative, enter*) and (*aggressive, stay out*). Both satisfy the defining condition of a Nash equilibrium: unilateral deviations from these outcomes are not beneficial for the deviating player.[24]

Let us now look at the extensive-form representation of the game (Figure 5.4). The idea of a subgame perfect equilibrium is to exclude those Nash equilibria which call for strategy choices that are irrational in some subgames. A subgame starts at a decision node in the extensive form and contains all successive branches and nodes from that node onwards. In other words, a subgame traces the moves after a selected decision node. In Figure 5.4 there are two subgames. One begins at the node following the competitor's *enter* choice, that is, where the chain store chooses either a cooperative or an aggressive strategy. The other subgame contains the entire extensive form. Now, the (*cooperative, enter*) strategy is also a perfect equilibrium since the choices it calls for are rational in all subgames. The (*aggressive, stay out*) strategy pair, on the other hand, is not a perfect equilibrium, for it calls for the chain store to choose *aggressive* which would not be rational in the subgame that begins after the competitor has chosen to enter. In that subgame *aggressive* would result in 0 while *cooperative* would give 2 to the chain store. Hence, the (*aggressive, stay out*) strategy pair is a Nash equilibrium but not a subgame perfect one.

The idea of subgame perfection is based on the observation that the extensive form representation is in a way more informative than the matrix form. Especially the move sequences are represented in game trees (i.e. extensive forms) in a more transparent manner than in strategic forms. Subgame equilibria embody the common-sense wisdom that one should not accept policies that – under some contingencies – dictate irrational behavior.

The chain store game and the unacceptable (*aggressive, stay out*) Nash equilibrium suggest another consideration that plays an important role in determining which patterns of conduct can be deemed rational in games. To wit, the elimination of this Nash equilibrium rests on the observation that should the competitor choose to enter, the chain store would be better off not choosing the aggressive strategy. However, in the Nash equilibrium strategy pair, the chain store's strategy is paired with the *stay out* strategy of the competitor. Hence, the fact that the game has led to the node which follows the competitor's *enter* strategy choice is something of a surprise. Given the chain store's component of the

Nash equilibrium strategy pair, it is irrational. In view of this, it is to be expected that a strategy that is rational against a rational player does not necessarily work when one is faced with an irrational opponent.

This reasoning leads to the question of whether it is rational to assume that one's opponent is rational. Common sense would suggest that in general it is not. Especially in situations where the players make mistakes in choosing actions, perceiving the states of the environment and have only partial knowledge of the game, it is plausible to consider the possibility that one's opponent is not rational with probability 1. This suggests an equilibrium concept which is closely related to the subgame perfect equilibrium, namely the *trembling-hand perfect equilibrium* (Selten 1975). Trembling-hand perfect equilibria are strategy pairs that are not only best responses to each other, but also to small perturbations (mistakes) in the opponent's strategies.

To illustrate the notion of trembling-hand perfect equilibrium, consider the chain store game again. Consider the implausible (*aggressive*, *stay out*) equilibrium again. Suppose that the competitor makes a mistake with a very small, but nonzero probability ϵ, while the chain store sticks with its aggressive strategy. This yields the chain store the expected payoff:

$$(1 - \epsilon) \times 5 + \epsilon \times 0 = 5 - 5\epsilon$$

if it plays aggressively. If, in the face of those mistakes, the chain store chose to play cooperatively, its expected payoff would be:

$$(1 - \epsilon) \times 5 + \epsilon \times 2 = 5 + 3\epsilon$$

which is larger than the payoff resulting from aggressive strategy no matter how small the value of ϵ. Hence, even the smallest perturbation of the competitor's strategy in the implausible Nash equilibrium destroys the equilibrium. Therefore, (*aggressive*, *stay out*) is not a trembling-hand perfect equilibrium.

The other Nash equilibrium, i.e. (*cooperative*, *enter*), in contrast, is a trembling-hand perfect one. This can be seen performing the same calculation as above under the assumption that either player makes trembles, that is, makes a mistake with a small probability. If the competitor trembles with nonzero probability δ, the chain store's expected payoff is:

$$(1 - \delta) \times 2 + \delta \times 5 = 2 + 3\delta$$

if it plays the cooperative strategy, while the aggressive one would yield 5δ. Thus, choosing the cooperative strategy leads to a higher expected payoff for the chain store for any tremble probability.

Similarly, if the chain store trembles at the (*cooperative*, *enter*) equilibrium with a nonzero probability δ, the expected payoff for the competitor is $(1 - \delta) \times 2 = 2 - 2\delta$ if it chooses to enter, while it is $(1 - \delta) \times 1 + \delta \times = 1$ if its choice is to stay out. Thus, as long as the tremble probability is smaller than 1/2, the competitor is better off entering than staying out. Hence, the (*cooperative, enter*) equilibrium is a trembling-hand perfect one.

The *subgame perfect* and *trembling-hand perfect* equilibria are but two – albeit perhaps the best-known – refinements of the Nash equilibrium concept. In their specific ways they represent attempts to overcome the apparent shortcoming of the Nash equilibrium that it is too liberal in including intuitively implausible outcomes. Other refinements have the same goal, namely, to retain the nice properties of the Nash equilibrium but adding other desirable properties so as to exclude some Nash equilibria. We shall not discuss further refinements. The basic point of both the Nash equilibrium and all its refinements as well as other solution concepts is to predict what will happen or make intelligible what has happened in social interactions modeled as games. Armed with some basic solution concepts we now move on to some particular game types that have played and continue to play an important role in applications of game theory. It is what the game-theoretical analysis can contribute to our understanding of these important game settings that determines the current value of game theory for political economy.

5.5   Special games

In the preceding we have not followed the classic distinction between zero-sum and *non-zero-sum games*, but discussed both types of games in parallel. Yet, there is obviously a clear difference between zero-sum and non-zero-sum settings, or rather, between situations where these basic game types are the most appropriate models. In zero-sum settings the players essentially extract payoffs from each other, while in non-zero-sum settings at least some joint losses or gains can result from certain strategy pairs. The very possibility of joint gains or losses has motivated the characterization of non-zero-sum games as *mixed motive* ones. The class of non-zero-sum two-person games is extremely heterogeneous, ranging from pure coordination settings to highly conflictual ones. In fact, the very heterogeneity of these games has given rise to literature that tends to focus on special game types rather than general features of non-zero-sum settings. Two-person games where each player has two strategies are called 2 × 2 games. There are altogether 78 different 2 × 2 non-zero-sum ordinal games, that is, games in which the payoffs have only ordinal significance and which differ from each other in terms of the strategic uncertainty faced by the players. In other words, there are 78 strategically different games if the players are capable of putting the four outcomes into strict preference ranking (see Rapoport and Guyer 1966; Brams 1983; Brams and Wittman 1981). Of these 78, by far the most extensively studied game is the *Prisoner's Dilemma* (PD, for short), but Chicken has also often been used as a model of certain kinds of interaction situations. In the following we shall approach the games by characterizing the general features of those settings in which various game types seem most appropriate.

5.5.1 Collective action games

It is quite common to assume that people join interest groups in order to receive the collective benefits or goods that these provide. One of the central arguments in Mancur Olson's ([1965] 1971) *The Logic of Collective Action* is that this is not the case, at least not among rational actors. In other words, Olson maintains that rational people do not join organizations in order to receive the public goods that these organizations provide. In other words, wage earners do not join labor unions, entrepreneurs do not join employers' unions, countries do not join military or economic unions if they are rational and the good or service provided by those organizations is genuinely public (see also Sandler 1992, 2004). According to Samuelson's (1954, 1955) definition, a good is a *pure public good* if two conditions are met: (i) when the good is available, no member of the group in question can be excluded from its consumption, and (ii) a group member's consumption of the good does not restrict the consumption opportunities of other members. The former condition is known as *non-excludability* and the latter *jointness of supply*. If only condition (i) is satisfied, the good is called public. So, pure public goods involve no scarcity or competition among consumers.

Mancur Olson Jr. (1932–1998), an American economist, was one of the founders of the public choice school of thought. This tradition emphasizes the role of economic reasoning, especially the utility maximization calculus, in social affairs in general and, most importantly, in political life. Olson's best-known work *The Logic of Collective Action* ([1965] 1971) applies economic reasoning to collective action and interest groups. *The Rise and Decline of Nations* (1982) extends the analysis to national economic systems, their adaptability to technological change and their growth potential. His last – posthumously published – book, *Power and Prosperity* (2000), draws upon lessons from the transformations of the former socialist systems in Europe.

Olson argues that if the benefit provided by the interest groups is of the nature of public good (salary increase for certain groups of wage earners, tax or tariff exemptions for certain types of firms, etc.) a rational actor does not contribute to the provision of that good if she can receive the same benefit without contributing. This argument can be expressed in the form of a two-person game.[25] To illustrate, we assume the simplest possible setting of a two-person society which faces a security threat calling for a joint investment on a pure public good, e.g. an alarm system warning of intruders. Suppose that the investment needed for the installment of the system is A units. Once the system is operational, its benefit to each member of the society is equivalent to B units. Since we are dealing with collective security, the benefit that the system provides for one member does not diminish the benefit available to the other member, i.e. the good is a pure public one. In case both players contribute, the cost A is divided equally between them. If just one player contributes, she pays the entire cost.

If neither contributes, there will be no alarm system, that is, the *status quo* continues.

Paul A. Samuelson (born 1915) is one of the most influential economists of the 20th century. His contributions extend over an unusually wide area in economics. Perhaps the most notable fields are public economics, consumer choice, macro-economics and international trade. In addition to his many publications in leading journals of economics, Samuelson has also written several very influential books, among them the most widely used economics textbook ever, *Economics* (first edition 1948) and *Foundations of Economics* (1947). Samuelson became the Nobel Memorial Laureate in economics in 1970.

Let us assume that the circumstances prevent the players from making binding contracts. In other words, the players cannot commit themselves to making any specific choices, e.g. to cooperate. This means that the game is *non-cooperative*. They have two choices: either to contribute to the provision of the security or refrain from contributing. Let us denote the first choice by C and the second by D. This enables us to represent the decision situation in matrix form (Table 5.9).

Table 5.9 Collective goods provision game

		Player 2	
		C	D
Player 1	C	$B - (A/2), B - (A/2)$	$B - A, B$
	D	$B, B - A$	$0, 0$

We denote the *status quo* payoff by 0. Looking at the game from player 1's point of view, we observe that if 2 were to choose C, 1 would be better off choosing D since the latter would give her B while the former would give something less than that. Were 2 to choose D, 1 would be better off choosing C or D depending on whether $B - A > 0$ or $B - A < 0$.

If $B - A < 0$, the game we are dealing with is the PD, whereas if $B - A > 0$ it is Chicken. These are by far the best-known games in the two-person non-zero-sum game theory. Supposing that the public goods provision game is the PD, then it can be seen that the individually rational choice leads to a non-optimal outcome. This follows directly from what was just stated, that regardless of whether 2 chooses C or D, 1 is better off choosing D. The same reasoning applies, of course, to 2. In other words, both players have a dominant strategy which is D. Thus, the outcome will be $(0, 0)$, i.e. the *status quo*. This is not optimal since there exists an outcome that would be better for both players than $(0, 0)$, namely $(B - (A/2), B - (A/2))$.

The dilemma in the PD is that coordination of choices would be beneficial for both players, but this requires something external to the game itself: an enforcer of promises, norms that modify the 'pure' payoffs or embedding the game into a larger context of larger games. The role of the state has often been seen in the enforcement of contracts between individuals or groups. The state or rule of law eliminates the inefficiency of anarchy (Hillman 2003: 28–29). Thus, the PD provides a kind of explanation for the emergence of the state.[26]

The dilemma in the PD takes on degrees which are not apparent in the definition that pays attention to order of preference of payoffs. Consider the two PD games of Table 5.10 and assume that the payoffs are sums of money. Both games qualify as PDs since the order of payoffs is that the highest payoff is received by unilateral non-contribution, the next highest by mutual contribution, the third-highest by mutual non-contribution and the lowest by unilateral contribution. Yet, there is a marked difference between these games. In *PD* 1 the best payoff total is obtained through mutual contribution $(3 + 3 = 6)$, while in *PD* 2 the largest payoff sum is reached when one and only one player is contributing $(7 + 1 = 8)$.

Table 5.10 Two PD games

PD 1

	C	D
C	3, 3	1, 4
D	4, 1	2, 2

PD 2

	C	D
C	3, 3	1, 7
D	7, 1	2, 2

Due to this difference in payoff sums, the players playing *PD* 2 may strike a deal to play C and D in alternating fashion so as to maximize the joint payoff. This deal would give both the average of 4 in each game, whereas cooperation in *PD* 2 would give them only 3. However, this kind of deal only makes sense in sequential PD games, i.e. in situations where the players can monitor the compliance of the other player. In a one-shot PD the player who – according to the deal – is supposed to cooperate may not find it worth her while to do so since, by definition of non-cooperative games, the contracts are not enforceable.

Despite the difference between *PD* 1 and *PD* 2, the crucial characteristics of PD are the following:

- that the non-cooperative strategy is the dominant one for both players,
- that the dominant strategy equilibrium is accompanied with a smaller payoff to both players than the outcome resulting from both players changing their strategy, and
- the dominant strategy equilibrium is the only *Pareto suboptimal* outcome in the game.

Some comments on these points are in order. The first observation can be verified readily upon inspecting the PD matrix. The second point states the basic dilemma of the PD – namely, cooperation would be beneficial since it would increase the payoff of both players from the equilibrium payoffs. At the same time this change would require both players to abandon their dominant strategies. This, however, is made unlikely by the fact that assuming that one's opponent is playing cooperatively, one's own payoff maximizing choice is the non-cooperative strategy. This is but an implication of the dominance relation between cooperative and non-cooperative strategies.

To elaborate the last point, let us first define a *Pareto optimal change* or *Pareto improvement* from one outcome to another. It is a change that brings about an increase in payoff of at least one player without diminishing the payoff of the other players.[27] Thus, in the PD the change from the equilibrium outcome to that resulting from both players choosing the cooperative strategy is a Pareto improvement since it brings about the payoff 3 instead of 2 to both players. The outcome is *Pareto optimal* if no Pareto improvements from it are possible. In other words, all changes of strategy in a Pareto optimal outcome lead to a smaller payoff to at least one player.

The PD illustrates in a very concise way the conflict between individual and collective rationality. If the former is understood as dictating the choice of a dominant strategy whenever there is one and the latter is viewed as the Pareto optimality requirement, then the PD shows that these two can be incompatible. Indeed, the conflict between these two rationalities is about as drastic as it can be. To wit, looking at the PD matrix form we see that there are three Pareto optimal outcomes: all those outcomes that result when at least one player chooses the cooperative strategy. In *PD* 1 these lead to $(3,3)$, $(4,1)$ and $(1,4)$ payoffs. Given any of these outcomes, no Pareto improvement is possible. Hence, we see that the individually rational equilibrium outcome is the only one that is Pareto suboptimal, i.e. not Pareto optimal.

Interchanging the smallest and next to smallest payoffs – or replacing the $B < A$ assumption with the $B > A$ one in Table 5.9 – in the PD payoff matrix turns the game into Chicken, another extensively discussed game of collective action. In Chicken, there are no dominant strategies and the worst outcome for both players results from both choosing the non-cooperative strategy. As in the PD we can construct variations of the Chicken game where the players are better off choosing cooperative and non-cooperative strategies in alternating fashion.

The crucial characteristic of Chicken:

- no dominant strategy for either player,
- there is an outcome that yields both players their lowest payoff,
- there are two Nash equilibria, and
- there are three Pareto optimal outcomes.

As in the PD, the outcome resulting from both players choosing the non-cooperative strategy is the only Pareto suboptimal outcome. However, in contradistinction to the PD, the incentives for choosing the non-cooperative strategy are essentially weaker: only if the opponent is likely to 'give way' yields this strategy a better payoff than the cooperative one.

The difference between the PD and Chicken pertains to the order of the smallest and next-to-smallest payoffs. Another game that has also been widely discussed differs from the PD in terms of the highest and next-to-highest payoffs. It is presented in Table 5.11.

Table 5.11 Assurance game

		Player 2	
		C	D
Player 1	C	4, 4	1, 3
	D	3, 1	2, 2

This game shares two properties with Chicken: (i) there are two equilibria, and (ii) there are no dominant strategies. In contradistinction to Chicken in this game – which is known as the Assurance game – one equilibrium is a Pareto improvement over the other. There are strong incentives for the players to choose C since the largest payoff is obtained by both players when they choose C. However, should the other player for some reason choose D, then D would be the best response to it.

The Assurance game has sometimes been considered as a proper model of a situation preceding the adoption of some joint standard of measurement of weight, length or value. Adhering to an established standard reduces transaction costs and makes communication between trading partners easier. However, if one's partner turns out to defect from the standard that one abides by, then the outcome is next best for the defector and worst for the adhering party. The state of affairs where no standard is established is next to worst to both players. Obviously, the Assurance game can also be seen as a game of collective action. In this case, however, the universal acceptance of the norm or standard is valued highest.

Both the Assurance and the Chicken games demonstrate that the assumptions regarding the rationality of one's opponent is an important ingredient in determining the best game strategy. If one can assume that the opponent is rational in the sense of trying to avoid the most disastrous outcome in Chicken, then the payoff-maximizing way to proceed is to play D. If, however, there is a good chance that the opponent plays D regardless of the consequences, then C is the sensible strategy to play. In Assurance the best way to proceed is to choose exactly as your opponent does. Obviously, if she aims at the highest payoff, she plays C which means that C is the best response. If, however, she aims at maximizing the security level payoff, she chooses D to which D is the best reply. The security level is the minimum payoff associated with each strategy. Thus, in the Assurance game, the security level is 1 for C and 2 for D. Hence, the player who aims at maximizing her security level payoff chooses D – and, *eo ipso*, gives up any chance of receiving 4.

Let us now return to Olson's argument according to which rational people do not contribute to collective goods if by not contributing they can enjoy the same benefit. The undeniable fact that people do participate in large numbers in various kinds of collective activities is in Olson's view to be attributed to selective incentives which are of private nature. In other words, there are goods or services available only to contributing individuals and the appreciation of these accounts for the blossoming of various forms of collective action. The preceding discussion of various non-zero-sum games shows that Olson's argument is based on the view that collective action is representable as the PD. Yet, there are public goods provision settings which resemble more the Chicken game than the PD. In these settings we simply do not have a clear-cut recommendation for individually rational way of acting. The same ambiguity characterizes the Assurance game situations.

But even in PD-like contexts, there are considerations that speak in favor of the cooperative strategy. Several arguments supporting the cooperative choice have been presented in the literature over the past decades. Perhaps the earliest one of these 'solutions' to the PD is Howard's (1971) *metagame* argument. It is based on the idea that the players are in effect choosing between metagame strategies rather than between C and D. A metagame is constructed by looking at player choices as responses to each other. Thus, for example, player 1 chooses between four strategies:

1. to play C against a C-playing opponent and against a D-playing opponent, that is, to play C unconditionally,
2. to play exactly as the opponent,
3. to play in exactly the opposite way as the opponent, that is, if she chooses C, choose D, and if she chooses D, choose C, or
4. to play D regardless of the opponent's choice.

These player 1 strategies are thus conditional on player 2's choices. Forming now a 4×2 payoff matrix where the columns represent player 2's two strategies and rows player 1's four strategies, we observe that the equilibrium remains one where both players choose D. In the metagame it is at the intersection of the unconditional D strategy of player 1 and the D choice of player 2.

However, if one moves one step further and constructs a metagame where player 1's strategies are those four just mentioned and player 2's strategies are conditional upon these, we get a 4×16 matrix where the columns are vectors with four components each representing a response to player 1's strategy choice. Thus, for example (C, C, D, D) represents player 2's metastrategy that dictates C if player 1 plays strategy 1, C if player 1 plays strategy 2, D if player 1 plays strategy 3, and D if player 1 plays strategy 4. Since there are four metastrategies of player 1 and to each player 2 can respond in two (C or D) ways, there are altogether 16 player 2 metastrategies.

In the ensuing 4×16 payoff matrix, it turns out that there are two equilibrium outcomes: one resulting from player 1 choosing metastrategy 2 and player 2 choosing (C, C, D, D), and the other resulting from player 1's choosing the metastrategy 2 and player 2's choice of (D, C, D, D). Both of these yield the $(3, 3)$ payoff. In other words, the cooperative choice of both players leads to an equilibrium in the metagame. There is, thus, an admittedly complex, but nevertheless plausible, argument for the choice of the C strategy in the PD. It is, however, based on considerations deeper than those of simply choosing C or D in a one-shot PD. In fact, one might argue that this solution concept implicitly assumes that the game is repeated.

The common component in these two cooperative equilibria is player 1's strategy of choosing whatever the opponent chooses. This is known as the TIT-FOR-TAT strategy (TFT, for short), although its proper setting is a sequential rather than a one-shot game. The crux of the cooperative equilibrium is then that one of the players is committed to a strategy of simple reciprocation. A rational response to this commitment is then the choice of the cooperative strategy. It seems that the emergence of reciprocity in the form of TFT or some similar principle may constitute a fundamental explanation for the ubiquity and stability of cooperative activity in the provision of collective goods.

5.5.2 *Norms of reciprocity and coordination*

The metagame provides an interesting and undoubtedly relevant angle to the PD in invoking considerations that pertain to norms of action. When engaged in social interaction people often justify their actions by rules or norms of conduct. It is quite common to explain action by the norms that prevail in the community surrounding the actors. Hence, it makes sense to argue that also in PD situations the choices are not made purely *ad hoc*. The metagame strategies are nothing but norms – albeit simple – of conduct in interactions involving two actors. Thus, even in one-shot PDs, the players could be envisioned to be acting in accordance with general rules or norms. Even more appropriate is to assume that players involved in several consecutive PD games, so-called *sequential PDs*, resort to norms that specify choices to be made in each subgame of the sequential PD.

In the late 1970s Robert Axelrod (1980a, 1980b) conducted a survey among prominent game theorists about strategies applicable in the sequential PD. The idea was to find out which strategies would be successful when confronted with each other. The strategies were given in the form of computer programs which made the evaluation of their success a primarily technical exercise. The instructions to the designers of the programs included the description of the specific version of the PD which was to be used (Table 5.12) as well as the general

Table 5.12 The PD version of Axelrod's tournament

		Column	
		Cooperate	*Defect*
Row	*Cooperate*	3, 3	0, 5
	Defect	5, 0	1, 1

success criterion to be used: the cumulated payoff over a sequence of games against other programs submitted to the competition. The rules of the tournament indicated that the competition was, indeed, a tournament which means that all the programs were playing against each other. They also confronted their own twin and a program which makes purely random strategy choices in each game.

Before reviewing the tournament results, let us consider the setting where the length of the game sequence is fixed, say 10 rounds. With this information one could begin the program construction from the end, rather than the beginning, of the sequence. In the 10th PD the choice of *defect* dominates *cooperate*. Hence, it makes sense to defect regardless of what the other player does in the last game. So, what is to be done in the last game is in fact known on the basis of the dominance relation. Take now the preceding, i.e. ninth game. Since we already know what is to be done in the last game, we can simply assume that this is the last one. By the same (dominance) argument we can infer that the player will defect in the ninth game as well. We can continue this argument until the first game where the prescription is the same, i.e. defect.

What we have done here is to apply Zermelo's algorithm to the sequential PD of known length. The result is disastrous: if both players follow the algorithm they acquire a payoff sum of 10 each even though the sum of 30 would have been achievable. Surely, the *defect always* strategy – ALL-D as it is called by Axelrod – is not the best way to accumulate payoffs. Yet, at the same time, it is impossible to beat ALL-D (AD, for short). If one does something else than AD, one is bound to play *cooperate* at some point when the AD program plays *defect*. In that game the AD player receives the payoff of 5 while the other player gets 0. The AD player thus beats – in the sense of receiving a larger payoff sum than – any other strategy she might be confronted with. Only when facing another AD player does this sequential game strategy break even with her (twin) competitor.

More precisely, AD is a collectively stable strategy. This means that no player resorting to any other strategy can receive a higher payoff sum when playing against an AD player than AD players get when playing against each other. In technical terms, no other strategy played by a single player can *invade* a population which consists of AD players.

In Axelrod's PD tournaments the success of a strategy was determined as the average of the payoffs obtained in playing 200 PDs with each of the participating programs, including the twin of the program. The programs (strategies) confronted by any given program were unknown to the persons invited to participate in writing the programs. Thus, tailoring strategies for certain types of opponents was not possible. Competing in the first tournament there were 15 programs, 14 submitted plus the program choosing *C* and *D* randomly. One of the submitted programs was TFT which in this setting amounted to the following two rules:

1. choose *C* in the first round of PD, and
2. from game 2 onwards, choose whichever choice was made by the opponent in the preceding round.

In terms of the payoff averages the TFT, submitted by Anatol Rapoport, was victorious. Its success was to a large extent accountable by the fact that a majority of the submitted programs were 'nice' in the sense of not choosing D first. Obviously, TFT does not choose D first either, which means that in a sequential PD where TFT faces another nice program, both receive the payoff 3 on every round. Yet, it is equally obvious that TFT cannot invade AD since the latter receives the highest payoff 5 in the first round, while TFT receives 0. Thereafter both get 1 in each subsequent round. This means that no matter how long the game sequence, AD gets a payoff sum which is 5 units larger than that of TFT. Thus, had the tournament submissions been more of the AD variety, TFT would not have been victorious.

All the more surprising, then, is the observation that TFT also won the other tournament arranged by Axelrod shortly after the first one. In this contest there were more than 60 submitted programs. The participants knew of the success of TFT and could, thus, anticipate that it would be present in the second tournament. It turns out that it is very difficult to envisage a metagame strategy that could exploit TFT after the first round. Thus, the longer the sequence of games, the less the weight of the first payoff in the overall payoff sum. Hence, even though TFT can be 'fooled' in the first round, it cannot be exploited thereafter. This follows from the simple logic of reciprocity that underlies it. If the 3, 3 outcome is not reached in any given round, the outcome is 0, 5 where TFT gets 'the sucker's payoff' 0. The only way out of the subsequent 1, 1 is through 5, 0. In a manner of speaking TFT takes back what it lost in the initial defection by its opponent program.

TFT seems to capture the norm of reciprocity in a very succinct way. The success of the program in the PD tournaments where a wide variety of different strategies are confronting with each other seems to suggest that reciprocity is so prevalent in human societies because it guarantees high payoff levels to those who adopt it. Theoretical support for this argument is provided by Axelrod's (1981) two theorems (see also Axelrod 1984). The first pertains to the conditions under which TFT can be a collectively stable strategy. These depend on the valuation of future payoffs by players. As the concept of collective stability involves a comparison of accumulated payoffs of players in an indefinitely long sequence of PDs, the weight of future payoffs in each player's payoff calculus is of crucial importance. It determines whether a 'newcomer' strategy receives a higher payoff against a player resorting to the prevailing strategy than the payoff accruing to those players who play the prevailing strategy against each other.

Consider TFT as the prevailing strategy and AD as the potential invader. It is reasonable to assume that each player has a *discount parameter*, denoted by w, which is used to multiply the present value of a payoff obtained after one time period. A payoff x after one time period has the present value of wx. The parameter takes on values in the [0, 1] interval. A payoff y obtained after two periods has the present value of $w^2 y$, etc. Suppose now that $w = 0$, that is, no payoff received after the first PD game has any value in the player's calculus. In this case AD invades TFT since in the first game against a TFT player AD receives 5 while the TFT player gets 0. The TFT players get 3 when playing against each other. Hence, the invasion succeeds since no payoffs after the first game are taken into account.

But obviously, the clever aspects of TFT never show up if only the first game counts. So, in the following we assume that the players have a non-zero discount rate. Instead of fixed cardinal number payoffs, we shall – following Axelrod – consider the general PD payoff matrix of Table 5.13 where $T > R > P > S$. For TFT to be collectively stable it is necessary and sufficient that any other strategy, when played against TFT, receives a discounted payoff sum that is smaller than the sum accruing to the TFT players when playing with each other.

Table 5.13 The general PD in matrix form

		Column	
		Cooperate	*Defect*
Row	*Cooperate*	R, R	S, T
	Defect	T, S	P, P

Consider now a strategy that in itself is collectively stable, namely AD. Let us denote the discounted payoff sum of players adopting strategy x against players adopting strategy y as $V(x|y)$. In finding out whether TFT is collectively stable against AD we need to compare $V(AD|TFT)$ and $V(TFT|TFT)$. Let us expand these two:

$$V(AD|TFT) = T + wP + w^2P + \cdots = T + \frac{wP}{1-w}.$$

$$V(TFT|TFT) = R + wR + w^2R + \cdots = \frac{R}{1-w}.$$

Now, AD invades TFT if the former payoff is larger than the latter, that is, if

$$T + \frac{wP}{1-w} > \frac{R}{1-w}$$

which amounts to

$$w < \frac{T-R}{T-P}.$$

The opposite condition, that is, $w > (T-R)/(T-P)$ gives the values under which TFT is collectively stable under AD attacks.

In the payoff matrix of Table 5.12 we get the cut-off value 1/2 for w. In other words, if the discount parameter is larger than one-half, then TFT cannot be invaded by AD if the payoffs in each game are those used in Axelrod's PD tournaments.

The far-sightedness of players thus provides one explanation for the survival of norms of reciprocity. But how does this norm become prevalent in AD-type environments? A partial answer to this question is provided by Axelrod's (1981) second theorem. It connects the invasion success of TFT with the properties of the group of TFT players that is immersed in the AD community. It is clear that a single TFT player cannot invade an AD community because her payoff will never reach the level of that obtained by AD players in their mutual interactions. The only way in which TFT may become the prevailing strategy or invade AD, is that a sufficient number of TFT interactions take place with other TFT – or otherwise 'nice' – players. Thereby the losses incurred in AD interactions may be offset by gains in the TFT ones.

Consider a setting where a group of TFT players is scattered among the prevalent AD player community. Assume that with probability q a TFT player encounters another TFT player and with probability $1-q$ an AD player. We also assume that the TFT group is relatively speaking so small that when computing the payoffs of the AD players, the interactions with TFT players can be ignored. Let us see what the expected payoff $E(TFT)$ for the TFT player is:

$$E(TFT) = qV(TFT \mid TFT) + (1-q)V(TFT \mid AD)$$

$$= q\frac{R}{1-w} + (1-q)(S + wP + w^2P + \cdots)$$

$$= q\frac{R}{1-w} + (1-q)\left(S + \frac{wP}{1-w}\right)$$

The expected payoff for the AD players, on the other hand, is $E(AD) = P + wP + w^2P + \ldots = P/(1-w)$.

The invasion of TFT succeeds if $E(TFT) > E(AD)$ which amounts to

$$q\frac{R}{1-w} + (1-q)\left(S + \frac{wP}{1-w}\right) > \frac{P}{1-w}.$$

Solving for q yields:

$$q > \frac{P - S - w(P - S)}{R - S - w(P - S)}.$$

Given the PD payoff matrix and the discount parameter this expression tells us the relative frequency of those interactions that have to take place with other TFT players for a group of them to succeed in invading an AD community. As an illustration, consider Axelrod's tournament payoffs and assume that the discount parameter is 0.8. The above inequality then indicates that whenever $q > 1/11$, the invasion succeeds. In other words, of the interactions of the TFT players not more than 10% need to be with other TFT players to guarantee a higher expected payoff than that enjoyed by the AD players when playing against each other.

The emergence and prevalence of reciprocity can thus be seen as a result of a mechanism that makes intuitive sense. The particular version of reciprocity, TFT, may, however, be questioned. It has been argued that as a principle of criminal justice, this strict version belongs to a (hopefully) bygone age. It is simply not deemed acceptable in modern civilized world to punish criminal offenders on a strictly TFT basis. For example, criminals who have caused other people some bodily harm are not harmed in the same way by the representatives of the criminal justice system. This does not, however, diminish the importance of Axelrod's analysis of the reasons for emergence of some type of reciprocity in societies. Once the reciprocity norm has been adopted, it may undergo changes due to other factors than those discussed in the tournament setting.

There are other reasons to question the applicability of the TFT as a model of how norms evolve in sequential PD settings. To wit, if sequential game strategies are conditional on each other, they must be based on observations of other players' actual choices over time. The observations cannot plausibly be assumed to be error-free. Rather, over extremely long sequences of plays some observation errors are bound to happen. In the simple PD setting, these are of the type that an opponent's C choice is interpreted as a D choice or vice versa. Per Molander (1985) shows that the success of TFT in long sequences of PDs is crucially dependent on the absence of 'noise' in the channel of communication between players. More specifically, arbitrarily small probability of interpreting the C choice as the D choice is accompanied with a dramatic decrease in average payoff: from R to $(T + R + P + S)/4$. As a countermeasure against this decrease Molander suggests a small increase in the level of unconditional cooperation probability from that dictated by TFT. In other words, when the level of disturbance in communication is low, the introduction of pure generosity or altruism seems a prudent strategy for risk-averse players, that is, players who strictly prefer a certain payoff x to a lottery with the expected value equal to x (see also Axelrod and Dion 1988: 1387). So, it seems that deviating from strict TFT in the direction of generosity or altruism has a rational foundation.

Thus far we have largely ignored a feature that intuitively seems important in game-like settings, namely the perception that the players have of each other. It is known that institutions of various type – firms, parties, universities – spend a lot of time and effort in building an image of themselves. This image may be distorted or truthful but in any case it is seen as a factor in determining the success of the institutions. We shall now turn to one aspect of the image that has been given considerable attention in game theoretical literature: reputation.

5.6   Reputation makes a difference

In the above chain store example we dealt with the game situation where a chain store is faced with a potential competitor in one of the several locations it is operating. In Selten's (1978) chain store paradox we take a broader look at the situation involving potential competitors of the chain in several locations. As we saw, there are two Nash equilibria in the chain store game with one entrant.

Only one of them, however, is subgame perfect. This calls for the competitor to enter and the chain to cooperate. The outcome in each game is, thus, 2 for both players. Suppose that there are 20 locations where this game is being played in a sequence and that what we have just considered is the last one. Suppose that the competitor decides to enter. Since it is the last game, the chain does not need to think about any long-term repercussions of its choice, but it can simply pick whichever alternative yields a higher payoff. Clearly, it is *cooperate*. Knowing this, the competitor is, indeed, better off by choosing *enter*. Thus, we end up with (*cooperate*, *enter*) in the last game.

In the 19th game both players know what will happen in the last, 20th, game. So, in essence the 19th game is the last 'undecided' game. By the same argument as above, it makes sense for the competitor to enter and for the chain to cooperate. So, even the 19th game is a foregone conclusion as far as the outcome is concerned. Now, this argument can be traced back to the very first game with the same conclusion: *enter* is the rational thing to do for the competitor and *cooperate* the rational response.

But clearly this does not make sense for the chain. In 20 games it gets the modest payoff of 40 which is clearly much less than it could acquire. In particular, if it announced before the first game that at least in the early games it will respond aggressively to each and every entrant, it could possible gain much more. Selten calls this way of proceeding the *deterrence theory*. Suppose that the chain announces that in the first 18 games it will punish every entrant with aggression. Suppose, furthermore, that its policy will be tested in some of these games. Say, entrants 3, 5, 7 and 11 decide to enter despite the chain's announcement. This means that in these four games the chain's payoff drops to zero. However, in the 14 games where it is not tested the chain receives 70 units of payoff, i.e. a lot more than it would have received in the sequence of 20 games had it followed the backward induction argument. And it still has two games left to play. In these games it may settle with the induction argument and receive an additional 4 units. Thus, by deterrence one might do considerably better than following the induction argument.

Of course, the success of the deterrence depends on whether the other players are deterred. If they are not, then the chain ends up with the meager 4 which it gets in the last two games where it plays cooperatively. This is just 10% of what the induction strategy would have given it. Obviously the chain's success in resorting to deterrence depends on the *credibility* of its threat of aggression, but there is another even more direct consideration, namely the *effectiveness* of the threat.[28] This increases with the absolute difference in the payoffs of the threatened player ensuing from (i) her defying the threat and (ii) her complying with the threat. The larger the difference, the more effective the threat. Credibility, on the other hand, depends on the consequence that carrying out the threat would have on the threatener herself. Suppose that in the chain store-competitor game the former announces a threat to take aggressive measures against each competitor that enters the market. The efficiency of such a threat depends on the difference between outcomes we have denoted by 1 and 0 in Table 5.8. This is the difference in payoffs of the competitor in case she complies with the threat versus her payoff, should she decide to challenge it. The credibility of the threat, on the other hand, is measured by the difference between payoffs 2 and 0, that is, between carrying out the threat versus ignoring the challenge.

As stated, the threat does not seem credible. If the competitor enters, the chain store only loses by aggression. Suppose the chain issues a probabilistic threat: if a competitor enters, the chain will respond aggressively with probability p and cooperatively with probability $1 - p$. Let us now do the payoff calculus for the competitor. If she stays out, her payoff will be 1. If she enters, her expected payoff is $p \times 0 + (1 - p) \times 2 = 2(1 - p)$. This is smaller than 1 if $p > 1/2$. In other words, if the chain will retaliate with a probability larger than 1/2, then the competitor is better off (in expected payoffs) by staying out. The probabilistic threat is more credible than the deterministic one. After all, it does not commit the threatener to acts that are disastrous to both parties. In Chicken games probabilistic threats make a great deal of sense just because they do not commit the threatener to suicidal acts.

The implausibility of the unique subgame perfect equilibrium in the chain store game where the chain cooperates and the competitor enters suggests that there may be something relevant missing in the game description. Rosenthal (1981) questions the plausibility in assuming that the potential entrants know the payoff structure of the chain. Suppose that several entrants have experienced to their disappointment that the chain store does not respond to entrance with cooperation but with aggression. Certainly this experience would diminish the plausibility of a new competitor's assumption that the chain will cooperate and that the competitor should thus enter. At some point it is likely that the competitor questions whether her assumptions regarding the chain store's payoffs are correct. Kreps and Wilson (1982b) combine this observation with the solution concept known as the *sequential equilibrium* (Kreps and Wilson 1982a).

The characteristics of sequential equilibrium:

- When making her choice, each player has some assessment regarding what has happened in the past and – in particular – at which node she is located in the game tree. This assessment is expressed in probability distribution.
- For any strategy to be an equilibrium, it must be consistent with this assessment.
- Starting from every information set, the player makes the choice that is optimal against the opponent's strategies. The optimal choice reflects the past moves of the opponent as well as the assessment concerning the payoffs of the opponent.

If the chain store responds with aggression to entrants, then the assessment of its payoffs is to be modified from the one of Table 5.8. This modification, in turn, calls for modification of the optimal action to be taken, etc. Kreps and Wilson consider the setting in which the entrants are facing either a weak or tough chain store. The difference between these two is in the payoffs. The weak chain store has the payoffs indicated in Table 5.8, while the tough one interchanges the payoffs 0 and 2. That is, the tough chain puts a premium on appearing competitive. This makes aggression the dominant strategy for the chain and thus the competitor is better off staying out. In the course of the play, the entrants update their beliefs about whether they are facing a tough or weak chain store. Their optimal response is modified accordingly. In equilibrium the assessments of the opponent, the beliefs about the game history and the strategies chosen are consistent.

In updating the beliefs regarding the opponent the most common rule stems from *Bayes' theorem* which enables the conversion of *a priori* probabilities into *a posteriori* ones. The theorem is a rule for updating one's probability assessment in the light of evidence. To illustrate, let us assume that a competitor knows from previous experience that 40% of chains that resort to aggressive strategies contact the top personnel of the competitors and offer them lucrative positions in the chain's organization. Also some cooperative chains do that, but their share is only 10% among the cooperative chains. Previous experience also indicates that about 70% of the chains fight aggressively their prospective competitors. Let us denote the event that the chain contacts the competitor's top personnel with attractive job offers by E and the event that the chain is tough by A. What the competitor thus knows is that

$$P(E|A) = 0.40$$

and

$$P(E|A') = 0.10$$

where A' denotes the absence (or complement) of event A, in this case the event of being a cooperative chain. Now, suppose that event A is observed, i.e. the chain representatives contact the personnel of the competitor with job offers. What is the likelihood that the competitor is facing a tough rather than cooperative chain? The answer is given by Bayes' formula:

$$P(A|E) = \frac{P(A)P(E|A)}{P(A)P(E|A) + P(A')P(E|A')}$$

which in our example yields:

$$P(A|E) = \frac{0.70 \times 0.40}{0.70 \times 0.40 + 0.30 \times 0.10} = 0.90.$$

Thus, on the basis of this evidence the competitor is advised to update her probability of being faced with a tough chain from 0.7 to 0.9. This, in turn, implies that the optimal strategy gives more probability weight to staying out than before the updating.

The solution concepts touched upon above – subgame perfect, trembling-hand and sequential equilibrium – are a sample of refinements of Nash equilibria (see e.g. Osborne and Rubinstein 1994; Van Damme 1987; Van Damme 2002, as well as Hillas and Kohlberg 2002 for comprehensive discussions). In other words, they are all Nash equilibria, but sometimes constitute proper subsets of the latter. The basic motivation of these and other refinements is typically the implausibility of some Nash equilibria. Sometimes acting in accordance with the dictates of Nash is downright irrational. Especially, in situations which are not supposed to arise at all, following Nash equilibrium strategy may be irrational. Which paths in the game tree are most likely is to a large extent determined by the reputation of the players. The evidence gathered in the course of the play may, in turn, modify the reputation. The recognition that the belief systems and their evolution play a central role in determining optimal strategies has been one of the main features underlying modern game theory.

5.7   ... and much hinges upon the quality of information

Reputation is but one of the factors that – in addition to the strategy sets and payoff function – complicates reasoning over what would constitute a rational play of the game.[29] Reputation pertains to the information the players have about each other and the circumstances under which the game is being played. In modern game theory it is customary to make two seemingly closely related distinctions: (i) one between games of perfect and imperfect information and (ii) the other between complete and incomplete information. The former distinction is related to the rules of the game. In *games of perfect information*, each information set contains just one node (Binmore 1992: 501). In other words, when making her choice, each player knows precisely what has happened earlier in the game. She also knows all the possible consequences of her choice contingent on the choice of the other player. In games of imperfect information at least one information set consists of several nodes.

Games of incomplete information are, in fact, not games at all in the game-theoretic sense.[30] That is, they do not contain all the information needed to construct a strategy set for each player and the payoff function specifying the payoffs to each player as a function of the strategy choices made. When dealing with games of incomplete information, we typically lack information about player preferences or beliefs. In some cases also the rules of the game may be in doubt. The so-called *Harsanyi transformation* maps the games of incomplete information into those of imperfect one (Harsanyi 1967, 1968a, 1968b). More specifically, it assumes a set of player types and probability distributions over these types. Given that the players do not know which kind of player they are confronted with, they assign each player type a probability. The type, in turn, determines (or is defined by) the preferences and beliefs of the player. Thus, each player has a probability distribution which tells her the probability of being paired with a player of a specific type. This assumption thus transforms an incompletely specified game into a set of games, each with a specific probability of appearing.

Among games of incomplete information of special interest for political economy are games where the *information is distributed asymmetrically*. In those games one player is in possession of information that the other does not have. The information may be related to the properties of the player (her skills, attitudes, values, physical or mental strength, etc.) or some acts she has performed. For example, if you are to hire a research assistant, the skills, motivation and working habits of the applicants are probably of great interest to you. Yet, it is possible that not all relevant information is disclosed in the application documents. Similarly, it may happen that some of the persons applying for the job have already received offers from elsewhere, unbeknownst to you. The distribution of information is asymmetric to the extent that the applicants know their own properties and acts better than you do.

Not all games of asymmetric information are those of incomplete information. Suppose that your friend says that she would like to withdraw from the distractions of her office to her vacation home deep in the wilderness in order to finish the book she has been working on for some time. She does not own a laptop computer and turns to you, the proud owner of a brand new device. The two of you strike a deal whereby she pays you $50 per week for the laptop. Both of you know the properties and condition of the computer. At the time of striking the deal you do not know how careful your friend is going to be in handling your computer. She may return it after one week, pay you $50 as agreed and the computer might be a complete wreck. Or she might return your laptop in perfect condition after a few weeks. It all depends on how gently she has handled the computer. Settings like this are quite common in everyday life. They are called *moral hazard*. Its essential features are that at the time of the agreement, both players know that the eventual payoffs depend in part on what will happen in the future and one of the players has more control on the developments than the other. Examples of moral hazard include insurance, share holder and management interaction and many other kinds of principal–agent games. In these games one player, the principal, hires another, the agent, to do certain tasks for her. To the extent that hiring contracts are made, as they typically are, in advance of the actual performing of the tasks, these contracts always involve a moral hazard.

Sometimes a distinction is made between two types of moral hazard. On the one hand we have settings where the lack of information pertains to properties of players (skill, ability to learn languages, etc.) rather than to their acts. These are called moral hazard with hidden information. On the other hand, we have moral hazard settings due to hidden actions (Rasmusen 1989: 133). Our example above is of the latter variety. The usefulness of the distinction between these two types is somewhat questionable. In fact, it is often difficult to draw a line between moral hazard due to hidden information, on the one hand, and some settings of incomplete information games.

Informational asymmetries feature also in games of incomplete information (Rasmusen 1989: 181–222). The paradigmatic setting is called *adverse selection*. It is the basic contract setting where one of the parties does not know the strategies and/or payoffs of the other. Typically, the former player is the principal who at the time of signing the contract does not know the agent to whom she assigns some tasks. The eventual payoff of the parties depends on the performance of the agent, but in the agent's case also – to an extent unknown to the principal – on other factors. An example is the interaction between a voter and the MP who represents her in the parliament. At the time of voting the voter may have some information about the values and interests that the MP – if elected – would pursue in the parliament, but over the election term new issues will appear in the agenda. Since the overall performance of the MP in the voter's opinion depends partly on these unknown issues, the 'type' of the MP is fundamentally unknown for the voter at the time of the election. This setting is nearly indistinguishable from moral hazard.

A special class of adverse selection games consists of situations where the players may send information about themselves to the other player. These situations are called *signaling games* (see Banks 1991 for a survey). The signals transmitted may concern policy plans, budget requests, educational choices or other kind of information which is deemed relevant for the payoffs. The information may or may not be accurate and the signaling act itself costless or costly. An example of signaling game models is one constructed and analyzed by Banks (1989). It is based on Niskanen's (1971) theory of budgetary process whereby agencies send budget requests to a committee. In this model the agency makes a budget proposal which the committee can accept, reject or subject to an audit. If it accepts, the proposal will become the budget of the agency, and if it rejects, there will be no transaction. If the committee decides to submit the agency to an audit the outcome of the audit determines the budget. The audit is, however, costly. Two procedures are considered: the closed one and the open one. In the former, the committee is restricted to the above three alternatives. In the open procedure, on the other hand, it may present its counteroffer which the agency may accept or reject. Under specific assumptions regarding utility functions of the players and varying the costs of auditing, Banks shows that in the closed procedure there is a fundamental tradeoff between equity and efficiency which is determined by the cost of auditing. Efficiency loss may occur due to either no exchange or to auditing. If there is no exchange, both players would suffer, while if there is an audit, the committee would receive the same budget but without the cost of auditing. Equity refers to the distribution of surplus between the committee and the agency. If the auditing costs are high, the agency benefits from inflated budget requests, while if the costs are very low, the committee takes the entire surplus.

With open procedure, it turns out that the budget requests have no significance in determining the agency's budget in equilibrium. Indeed, they have no informational role at all. Instead the auditing costs are crucial in determining the outcome. Somewhat paradoxically, Banks shows that in the equilibrium the closed procedure is more preferable to the committee than the open one, despite the fact that in the latter it can make counteroffers.

5.8   The role of two-person game theory

When the rules of the game, strategies and payoffs are all common knowledge among the players, we are dealing with *games of complete information*. It is useful to study these games since they enable us to focus on the basic elements of strategic behavior, strategies, outcomes, payoffs and various solution concepts. From the viewpoint of practical application, the games of complete information may, however, be unrealistic. Knowing another person's preferences or her beliefs regarding which actions are available to her or even her beliefs of the causal mechanism whereby actions result in outcomes, is a strong assumption, indeed. Consequently, when predictions concerning outcomes fail, this may be due to several things. Firstly, the actors may simply be irrational and thus contradict the behavior predictions based on rationality assumption. Secondly, their view of the interaction situation may differ from the one that the analyst comes up with. In particular, the players may believe that outcomes ensuing from the strategy choices are not those envisioned by the analyst. Thirdly, the players may assign the outcomes subjective values that differ from the analyst's payoff assignments. Fourthly, the players' knowledge of each other's preferences and/or strategy sets may be cursory or downright incorrect. In other words, various types of informational asymmetries may be involved and/or the game may be one of incomplete information.

So, there are many reasons for predictions based on two-person game theory to fail in real world games. Indeed, it is not common to see the theory being applied in purely predictive settings. Although international conflicts, labor disputes, plea bargaining, etc., feature in game theory texts, it is not typical that the theory would be used as a tool for predicting what is still unknown. Rather the theory is used as a benchmark against which empirical data are being evaluated. Thus, one compares the outcome of the interaction with various solutions to the corresponding game. The role of the theory is rather in explaining than predicting facts. The theory provides a structure for analyzing and accounting for events that have occurred in terms of goals of actors, their options, knowledge and beliefs.

To explain why the US and its allies invaded Iraq in the spring of 2003, it is illuminating to know the interests and goals of the US and Iraq, their strategic options and crucial beliefs: in the case of the US the strategic options included strengthening of the trade embargo, military operations of limited scope, and an all-out invasion. The primary interest of the US (at least in media reporting) was to fight terrorism or, more specifically, its particular movement, al Qaeda, which was believed to be responsible for the September 2001 attacks on the US. The crucial belief of the US was that Iraq was involved in the al Qaeda activities and was, therefore, a threat to the US and its strategic allies through its programs to develop and produce weapons of mass destruction. Iraq's strategic options included cooperation with the UN inspector teams, making concessions in the form of disarming some of its forces and dismantling weapons programs   or ignoring the UN resolutions and assuming a nonconciliatory posture in negotiations. Iraq's crucial beliefs, in turn, may have included one according to which the US's threshold for going to war against it is critically higher than in the case of invasion to Afghanistan.

Of course, seeing the US and Iraq as players involves an enormous simplification since in both countries there were several conflicting or mutually reinforcing political forces that could with equal justification be called players. Yet, for the analysis of the conflict on the level of powers most directly involved it is useful to regard the country leaderships as players. This does not exclude the possibility to consider the policy formation within both countries as a lower-level game between various power-holders.

To account for an event by invoking considerations that made its occurrence inevitable in the light of the actors' preferences, knowledge, beliefs and strategies is basically what we normally do in trying to make certain types of events intelligible. Game theory adds to this commonplace activity a standard language and a set of analysis techniques. Siebe (1992: 180) writes of an encounter with an ambassador who had been involved with many an international negotiation and enjoyed considerable esteem among his peers because of his success in those negotiations. Yet, this ambassador had never heard of game theory. The story is in a way telling. Like the proverbial person who had been conducting his conversations in prose throughout his life without knowing the meaning of the word 'prose', people use game theoretic reasoning quite instinctively without realizing that there might be an abstract theory which sheds more general light on why certain negotiators are successful and others are not. Especially in the field of diplomacy the game theoretic reasoning is quite natural and often employed without direct reference to the theory. Notions like strategy, goals, options, beliefs, regarding the opponent's preferences, etc., belong to the normal parlance of diplomacy and news reporting.

So, the two-person game models are more often to be found in accounts that aim at explaining why some things happened than in predictive settings. It is simply easier to distinguish strategies, beliefs and preferences after the fact than before it. Game situations in the real world are always embedded in larger contexts. The labor negotiations are rarely a once-for-all encounter. Similarly, international political conflicts are rarely 'purely political', but often involve economic, cultural and human rights issues. Thus, game situations encountered in the real world are typically nested: what seems to be irrational and even self-destructive strategy in one game may be just one necessary step in an effort to maximize payoff in the larger game. The analogy of losing a battle in order to win the war is often an apt one.

The two-person game models have, however, another role in political economy, namely that of providing a test-bed for evaluations. The evaluations may pertain to strategies resorted to by the players, but more often to the norms or arrangements underlying the game. A case in point is the enormous interest that the Prisoner's Dilemma game aroused in the scholarly community. The reason for this interest is mainly due to the fact that this simple game situation enables us to analyze the consequences of adhering to conflicting norms of behavior. At the same time this conflict has been seen as common in many spheres of social life. So, understanding this simple game opens vistas for accounting for significant aspects of social, political and economic systems. Indeed, one could argue that a crucial activity of the public sector is to provide cooperative solutions to PD's. Ullman-Margalit (1977) analyzes the norms that have been devised to resolve PDs. Thus, seeing norms and institutions in the light of the PD or some other game model provides a new angle towards understanding what norms and institutions do or what they are good for.

Much of the early criticism of game theory was directed towards its alleged normative bias. Since many examples – notably the Battle of the Bismark Sea – were models of military confrontations, it was felt that this theory was just another weapon in the arsenal of the big powers.[31] Thus, the whole enterprize was deemed morally questionable. Today these suspicions are less commonly encountered and for good reason. The simple 2×2 games do not provide strategic actors with new insights. These models do not 'teach' them anything they do not already know. To the contrary, the real world actors have provided game theorists good reasons to modify, elaborate and refine their concepts, especially solutions. The fact that the players sometimes stick to cooperative strategies in Chicken or PD games and sometimes fail to do so begs the question of whether the game models contain all relevant information about the situations in which the players find themselves. Especially the assumptions that the players make of each other's preferences and beliefs, the information they have of each other's behavior patterns as well as the long-term payoff opportunities are all considerations that have been suggested by contrasting simple game models with the real world behaviors.

The understanding that game theory gives of political economy is inherently reductionistic in the sense that the states of affairs, processes, structures and patterns of behavior are accounted for by seeing them as outcomes of strategic interaction involving agents with at most partial control over the outcomes. Given the players, their strategy sets and assumptions concerning the principles governing their behavior (e.g. rationality), the theory enables us to simulate games that have not yet been played. This is perhaps the most important role of game theory especially when it comes to designing institutions.

5.9   Suggested reading

The classic opus in game theory is von Neumann and Morgenstern (1944), but it makes difficult reading for a beginner. Much more accessible is Luce and Raiffa (1957). Brams (1975) is also a very useful text for a reader interested in political applications of game theory. More up-to-date and advanced general texts on game theory are Fudenberg and Tirole (1991), Myerson (1991), and Owen (2001). Dutta (1999) and Osborne (2004) as well as Osborne and Rubinstein (1994), in turn, are of introductory nature and, especially the two first-mentioned ones, appropriate as first texts in game theory. Collective action is dealt with in Hardin (1982) and (1995). While most literature focuses on finding reasons for the emergence of 'beneficial' cooperation, the latter book also discusses cases where cooperation is arguably not beneficial for the excluded parties. For readers of German language, Holler and Illing (2003) is a cogent introduction and overview of game theory. It is written mainly for students of economics, but can be used in other academic fields as well. Good introductions to asymmetric information games are Banks (1991), Calvert (1986) and Rasmusen (1989).

6 Bargaining and coalitions

Two-person games discussed above are non-cooperative. In other words, it has been assumed that the players are not able to make enforceable commitments regarding their future strategy choices. They may announce plans to play certain strategies, but by definition these announcements are not binding. Many negotiation, deal-making and bargaining activities take place under circumstances where binding commitments can be assumed. In other words, in these situations the parties typically keep their word once the deal has been made. For example, in labor negotiations of the modern developed world the parties know that they will be facing each other again in the not-too-distant future and that it therefore makes no sense to renege from one's commitments given at the negotiation table. In other contexts, there may be a contract-enforcing body with adequate powers to ensure that contracts are being adhered to. It thus makes sense to study rational behavior under cooperative settings.

6.1 Classic solutions

Let us begin with a fictitious example of a two-person negotiation. The negotiation parties are Union 1 and Union 2, the former representing employees and the latter employers. The subject of negotiation is a five-year contract on general standards to be followed in individual labor contracts within an industry. In the course of lengthy negotiations five proposals have been put on the table. The first – alternative 1 – is Union 1's favorite, guaranteeing a sizable wage increase as well as strengthening of employment security and health insurance benefits. Alternative 3 is Union 2's proposal containing a small wage increase accompanied with a slight deterioration in occupation related benefits. Alternative 2 has been presented as a take-it-or-leave-it proposal by Union 1 once it has become apparent that the time reserved for negotiation is running out and strike is imminent. This proposal involves a somewhat smaller wage increase than alternative 1 combined with keeping the benefits on their present level over the contract period. Alternatives 4 and 5 represent early proposals involving relatively small changes in the *status quo*.

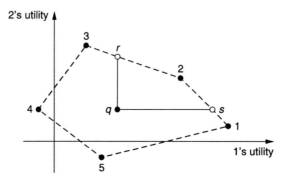

Figure 6.1 Two-person bargaining.

In Figure 6.1 the alternatives 1–5 are represented as points in a two-dimensional space. The horizontal axis stands for Union 1's utility values and the vertical axis for Union 2's values. The utility values are purely fictitious, but reflect the fact that alternative 1 is Union 1's favorite, alternative 3 Union 2's, and alternative 2 is a compromise between these two. The assumption that Union 1 has made the compromise proposal is reflected by the horizontal distances between 1, 2 and 3: the compromise alternative is closer to Union 1's than Union 2's favorite. The point *q* in Figure 6.1 represents the utility values for unions in case no agreement is reached. It is called the *threat point*.

The dotted lines represent theoretical alternatives. Consider the line segment connecting point 1 to point 2. The coordinates of the points on this line segment are weighted averages of the coordinates of the end points of the line (i.e. 1 and 2). If we assume that the bargaining process is repeated indefinitely many times and the parties choose outcome 1 half of the time and alternative 2 half of the time, their payoffs (expected utilities) are represented by the point in the midway between the end points of the dotted line connecting 1 and 2. If they choose alternative 1 more often than alternative 2, then the expected utilities are closer to point 1. In fact, all points in the dotted line represent the expected utility of some probability mixture of alternatives 1 and 2. And vice versa, all probability mixtures of 1 and 2 can be represented by a point on this line.

Thus, if the parties agree on an outcome that is represented by some point on the line segment 12, then they can presumably also agree on how to achieve this, given that 1 and 2 are achievable outcomes. The same applies to points along the line segments 23, 34, 45 and 15. That is, the outcomes along these line segments represent probability mixtures of the outcomes represented by the end points. In other words, given that the parties are engaged in a cooperative game, all these outcomes can be achieved. The outcomes on the dashed-line segments between end points, however, are theoretical in the sense of representing expected values. They are of the same nature as mixed strategies.

Not only the vertices and edges of the Figure 6.1 pentagon but also the points located inside it represent probability mixtures of alternatives. Thus, for example, the coordinates of point q can be computed as a weighted average of the coordinates of points 1–5. The same applies to every point in the interior of the pentagon. This is due to the construction of the pentagon. The dotted lines together with the vertices define a *convex hull* generated by points 1–5 in two dimensions. This is by definition the set characterized by three conditions:

- all generating points (1–5) belong to the set,
- every line connecting any two points of the generating point set also belongs to the set, and
- no proper subset of the set satisfies the two preceding conditions (i.e. the constructed set is the smallest possible one),

The earliest solution concept for two-person bargaining games has been attributed to von Neumann and Morgenstern (Luce and Raiffa 1957: 118; Riker and Ordeshook 1973: 232). It invokes two intuitively reasonable considerations. Firstly, neither player settles for smaller payoffs than she would receive without negotiations. Secondly, the players do not accept *Pareto inferior*, i.e. Pareto suboptimal outcomes. The first requirement boils down to individual rationality: if one has to choose between two options, it is rational to choose the preferred one. If one knows that through negotiations the outcome is worse than without them, one walks away from the negotiation table. This requirement is often used as a justification for breaking negotiations.

John von Neumann (1903–1957), a Hungarian-born mathematician was – together with Oskar Morgenstern (1902–1977) – the founder of modern game theory. His exceptional mathematical talent was recognized very early on in his career. In his early thirties he became one of the professors of mathematics in the new Institute of Advanced Study in Princeton. This institution was to become quite central in the development of game theory. von Neumann was also one of the pioneers of modern computer science (automata theory), mathematical logic and the theory of measurement. The range of his scholarly activities is truly astonishing. His best-known work in game theory is *Theory of Games and Economic Behavior* (with Oskar Morgenstern) (1944).

The second consideration, on the other hand, appeals to collective rationality: the players should not settle for outcomes that are not *Pareto optimal*. The argument is straightforward: if either player proposes a Pareto suboptimal outcome, the other player can always propose another outcome that guarantees the first one at least the amount of her proposal and the second player strictly more than in the suboptimal proposal.

R. Duncan Luce (born 1925) is an American mathematical psychologist. In addition to his work on decision and game theory he has made major contributions to the theory of measurement as well as to the theory of choice. His main book-length works are *Games and Decisions* (with Howard Raiffa) (1957), *Individual Choice Behavior* (1959), *Foundations of Measurement, Vol I* (with P. Suppes, D. Krantz and A. Tversky) (1971), *Foundations of Measurement, Vol II* (with P. Suppes, D. Krantz and A. Tversky) (1989), *Foundations of Measurement, Vol III* (with P. Suppes, D. Krantz and A. Tversky) (1990) and *Response Times* (1986). In 2003 he was awarded the National Medal of Science by the president of the United States.

The outcomes that satisfy these two requirements, individual rationality and Pareto optimality, constitute the *negotiation set*. Outcomes in the negotiation set guarantee each player at least the same payoff as the threat point. Moreover, these outcomes are Pareto optimal, i.e. an improvement in either player's payoff can be achieved only at the cost of reducing the payoff of the other player. In Figure 6.1 the negotiation set consists of line segments *r2* and *2s*. The horizontal and vertical lines through point *q*, the threat point, delineate the area in the two-dimensional space which satisfies the individual rationality condition: outcomes above the horizontal and to the right of the vertical lines represent individually rational payoffs. The individually rational area within the convex hull can further be restricted by the Pareto optimality requirement. All outcomes inside the area are Pareto dominated by at least one point along the line segments *r2* and *2s*. In other words, for any outcome *x* inside the quadrangular area *qr2s* there is another outcome on the two line segments that gives both players at least as high payoff as, and to at least one of them strictly higher payoff than, *x*.

Howard Raiffa (born 1924) is an American decision theorist who has made major contributions also to study of negotiations, auctions and other allocation mechanisms. Raiffa is one of the founders and the first director of the International Institute of Applied Systems Analysis (IIASA) in Austria. His most important books are *Games and Decisions* (with R. Duncan Luce) (1957), *Decision Analysis* (1968), *The Art and Science of Negotiations* (1982), *Negotiation Analysis* (with John Richardson and David Metcalfe) (2002) and *Smart Choices* (with John Hammond and Ralph Keeney) (2002).

The plausibility of the negotiation set as a solution concept for two-person bargaining games is obvious. Its major drawback is that it specifies a large number of outcomes as solutions. To restrict the number of solutions has led to several theoretical approaches to what is known as the *bargaining problem*. The earliest one resulted in the *Nash solution* (Nash 1950). This has nothing to do with the Nash equilibrium which pertains to non-cooperative games. The Nash solution to the bargaining problem is obtained by imposing restrictions – called axioms – on outcomes. In the same way as individual rationality and Pareto optimality can be seen as restrictions on plausible outcomes, one may try to find further restrictions which are mutually compatible and lead to manageable set of solution outcomes. Nash shows that there is a set of such restrictions which does even better, that is, it leads to a unique solution to the bargaining problem. The approach Nash resorts to is known as axiomatic method. This has been used extensively in many branches of science, notably in the foundations of measurement in general and the measurement of probability and preference, in particular (e.g. Krantz *et al.* 1971; Luce 1967; Roberts 1979; Fishburn 1970). In the following we shall briefly outline the Nash axioms.[32]

The first axiom we have already encountered: Pareto optimality. The second is *independence of linear transformations*. It states that if the utility scales of players are linearly transformed, so are the solutions. For example, suppose that the players' utilities are identical with monetary payoffs. Let the point (x_0, y_0) be the solution when the values are expressed in US dollars. Transform now the payoffs (linearly, that is, by multiplying each value with the same constant) into South African rand and compute the solution. Denote it by (v_0, w_0). Independence of linear transformations requires that the decision alternatives which bring about the (x_0, y_0) outcome in the first case are identical to those associated with the (v_0, w_0) one in the second.

The third axiom is called *symmetry*. It pertains to solutions in games that are symmetric in the sense that whenever the point (x, y) represents a possible outcome in the game, point (y, x) also does. Assuming that q is on the diagonal, the symmetry axiom requires that in symmetric games the solution payoffs to players must be identical. The fourth axiom is also familiar from the preceding: individual rationality. These four axioms characterize several plausible solution concepts. Adding the following fifth one puts the Nash solution into a class of its own. This axiom is known as *independence of irrelevant alternatives*. It states that if the solution outcome belongs to a subset of decision alternatives, then it should also be a solution in case all other alternatives except this subset were excluded. To illustrate, assume that the players negotiate about the amount of funds to invest in a joint venture. The amounts considered range from USD 5000 to USD 10,000. Assume that the solution is associated with amounts of 7000 from each player. The independence of irrelevant alternatives requires that in case it turns out that one of the players can only invest from 5000 to 7000, the solution should still remain the same, i.e. 7000 from each.

The axioms are not of much assistance in determining the Nash solution in a given two-person bargaining game. What is needed is the computation formula. It is based on distances of Pareto optimal points from the threat point. More specifically, the Nash solution singles out that particular point from the set of Pareto optimal outcomes that maximizes the product of the horizontal and vertical distances from the threat point. This is intuitively plausible since the larger the horizontal (vertical, respectively) distance, the larger player 1's (player 2's) payoff with respect to the threat point. Let the coordinates of the threat point be (q_1, q_2) and denote by S the convex hull generated by the decision alternatives.

Then for any point (x_i, y_i) in S, the expression $(x_i - q_1)(y_i - q_2)$ is the Nash product associated with the point. The Nash bargaining solution is the point in S which maximizes this product.

The plausibility of the Nash solution hinges on the axioms underlying it. More informally, it can be defended on the grounds that:

- it is always a point in the negotiations set,
- it does not depend on the particular utility units used in measuring player preferences,
- it is anonymous, i.e. the names of the players do not affect the solution,
- small errors in measuring utilities are not accompanied with large errors in the solution, and
- the threat capabilities of players should be reflected in the solution (Luce and Raiffa 1957: 123; see also Osborne 2004: 481–489).

Yet, the axiom that is specific to this solution, namely the independence of irrelevant alternatives, can, with some justification, be held in doubt. An often-cited example of Luce and Raiffa (1957: 133) illustrates these doubts. Its slightly modified version is shown in Figure 6.2.

The figure depicts two bargaining games. The origin represents the threat point in both games. As in the preceding, the coordinate axes measure the utilities of various outcomes for player 1 (horizontal axis) and player 2 (vertical axis). The negotiation set is spanned by points A, B and C in the left game and by points D, B and C in the right one. B is the midpoint on the line from A to C. It is the Nash solution in the left game.[33] In the right game the outcome A is infeasible. Thus, the outcomes spanning the convex hull of feasible outcomes are C, B and D. This does not affect the Nash solution: it is still point B since at this point the Nash product is maximized. This stands to reason: since the product is maximized at B in the original, larger, set of outcomes, it is also maximized at the same point when a proper subset of outcomes is considered. Yet, this is implausible, argue the critics. The Nash solution in the right game gives player 2 her maximum attainable payoff, while player 1 has to settle for much less than her maximum.

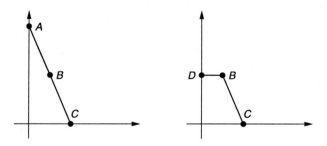

Figure 6.2 Is independence plausible?

The argument can be strengthened by assuming that player 1's maximum feasible payoff is very small, say one percent, compared to the maximum payoff of player 2. Under these circumstances it may, indeed, seem unreasonable that in the right game the worse-off player has to settle for less than her (very small) maximum, while the better-off one gets all she can get at the Nash solution.

Considerations like these call into question the independence of the irrelevant alternative axiom. However, an obvious counterargument would point to the fact that if one deems the maximization of the Nash product desirable in the first place, then inter-player payoff comparisons should not play any role in determining the solution. If they do, they should be introduced as axioms.

The Nash solution has, indeed, found competitors in the literature. In most cases the competing solution concepts have retained all but one of the Nash axioms, i.e. the independence of irrelevant alternatives. The *Kalai–Smorodinsky solution* replaces the independence axiom with one known as *restricted monotonicity* (Kalai and Smorodinsky 1975). This axiom states that if the maximum attainable payoffs for both players are the same in two games, one of which consists of a proper subset of the outcomes of the other game, then the payoffs associated with the solution of the larger game may not be smaller than those of the smaller game. In other words, adding strategic opportunities of players is never accompanied with smaller payoffs at the solution.

To find the Kalai–Smorodinsky solution to a two-person bargaining game one first finds the maximum achievable payoffs for both players. Call these values c_1 and c_2, respectively. One then draws the vertical and horizontal lines $x = c_1$ and $y = c_2$. These intersect at (c_1, c_2). One then draws the line from this point to the threat point q. The point at which this line intersects the negotiation set is the Kalai–Smorodinsky solution. The point (c_1, c_2) is sometimes called the *utopia point* for the obvious reason that it represents the outcome where both players get the maximum achievable outcome. This is feasible only under very special circumstances, namely when the convex hull spanned by the decision alternatives forms a quadrangular area. Hence the label of utopia point is, in general, appropriate.

Figure 6.3 illustrates the behavior of the Kalai–Smorodinsky (KS) solution. The feasible outcomes are the same as in Figure 6.2. The arrows point to the KS solution which in the right game is different from the Nash one. In other words, the KS solution does not satisfy the independence of irrelevant alternative axiom. That the KS solution satisfies the restricted monotonicity axiom cannot be verified on the basis of this example since the maximum achievable payoffs are not the same for player 2 in the two games.

From the axiomatic point of view, the KS solution differs from Nash's in satisfying restricted monotonicity instead of independence of irrelevant alternatives (Roth 1979). Several other solutions to two-person bargaining games have been introduced and axiomatized. Most of them boil down to specifying a general principle to single out a unique outcome from the negotiation set (see Moulin 1988a; Roth 1979; Salonen 1987; Thomson 1981; Thomson and Lensberg 1989). As in the example of Figure 6.2 the principles are related

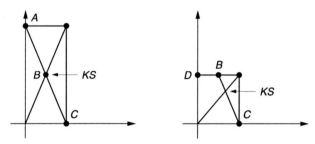

Figure 6.3 The Kalai–Smorodinsky solution.

to various criteria one can impose on reasonable or fair outcomes. Thus, the two-person bargaining game setting allows us to analyze – in highly simplified models – the issues related to justice. However, in order to persist, these principles have to possess another feature in addition to fairness, i.e. stability.

6.2   Stability, core and bargaining sets

A defining characteristic of equilibria is some kind of stability. In the case of the Nash equilibrium this amounts to the requirement that the strategy choices of players are best responses to each other. In multi-player games, generally known as *n*-person games, stability considerations also play an important role. The earliest solution concepts to *n*-person games are the *core* and the *stable set*. To outline them, we need some conceptual apparatus. Multi-person games are typically about coalitions that the players form and about the way they distribute the payoffs among themselves. Sometimes these games deal with other strategies in addition to coalition building ones, but the classic solution concepts concern just coalitions. The multi-person or *n*-person games are usually divided into those with transferable (TU) and those without transferable utility (NTU). The former are games in which the payoff accruing to a coalition is divisible in arbitrary ways among the coalition members. In the NTU games, the payoffs are not arbitrarily divisible, but each coalition is associated with consequences, each of which is a fixed division of the payoff among the coalition members (Osborne and Rubinstein 1994: 268). Our focus is on the TU games.

The *n*-person games are defined in terms of a *characteristic function*, typically denoted by $v(S)$ where S is a coalition, i.e. a distinct group of players.[34] Given any coalition S, the function v indicates the value, worth or payoff of this coalition. It is something that the members of S (individual players or sometimes smaller groups of them) can divide among themselves independently of what other players – that is, those not belonging to S – do. The main goal of *n*-person game theory is to suggest solutions to games defined in terms of characteristic functions. Solutions contain a specification of both the coalitions that will form and the payoff distribution among players. It is common to assume that the games studied are *cohesive*, that is, the value $v(N)$ of the coalition consisting of all players is larger than or equal to the sum of the values of all coalitions in any *partition* of the player set N. A partition is an assignment of each player into one of mutually exclusive and exhaustive subsets (coalitions). In cohesive games, then, the largest value that the players can obtain is by forming the grand coalition of all players.[35]

The *core* of a (TU) voting game is a coalition structure and a payoff distribution over players which has the property that no group of players can form a new coalition that guarantees its members a strictly larger payoff than the prevailing one. In other words, each player group lacks either the will or desire to form a new coalition. In this sense the coalition structure represents the best response of each coalition to the prevailing coalitions formed by other players. Thus, the core is very much in the spirit of the Nash equilibrium.

To illustrate the core concept, let us consider a three-person game discussed by Young (1994: 85). Three towns, A, B and C are planning to build a joint water distribution system. They can build completely separate systems, but would make substantial savings if they cooperate with one or both of the other players. The costs expressed in millions of dollars are $c(A) = 11$ for A, $c(B) = 7$ for B and $c(C) = 8$ for C. If two towns join hands the respective costs are $c(AB) = 15$, $c(AC) = 13$, and $c(BC) = 10$, while it is $c(ABC) = 20$ if all three join in. We are here dealing with a cost-sharing game where the definition of the core can be expressed as the requirement that no player or coalition pays more than its stand-alone cost, i.e. the cost indicated above for each town and town coalition. Thus, for a distribution to be in the core, it would have to charge B and C together no more than 10 million. Similarly, A and C can be charged jointly no more than 13 million, while A and B can pay jointly at most 15 million. Denoting the cost allocations at the core by $x(A)$, $x(B)$ and $x(C)$, respectively, we thus get the following system of inequalities:

$$x(A) + x(B) \leq 15$$

$$x(A) + x(C) \leq 13$$

$$x(B) + x(C) \leq 10$$

The two first inequalities amount to: $x(B) \leq x(C) + 2$. Substituting this to the third one yields: $x(C) \leq 4$. Thus, at the core $x(A) < 9$, $x(B) \leq 6$ and $x(C) \leq 4$, but this is not compatible with $c(ABC) = 20$. Hence, there is no core in this cost-sharing game.

A slight modification of the coalition costs transforms this game into one with a core. To wit, assigning town coalitions AC and BC the costs 14 and 13, respectively, restores the compatibility between the cost-share restrictions. It can be argued, however, that the outcomes in the core are not always plausible. In fact in some cases one can be almost certain that the core outcomes will not materialize. Raiffa *et al.* (2002: 444–446) gives one example involving three parties A, B and C. The characteristic function assigns each singleton coalition the value 0. The coalitions AB, AC and ABC are given 10, while BC is given 0. Thus, A has to be present in any coalition if it is to have non-zero value, but A needs at least one partner. There is a core in this game. In fact, it is the unique distribution of payoffs that gives A, B and C 10, 0 and 0, respectively. This outcome would, however, seem highly unlikely since, unless A is joined by at least one other player, she will receive nothing. One could argue that this fact necessitates that the other players are given some payoff in the outcome.

In the debate on the core as the solution concept it has also been maintained that the mere impossibility of deviation from a given coalition structure and the associated payoff distribution is not all that determines the stability of the outcome. It may happen that even though deviation is possible it is likely to trigger a process of countermoves that results in outcomes that are inferior to the players making the first move. Considerations like this have given rise to two types of solutions: (i) the *stable set*, and (ii) the *bargaining set* (Osborne and Rubinstein 1994: 277–283).

To define the stable set, consider a payoff distribution that gives every player at least the payoff that she would receive if she formed a coalition alone. These kinds of distributions are called *imputations*. Consider two imputations x and y (both are vectors indicating the payoff accruing to each player). The imputation x is an objection of the coalition S of players to imputation y if all members of S receive a strictly larger payoff under x than under y and if the sum of payoffs under x is no larger than $v(S)$. In other words, an objection amounts to pointing out that there is a better payoff distribution for the objectors and that this distribution is attainable given the characteristic function. The stable set consists of certain types of imputations, namely those which are stable both internally and externally. Internal stability of a set of payoff distributions means that no distribution within the set is an objection of any coalition to another distribution in the set. A set of imputations is externally stable if, given any imputation outside the set, there exists an imputation within the set so that the latter is an objection to the former by some coalition of players.

It turns out that there may be more than one stable set. However, the core is a subset of every stable set (Osborne and Rubinstein 1994: 279). As a solution concept the stable set is thus somewhat more generally applicable than the core. Even more applicable is the bargaining set. Originally introduced by Aumann and Maschler (1964), it deals with objections that various coalitions can present against each other in a given situation. Thus, the bargaining set concept is conditional on a given payoff distribution and a partition of the players into coalitions. Its crucial feature is an objection that a member of a coalition, say A, presents against another member of the same coalition, B, in this situation. The objection is a proposal for a new coalition structure (partitioning of players) and payoff distribution so that A's payoff is strictly larger than before and B is not a member of the coalition that A forms. In addition, all A's partners in the coalition get at least the same payoff as in the original situation. A counter-objection, in turn, is B's statement according to which B can build a coalition excluding A so that B is better off than in the original distribution and B's partners get at least the same payoff as in A's objection. The bargaining set consists of those coalition structures along with their associated payoff distributions where all objections can be countered, i.e. for any objection of player i against player j, there is a counter-objection of j against i.

To illustrate, consider a majority government formation in a multi-party system. There are 100 seats in the parliament and they are distributed among four parties A, B, C and D so that A and B have 30 seats each, C has 25 and D 15 seats. A viable majority government needs the support of at least 51 members of parliament. To keep the example simple, we assume that there are only five ministerial positions: one of prime minister (PM) and four ordinary minister (OM) portfolios. Each four are regarded equally valuable by all parties, but the PM post is deemed more important than two but less important than three OM portfolios. At the beginning of the negotiations a party D representative proposes a government coalition consisting of B, C and D with the portfolio distribution: B gets PM, while C and D get 2 OM portfolios each. Party A is excluded. Given this proposal, party B may present an objection against C and D by proposing a cabinet coalition of A and B so that A gets 3 OM and B the PM and one of the OM portfolios. This is feasible since A and B have more than 51 seats. Moreover, B's offer obviously gives A more than D's proposal and B gets one OM in addition to the PM it had in D's proposal.

This objection cannot be countered by C and D. To counter it they would have to keep their two OM posts each leaving only PM to be offered to the only available coalition partner A. This is, by assumption, strictly less than what B offers A in her objection. Thus, B's objection cannot be countered. We conclude that D's proposal is not in the bargaining set since there is an objection that cannot be countered.

Suppose that C proposes a two-party government BC where B gets the PM and one of the OM posts, while C gets three OM ones. This belongs to the bargaining set since all objections by the two partners can be countered. For example, if B objects by proposing AB so that A gets two OM's with B getting two OM's and the PM post, this can be countered by C who can offer A the PM post (which by assumption is more than B's objection gives A) and capture the four OMs to herself.

Two examples from Danish cabinet formation after the 1957 and 1960 parliamentary elections and from the Finnish one after the 1999 and 2003 elections in Tables 6.1 and 6.2, respectively, illustrate applications to multiparty politics. The former table is from Laver and Schofield's (1990: 174) book. The bargaining set can be given slightly different content by restricting the objections and counter-objections to individual players or coalitions. Laver and Schofield focus on those payoff distributions in which all objections of single players (parties) in the potential cabinet coalition against the coalition formed by the rest of the cabinet, can be countered (see also Schofield and Laver 1985: 149). The same principle is used in determining the bargaining set in Table 6.2.

In these cases the bargaining set 'prediction' – listed in the 'b. set' column – is either very close to or identical with the actual portfolio distribution. In fact, the

Table 6.1 Cabinet formation in two Danish elections

	1957 Elections			1960 Elections		
Party	*Seats*	*Posts*	*b. set*	*Seats*	*Posts*	*b. set*
Communists (DKP)	6	0	0	0	0	0
Socialists (SF)	0	0	0	11	0	0
Social Democrats (SD)	70	9	8	76	10	10
Radicals (RV)	14	4	5	11	5	5
Liberals (V)	45	0	0	38	0	0
Conservatives (KF)	30	0	0	32	0	0
Justice Party (DRF)	9	3	3	0	0	0
Others	1	0	0	7	0	0
Total	175	16	16	175	15	15

Source: Laver and Schofield 1990.

Table 6.2 Cabinet formation in two Finnish elections

	1999 Elections			2003 Elections		
Party	*Seats*	*Posts*	*b. set*	*Seats*	*Posts*	*b. set*
Social Democrats (SDP)	51	6	7	53	8	8
Centre (Kesk)	48	0	0	55	8	8
National Coalition p. (Kok)	46	6	5	41	0	0
Left Alliance (Vas)	20	2	2	19	0	0
Swedish People's p. (Rkp)	11	1.5	1.5	9	2	2
Green League	11	1.5	1.5	14	0	0
Christian Democrats	10	0	0	6	0	0
Others	3	0	0	3	0	0
Total	200	16	16	200	18	18

bargaining set has proven to be a very good predictor of government coalitions in Western European systems (Schofield and Laver 1985). On the other hand, it tends to be very inclusive in the sense that, given an electoral outcome, there is typically a large number of portfolio distributions that all belong to the bargaining set. This has led to various modifications of the concept (see Schofield 1978).

In Table 6.2 the performance of the bargaining set as a predictor is also very good. In looking at this table one should bear in mind that in Finland the number of cabinet portfolios is not fixed, but can vary in the 12–18 interval. This provides the government negotiators an additional instrument. Even so, sometimes rather unconventional measures have been resorted to. An example is from the 1999 negotiations which resulted in a time-sharing arrangement whereby the Swedish People's Party and the Green League shared the responsibility of one portfolio, i.e. one of them nominated the minister for the first and the other for the second half of the parliamentary term.

The bargaining set is based on an intuitively plausible reasoning: an outcome cannot be a solution if it can be credibly and irresistibly challenged. An objection is precisely a challenge to a proposed coalition structure and payoff distribution. A challenge is credible if it can be realized and irresistible if it cannot be countered.

6.3   Values for *n*-person games

If a game has a unique solution outcome, then the players – provided that the game is one of complete information – know what they are about to gain or lose by playing the game. The value of the game for them is then simply the payoff ensuing from the solution outcome. Given the plethora of solution concepts to *n*-person games and the fact that many of them do not in general result in unique outcomes, it is, however, difficult to use this principle in assigning values to games in general. Yet, efforts to define value concepts have been present in game theoretic literature from its beginning. In two-person zero-sum game theory, it is natural to define the value of the game as that minimum payoff that a player can guarantee to herself unilaterally. This principle could, of course, be extended to *n*-person games as well, should these be defined in strategic forms, i.e. by listing all strategy combinations of players with the ensuing payoffs. However, this method does not work if the games are defined – as they typically are – in terms of the characteristic function specifying the value of each coalition. For games in the characteristic function form, Shapley (1953) suggested a value concept which has – in a slightly modified version – found many applications in the study of voting power in collective decision-making bodies. The following example from Raiffa *et al.* (2002) illustrates it.

Three companies, let us call them Big, Medium and Small, have formed a limited-period cartel in the production of cement in a country. They face no domestic or international competition. Within the framework of the current arrangement their earnings in millions of dollars are: 32, 23 and 6. When the time has come to renegotiate the cartel agreement, the chief executives of the companies have decided to call upon an independent consultant to undertake an analysis of various merger possibilities, their advantages and disadvantages. Having finished her analysis the consultant summarizes her findings in Table 6.3.

Obviously forming a two-company merger would bring about higher earnings to the merge partners, but would hurt the third company. The largest total gain results from the total merger which increases the earnings by 16 million (from 61 to 77 million). What can the companies expect in this kind of merger game? In other words, what is the value of the game for each player?

Shapley's solution starts from the assumption that coalitions (or mergers) are formed over time. This means that the coalition's first member is the player who starts looking for partners. When she finds one, a two-player coalition is formed and the partner thus found makes a contribution to the value of the coalition.

Table 6.3 Company merger payoff table

Merger type	Earnings (in millions of USD)
All companies separate:	
Big	32
Medium	23
Small	6
Two merge, one separate:	
Big–Medium merge	59
–Small separate	5
Big–Small merge	45
–Medium separate	22
Medium–Small merge	39
–Big separate	30
Total merger:	
Big–Medium–Small	77

Source: Raiffa *et al.* (2002: 433).

Then the next partner joins the coalition and again makes a contribution to the value of the coalition. The process continues until all players have joined the coalition. The contribution that each new member adds to the coalition value is simply the difference between the value of the coalition after her joining and its value before her joining. For example, if company Big looks for merger partners and finds Small first, the contribution of the latter is $45 - 30 = 15$ million dollars. The more value a player contributes to various coalitions, the more valuable a partner she is and, hence, the more value she can expect to gain from the coalition game.

But what determines the sequence in which the coalition partners join each other? In general, one would expect that partners are first sought for and found among one's closest allies, i.e. among those who are 'closest' to one's views on the issue at hand. In politics this would naturally translate into ideological proximity. Also in company merger processes the partners are likely to be sought among those with shared views regarding the future of the market, technological development, etc. However plausible such search principles might seem, it is impossible to predict which principle will be the dominant one in the future. So, Shapley's insight is to deem all coalition sequences equally possible instead of focusing on just a few most likely ones. Table 6.4 lists all merger sequences in our example, all contributions that the players make to each coalition and the average contribution of each player (Raiffa *et al.* 2002: 445). For example, in the merger sequence Medium–Big–Small the starting point is one where Medium is alone in the merger. Its contribution is 22 since this is the value of the coalition consisting of just Medium, while Big and Small are in a separate coalition. If Medium manages to attract Big into a coalition, the latter's contribution is $59 - 22 = 37$ (the value of the Medium–Big coalition being 59). If Small then enters the coalition, its contribution is 18.

Table 6.4 Merger contributions of companies

	Contributions			
Merger order	Big	Medium	Small	Total
Big–Medium–Small	30	29	18	77
Big–Small–Medium	30	32	15	77
Medium–Big–Small	37	22	18	77
Medium–Small–Big	38	22	17	77
Small–Big–Medium	40	32	5	77
Small–Medium–Big	38	34	5	77
Average	35.5	28.5	13	77

Source: Raiffa *et al.* (2002: 445).

The value of the merger game for the players is their average contribution, argues Shapley. The values so obtained are, accordingly, called the *Shapley values* of players.

In games with small number of players, the computation of Shapley values can be done in the way outlined above. If, however, the number of players exceeds 4, it gets tedious. The general formula for computing the Shapley value f_i^{Sh} of player i in any n-person game is the following:

$$f_i^{\text{Sh}} = \sum_{i \in S \subseteq N} \frac{(s-1)!(n-s)!}{n!} \times \underbrace{[v(S) - v(S \setminus i)]}$$

In this complicated looking formula N denotes the entire set of n players, S a coalition of s players and v the characteristic function. The symbols "!" denote factorials defined as: $n! = n \times (n-1) \times \ldots \times 2 \times 1$. By convention $0! = 1$. The expression underlined by brace represents player i's contribution or value added to coalition S. $i \in S \subseteq N$ denotes all those coalitions to which player i belongs. Thus, the contributions of the player are summed over all coalitions which she is a member of. In the three-company example above, $N = \{Big, Medium, Small\}$ and thus $n = 3$. For Big we get the Shapley value:

$$f_{\text{Big}}^{\text{Sh}} = \frac{0!2!}{3!}(30) + \frac{1!1!}{3!}(37) + \frac{1!1!}{3!}(40) + \frac{2!0!}{3!}(38)$$

$$= 10 + \frac{37}{6} + \frac{40}{6} + \frac{76}{6} = 35.5$$

Thus, each different merger where Big is present – including the empty one – is considered, Big's contribution to it determined and the contribution weighted by a factor expressing the likelihood of this coalition emerging under the assumption that each sequence of merger partners is equally likely.

It could be – and has been – argued that the merger sequence should not be important in determining the value of each player. More important is her contribution or the net value added by her presence expressed by $v(S) - v(S \setminus i)$. An alternative approach to defining the value of player i is to consider all coalitions that do not include i and compute her contribution to each of them. Summing the contributions over all coalitions and dividing the sum by the number of coalitions that do not include i gives an unweighted average of i's contribution to various coalitions that she might join.

This idea underlies another well-known value concept, namely the *Banzhaf value* (Banzhaf 1965, 1966).[36] In the example of Table 6.4 there are $2^{3-1} = 4$ coalitions that do not include Big: empty coalition, Medium, Small and Medium–Small. Big's contributions to these are: 30, 37, 40 and 38 summing to 145. Dividing this with the number of coalitions that do not include Big gives 145/4 = 36.25. This is Big's Banzhaf value. In a similar way, the values for Medium and Small can be determined. These are 29.25 and 13.75, respectively. Summing the Banzhaf values yields 79.25, that is, more than the value of the game for the coalition of all players. If the 'cake' to be divided among players is 77 at the maximum, then the Banzhaf value obviously does not give everyone her realistic share. To overcome this problem one might sum up the Banzhaf values and divide each Banzhaf value with this sum. Thereby one would necessarily end up with portions so that multiplying 77 with player i's portion would give her value. This is called the normalized Banzhaf value. We shall take a closer look at it in the context of a much debated application, the Council of Ministers of the European Union.

6.4   Applications to European institutions

In practice, we often do not have the characteristic function of the game to begin with. Rather we know that certain players, when acting together, are powerful enough to impose their common will upon the others. For example, in legislatures the decision rules adopted indicate which groups of actors can in effect dictate the content of legislation. If the decision rule states that the legislative proposals are to be voted upon using the simple majority principle, then it is evident that whenever a coalition including more than a majority of voters is formed, the coalition determines which proposals may pass in the legislative process. It is hard to pin down a value to such coalitions, but in a sense they are all equally powerful: each one of them may enact laws, while no other type of coalition can. This intuitively plausible observation was utilized by Shapley and Shubik (1954) when they suggested a method for measuring power in collective decision-making bodies. The method is today known as the *Shapley–Shubik index*.

The index is a restriction of the Shapley value to a class of games, known as *simple* ones. In these games, the characteristic function has only two values, 0 and 1, the former being assigned to non-winning and the latter to winning coalitions. The contribution of each player then reduces to either 0 or 1 as well. In the latter case she makes a non-winning coalition winning by joining it.

In the former case the player's entry makes no difference to the status of the coalition.

The European Union has over the past decades grown from a six-member community of countries aiming at coordinating their policies related to coal and steel production into a 25-member one with ambitious plans for creating the world's most competitive economic power through common legislation combined with harmonization of national regulations. Over the years the role of the Union as target setter and coordinator has grown significantly. Yet, the institutions within which all these coordinating and policy-setting activities take place have remained largely the same. The Commission, Council of Ministers and European Parliament (EP) have been and are still the most central institutions. Of these, the Commission has the primary – and in most instances exclusive – role in initiating the Union legislation. In adopting, rejecting or modifying those proposals the Council of Ministers has thus far played a major role. The evolution of the EU decision rules has, however, considerably increased the legislative powers of the EP, particularly since the Treaty of Maastricht in the early 1990s. Before that the Council was, in fact, the prime mover of the Union policy making and legislation.

The Council consists of cabinet-level representatives of the member states. Each representative is given a number of votes that roughly reflects the size of her country's population relative to other members. In its decision making the Council resorts to various rules, the most important being the qualified majority. This has made the Council a very convenient object of power index studies (see e.g. Brams and Affuso 1985; Nurmi and Meskanen 1999; Widgrén 1994). Once the majority threshold for passing a motion and the distribution of votes are known, the Shapley–Shubik index can be computed. To say that the index value can be computed does not mean that it can be done with just paper and pencil. In principle one has to generate all possible 2^n coalitions that can be formed of n players and then determine whether each one of them is losing. Let the coalition under scrutiny be S consisting of s players. If S is losing, then one has to check if adding the player to S would turn it into a winning one. If it would, then one adds:

$$\frac{(s-1)!(n-s)!}{n!}$$

to the player's Shapley–Shubik score. Continuing through all coalitions yields the player's Shapley–Shubik index value. This follows from the fact that we are focusing on a simple game in which only those coalitions add a players' index value that are non-winning without the player's presence but become winning with her entry. In these types of coalitions the player has a swing, i.e. she 'swings' a losing coalition into a winning one.

Table 6.5 reports the Shapley–Shubik index values of the member states of the 25-member Union, or EU-25 as it is often called.[37] The table also lists two Banzhaf index values: the absolute and normalized one. The former is the number of swings of a player divided by 2^{n-1} while the latter is the number of swings divided by the sum of swings of all players. All indices in the table are based on the assumption that the majority threshold is 232 out of the total of 321 votes.[38]

Table 6.5 also reports two other power index values, the Deegan–Packel (DP) and the Holler (H) ones (Deegan and Packel 1978; Holler 1982). To define these, let us denote by $\mathcal{T}$ the set of *minimal winning coalitions* that can be formed from the player set N. A coalition is minimal winning if it is winning and if a removal of *any player* would make it non-winning. The two indices are, then, defined as follows:

$$DP_i = \frac{\sum_{S \in \mathcal{T}} 1/s[v(S) - v(S \setminus i)]}{\sum_{j \in N} \sum_{S \in \mathcal{T}} 1/s[v(S) - v(S \setminus j)]}$$

$$H_i = \frac{\sum_{S \in \mathcal{T}} [v(S) - v(S \setminus i)]}{\sum_{j \in N} \sum_{S \in \mathcal{T}} [v(S) - v(S \setminus j)]}.$$

Table 6.5 Some power index values in EU-25

Country	Voting weights	Shapley–Shubik	Abs. Banzhaf	Std. Banzhaf	DP index	Holler index
Germany	29	0.093	0.055	0.086	0.053	0.052
France	29	0.093	0.055	0.086	0.053	0.052
Italy	29	0.093	0.055	0.086	0.053	0.052
UK	29	0.093	0.055	0.086	0.053	0.052
Spain	27	0.086	0.052	0.081	0.051	0.050
Poland	27	0.086	0.052	0.081	0.051	0.050
Netherlands	13	0.040	0.027	0.042	0.040	0.040
Belgium	12	0.036	0.025	0.039	0.040	0.040
Czech Republic	12	0.036	0.025	0.039	0.040	0.040
Greece	12	0.036	0.025	0.039	0.040	0.040
Hungary	12	0.036	0.025	0.039	0.040	0.040
Portugal	12	0.036	0.025	0.039	0.040	0.040
Austria	10	0.030	0.021	0.033	0.038	0.038
Sweden	10	0.030	0.021	0.033	0.038	0.038
Denmark	7	0.021	0.015	0.023	0.036	0.036
Ireland	7	0.021	0.015	0.023	0.036	0.036
Lithuania	7	0.021	0.015	0.023	0.036	0.036
Slovakia	7	0.021	0.015	0.023	0.036	0.036
Finland	7	0.021	0.015	0.023	0.036	0.036
Cyprus	4	0.012	0.009	0.013	0.033	0.035
Estonia	4	0.012	0.009	0.013	0.033	0.035
Latvia	4	0.012	0.009	0.013	0.033	0.035
Luxembourg	4	0.012	0.009	0.013	0.033	0.035
Slovenia	4	0.012	0.009	0.013	0.033	0.035
Malta	3	0.009	0.006	0.010	0.028	0.029

The difference between these indices, on the one hand, and the Banzhaf and Shapley–Shubik ones is that the former restrict attention to only minimal winning coalitions, while the latter consider all winning coalitions, i.e. such coalitions which – if unanimous – can dictate the outcomes of the voting game. All four indices count the swings of the players and determine their voting power value accordingly. In the case of DP, each swing is multiplied by $1/s$, that is, the value of the swing is divided equally among the s players forming the coalition.

To see the difference between the winning and the minimal winning coalition, consider a 100-seat legislature that consists of three parties A, B and C with 40, 35 and 25 seats, respectively. Let us assume that the decision rule is 62, that is, 62 votes out of 100 are needed to pass a motion. The winning coalitions are: AB, AC and ABC. Thus, A has 3, B 1 and C 1 swing. Hence, the normalized Banzhaf index values are 3/5 for A, 1/5 for B and 1/5 for C. The minimal winning coalitions, on the other hand, are AB and AC since B or C can be removed from ABC without making it non-winning. Thus, A has two swings, while B and C have one swing each. The Holler index value distribution is, thus, 1/2, 1/4 and 1/4.

6.5 Power and preferences

The indices described above are all distinctively *a priori* measures of voting power. In other words, they pertain to expectations rather than actual influence exerted by players on the outcomes. They show the theoretical effects of changes in voting weights and decision rules assuming all players (countries) participate in each vote. Since the player coalitions that are formed in any given time interval are typically known only after the fact, these indices look at theoretical coalition formation processes. The Shapley–Shubik and Banzhaf indices focus on the value added by the player to each coalition she joins and give this value a weight that reflects the *a priori* likelihood of this coalition being formed. The weights differ in different indices and hence the power index values of players may differ in identical games. In Holler's index as well as in the Deegan–Packel one the attention is on special types of coalitions, namely minimal winning ones. Otherwise the idea is the same as in the Shapley–Shubik and Banzhaf indices. All these four indices base the computations on two types of data: (i) the distribution of resources (votes, shares, etc.) and (ii) the decision rule, i.e. the minimum required amount of resources (votes, shares) needed to back the proposal in order for it to be passed. But it can be argued that we often know more than that. In particular, we may have a pretty good idea of those types of coalitions that are likely to form and of those that are well-nigh impossible.

The fact that this eventual information is not utilized by the indices has been a source of criticism (Garrett and Tsebelis 1996; Tsebelis and Garrett 1996). In particular, it has been argued that neglecting information about which coalitions are most likely to form leads to a systematically distorted picture of the power distribution. Suppose, for example, that the players' opinions can be expressed in a one- or many-dimensional Euclidean space. Each policy alternative is represented as a point in the space, that is, the alternative is described by its values in the coordinate axes. Let the axes be, for example, the degree of competitiveness of the economy and the average yearly income level of the decile of the population with lowest income. The interpretation of the crucial variables (coordinate axes) depends on the alternatives under consideration, but in the spatial voting models those dimensions are assumed to be the same for all players. In addition to policy alternatives, the players can also, then, be characterized by points in the space. That is, each player has an ideal point which represents the best possible combination of variable values for the player. Since the space under consideration is assumed to be Euclidean it follows that the dimensions are independent. Furthermore, one can measure distances between policy alternatives and player ideal points using the Euclidean metric:

$$d_E(x, y) = \sqrt{(x_1 - y_1)^2 + \cdots + (x_k - y_k)^2}$$

where x and y are two points (ideal points or policy alternatives) in a k-dimensional Euclidean space.

Now, given that player opinions can be represented in this fashion in the policy space, it makes sense to assume that each player is more likely to form a coalition with players close to her than with players far apart from her ideal point. Garrett and Tsebelis argue that one can be more specific than this and say that only connected coalitions are likely to form (Garrett and Tsebelis 1996; Tsebelis and Garrett 1996). In one-dimensional space (line) case connectedness means the following. Suppose that a player B is located in the dimension between two other players A and C. This means that when one draws a line connecting A and C, B is located on this line. A coalition is connected if it includes all players between any two coalition members. If there are more than one dimension, the connectedness amounts to the requirement that if one constructs the convex hull of all ideal points $x_1, \ldots, x_i$ of players $1, \ldots, i$, then the coalition is connected if and only if the coalition includes all those players whose ideal points are in the hull. If, for example, player $i + 1$'s ideal point is in the hull, but $i + 1$ is not included in the coalition, then the coalition is not connected. Now, Garrett and Tsebelis maintain that connected coalitions are likely to form, whereas unconnected ones are not. This implies then that not all coalitions are equiprobable, an assumption that can be seen to underly the Banzhaf indices.

The conclusion that coalitions differ in terms of frequency is correct. However, as a criticism of the *a priori* power indices the argument misses the point. These indices are measures of the theoretical probability of having one's views represented in the collective decisions using only three predictors: the resource distribution, the decision rule (majority threshold) and the coalition formation process. The indices are fairly useful indicators and benchmarks in situations where the resources distribution (voting weights) and decision rules are under negotiation. In these settings the power distribution *per se* is not at issue. Rather, one is interested in the incremental indicator values, that is, how much difference in relative terms a change in resource distribution or decision rule is accompanied with. Thus, one compares the index values holding constant the coalition formations process.

It is quite possible to turn the *a priori* voting power measures into *a posteriori* ones by taking into account the differential formation probabilities of coalitions. A straightforward method of doing this is to use the empirical relative frequencies of coalitions formed in the past as weights for computing the weighted average of a player's contributions to various coalitions. This has been done by Lane and Stenlund (1989). Also Kirman and Widgrén (1995) suggest a method for calibrating the power index values to reflect the likelihood of coalitions. The question, however, is where to obtain these probabilities. The same question should also be asked in the case of spatial models. Specifically, how does one find out the spatial dimension or dimensions in terms of which the connected coalitions can subsequently be defined?

Steunenberg *et al.* (1999) suggest an approach to power measurement that – although similar in spirit to the one proposed by Garret and Tsebelis – runs directly counter with their injunction not to assume random distribution of policy preferences of players.[39] In fact, Steunenberg *et al.* go one step further than the classic power indices in assuming not only that the player coalitions or – in the case of the Shapley–Shubik index – player permutations are equiprobable, but that all states of the world are equally probable. Each state of the world is an $(n+1)$-tuple consisting of ideal points of the n players and a status quo point. The mean distance between equilibrium outcomes and a player's ideal point is used in defining the *strategic power index* value of the player. To achieve a degree of standardization Steunenberg *et al.* consider a *dummy player*, i.e. one that has no influence on the equilibrium outcomes. The strategic power index of a player i is computed as follows:

$$\Phi_i = \frac{\Delta_d - \Delta_i}{\Delta_d}$$

In the formula Δ_d is the mean distance between the equilibrium outcome and a dummy player's ideal point, while Δ_i is the mean distance between player i's ideal point and the equilibrium outcome.

For practical computation of the strategic power index values, Steunenberg *et al.* construct a dimension which consists of eight points. The players – Commission, the median member of the EP, five members of the Council, a dummy player – and the status quo are located at one of the eight points randomly and independently of each other. Since there are eight players and the status quo to be allocated, there are $8^9 = 134.2 \times 10^6$ different states of the world. For each state Steunenberg *et al.* determine the equilibrium outcome as well as its distances from ideal points. Obviously, the strategic power index is of *a priori* nature and thus comparable to the classic power indices. The new feature it incorporates is the notion of equilibrium outcome which plays no role in the classic power indices. Due to the random assignment of players to ideal points on the issue dimension it is subject to the same criticism as its classic counterparts.

The theory of n-person games extends some notions of two-person game theory to a new domain of multiple agents. It does so, however, at the cost of reducing the strategy repertoire of the players to a dichotomy: either a player joins a coalition or stays outside of it. It is possible to generalize this setting so that each player is endowed with a richer set of strategies than the restricted set of to join or not to join strategies. Thereby the theory becomes, however, essentially more complicated. We shall now turn to a special class of n-person games where a richer variety of choices by players is a standard assumption. The theory of this class of games is one of the cornerstones of modern political economy, namely the theory of voting. As we shall shortly see, voting can be considered as an n-person game where the voters have at their disposal strategies which, together with strategy choices of other voters and the voting rule, determine the electoral outcomes.

6.6   Suggested reading

Roth (1979), Moulin (1988a, 1988b) as well as Thomson and Lensberg (1989) are excellent texts on bargaining theory. However, they are all pretty technical. Raiffa *et al.* (2002), in contrast, introduces the theory via examples and is, thus, more accessible to beginners. Power indices have been studied for decades, but the institutions of the European Union have sparked a new wave of interest. Brams (1975) is a non-technical introduction to these indices. Felsenthal and Machover (1998) give an extensive analysis of the indices and their background. The power index approach has also met with some criticism. Garrett and Tsebelis (1996) as well as Tsebelis and Garrett (1996) base their objections on the assumptions underlying the power indices. Laruelle (2002) along with Napel and Widgrén (2004) introduce richer models containing spatial information. Hosli, van Deemen and Widgrén (2002) contain several articles applying game theory to the Union institutions.

7 Decision making in committees

The background of committee decision-making theory is in voting paradoxes, the first of which were discovered more than 200 years ago during the years preceding the French revolution of 1789. We discuss these as well as some other voting paradoxes of more recent origin.[40] We also outline two basic intuitions of what characterizes collectively best decisions. Many important results in the committee decision-making theory are of negative nature. They amount to showing incompatibilities between various desiderata one would intuitively like to associate with choice rules. Let us, however, begin with some basic concepts.

7.1 Basic concepts

The founding fathers of the modern committee decision theory (also known as social choice theory, group choice theory and collective decision-making theory) were Jean-Charles de Borda and Marquis de Condorcet who presented their basic insights, paradoxes and solution proposals in the pre-revolution France. Borda was a man with a practical, 'engineering' turn of mind. Condorcet, on the other hand, was one of the greatest social philosophers of the Enlightenment era. It has been argued that the foundations of the theory were laid much before that period (McLean and Urken 1995), but it seems that Borda's and Condorcet's work are the earliest ones with relevance that extends to the present day theorizing (see Kelly (1991) for a comprehensive bibliography of this vast field up to the beginning of the 1990s). The basic setting analyzed by these authors was the following: given a committee that consists of rational persons having consistent opinions about the issues to be decided, what is the best method of reaching a collective opinion about the issues? This is still the basic problem of the committee decision theory. Let us outline some components of this problem formulation in some detail.

First of all, a committee is a set of individuals forming a joint opinion regarding the course of action (policy) to be taken, candidate to be elected, a statement to be issued or a body of individuals to be nominated. The set of decision alternatives or issues is usually a fixed set A. Very often it is finite and consists of no more than a handful of alternatives. There exists, however, a fairly extensive literature on decision settings where each alternative is represented as a point in a multi-dimensional Euclidean policy space. If, conversely, every point in the space is regarded as a possible policy alternative, then we obviously have an infinite set of alternatives. In this book we shall, however, focus on non-spatial models and refer the reader to Enelow and Hinich (1984) for an introduction to spatial theory. Each member of the committee is assumed to have an opinion on the matters to be decided. This opinion is assumed to be consistent in the sense that member i's opinion can be represented as a complete and transitive binary preference relation R_i over A. Thus, our starting point is the same as in decision and game theory.

It is well known, however, that people are not always consistent in their opinions. Finding procedures that would produce good outcomes even in contexts involving inconsistent persons would of course be a goal worth pursuing, but the problem would be to define 'good outcomes' independently of the opinions of the persons involved. In the absence of such a definition we assume that the committee members are consistent in the above sense. After all, if people are inconsistent it would be a tall order to expect their collective decisions to be consistent. Hence, we assume that the set of individual preferences is given. To conclude our list of definitions we define a *preference profile*. A collection of individual preference relations over A is called a preference profile and denoted $R = (R_1, \ldots, R_n)$.

7.2 Aggregating opinions

The problem is to find a method for aggregating the opinions of voters or forming the collective opinion about the issue at hand. Sometimes the voting body is to decide which public policy alternative should be pursued. Sometimes a person or a group of persons is elected by the body to perform certain tasks. The opinion aggregation is necessary in order to pursue consistent public policy or declare a winner in an election. There are basically three different explications of what exactly the method ought to accomplish.

- *Social welfare function* maps each profile into a complete and transitive (collective) preference relation. This explication is the one that appears in the famous theorem of Arrow (Arrow 1963). The method, thus, transforms individual preference rankings into a collective one. In other words, one ends up with a collective opinion that not only specifies the alternatives held collectively best, but also the ranking between the remaining ones.
- *Social choice function (correspondence)* maps each profile and subset A' of A into the set of subsets of A'. This explication, in turn, gives the subset of best alternatives once the individuals have submitted their preference rankings.

Social choice functions are undoubtedly the most common explications of opinion aggregation methods in the modern social choice theory (Fishburn 1973).

- A *resolute social choice function* or *social decision function* is a singleton valued social choice function. Sometimes a mere subset of best alternatives is not sufficient, but one is looking for a single alternative as the winner (e.g. in presidential elections a tie will not do as an outcome). Then the resolute social choice functions are the constructs one needs.

Peter C. Fishburn (born 1936) is one of the leading decision and social choice theorists. His contributions cover an astonishingly wide area ranging from foundations of measurement through coding theory and utility theory to comparison of voting systems. Some of his most important book-length works are *Utility Theory for Decision Making* (1970), *Nonlinear Preference and Utility Theory* (1988), *The Theory of Social Choice* (1973), *Approval Voting* (with Steven Brams) (1983), and *Interval Orders and Graphs* (1985). In 1996 the Institute for Operations Research and Management Sciences (INFORMS) awarded him the John von Neumann Prize.

Voting is based on rules determining the validity of ballots. Some ballot rules require the voters to indicate a person, a party or a preference ranking over alternatives. A voting procedure is a method of counting ballots to determine the winner(s). A voting procedure is, thus, basically a social choice function.

7.3   New systems, new winners

The study of opinion aggregation methods is based on the observation that a whole range of methods exists in real-world elections. This variety can perhaps be best explained by historical contingencies. More important, however, is the fact that the voting procedures make a difference in collective decision making outcomes. This is demonstrated by the following example (Table 7.1). There are five candidates for the vacant post of department chairperson. They are A, B,

Table 7.1 Who should become the chair?

4 voters	3 voters	2 voters
A	B	C
E	C	D
D	E	E
C	D	B
B	A	A

C, D and E. There are nine voters who make the decision. Four candidates consider the scholarly excellence of primary importance and, on the basis of a thorough survey of citation indices and other pertinent material, these four rank the candidates so that A is first, E second, D third, C fourth and B last. The next three voters focus solely on the applicants' teaching skills. These turn out to be negatively correlated with the scholarly excellence so that A, who is best in terms of the latter, has the worst record as an instructor. In all, the three voters rank the applicants as follows: BCEDA. (Henceforth we drop the $\succ$ symbols for brevity and simply write preference rankings from left to right in the order of preference.) Finally, two voters see administrative experience as the only criterion relevant for the task at hand. Upon consulting the applicants' resumés they conclude that the ranking should be: CDEBA. Table 7.1 summarizes the views of the voters. The voter preference rankings are listed from top to bottom. This convention will be resorted to in other tables to follow as well.

Suppose that no established system of voting exists in the department. Rather, the voters are at liberty to decide which method of voting they use. In this example it turns out that assuming that the voters vote according to their preferences, five common voting procedures lead to five different winning candidates. In other words, any applicant can become the department chair, depending on the voting rule.

The *plurality* or *one-person-one-vote* system leads to candidate A, since A gets 4 votes, while the other candidates get strictly fewer votes. The *plurality runoff* system leads first to a runoff between A and B since no candidate gets more than 50% of the votes on the first round. On the second round B defeats A with 5 votes to 4 (the 2 voters on the right preferring B to A can be expected to vote accordingly). If the *amendment procedure* is used, one conducts pairwise comparisons between candidates according to a fixed *agenda* so that the loser in each comparison is eliminated and the winner continues the race. In this system the agenda often determines the winner, but under special preference profiles – such as the one we have here – one can predict the winner regardless of the agenda. The winner is C, because it is supported by majority of voters against any other candidate. C is, thus, the *Condorcet winner*.

The system proposed by Borda – nowadays known as the *Borda count* – yields candidate *E* as the chairperson. In the Borda count, the candidates are given points according to their rank in voter preferences. With k alternatives, each voter who ranks a candidate first adds $k - 1$ points to its Borda score. Each voter who ranks it second, adds $k - 2$ points, and so on. The winner is the alternative with the highest score. In this example it is candidate E. Finally, *approval voting* could be envisioned to produce yet another winner, namely D, provided that the 4 voters on the left vote for three top-most alternatives, while the other voters vote for their two top-ranked ones. In approval voting one can vote for as many alternatives as one wishes under the restriction that only 1 or 0 votes can be given to any alternative (see e.g. Brams and Fishburn 1983, Nurmi 1987, and Riker 1982 for a description and analysis of these and many other voting procedures).

William H. Riker (1920–1993) was one of the most influential political scientists of the 20th century. As the founder of the positive political theory he originated a research tradition which focuses on the strategic aspects of political behavior and develops research methods and techniques appropriate for the analysis of this kind of behavior. One of Riker's important contributions is the application of social choice theory to the analysis of political institutions. His ground-breaking book *Liberalism against Populism* (1982) has provided inspiration to numerous works on political institutions. His other major books are *The Theory of Political Coalitions* (1962), *Federalism* (1964), *An Introduction to Positive Political Theory* (with Peter Ordeshook) (1973) and *The Art of Political Manipulation* (1986).

Thus, all five candidates can become department chair persons in the example of Table 7.1 despite the fact that the voter opinions remain fixed. Voting systems do, indeed, make a difference. Real-world examples are more difficult to come by since the preferences of voters are often difficult to find out in detail. Often these have to be inferred from the voting behavior which, in turn, may embody strategic considerations along with the preferences. One real-world example of considerable practical importance can be mentioned, though: it seems evident that the parliamentary decision to move the German parliament and the federal government from Bonn to Berlin is an example of a context where the decision rule played an important role in the decision outcome (see Leininger 1993).

Steven J. Brams (born 1940) is one of the best-known political scientists of our time. He has written extensively on applied game theory, conflict analysis, fair division, coalition formation and voting systems. In the mid-1970s he – together with Peter Fishburn – introduced and analyzed the approval voting method. He remains a strong advocate of this system. Brams is the author or co-author of 15 books, including *Game Theory and Politics* (1975), *Biblical Games* (1980), *Theory of Moves* (1994) and *The Win–Win Solution* (with Alan Taylor) (1999).

7.4 Theory of committee voting in the olden days

The study of committee decision-making has from the very beginning been characterized by counterintuitive findings, puzzles and paradoxes (see Nurmi (1999) for an overview of voting paradoxes). The latter are particularly difficult and dramatic problems that contradict what one would normally expect in group choice settings. The classic paradoxes, discovered in late 18th century France, bear the name of the persons who first discovered and discussed them.[41]

Borda's paradox consists in the incompatibility of two intuitively compelling requirements that one can impose on social choices, that is, (i) that the alternative ranked first by more voters than any other alternative should be elected, and

Table 7.2 Borda's paradox

Voters 1–4	Voters 5–7	Voters 8,9
A	B	C
B	C	B
C	A	A

(ii) that the alternative defeated by a majority in pairwise contests against any other alternatives should not be elected. Table 7.2 summarizes the preferences of nine voters over three candidates: A, B and C. Candidate A is ranked first by more voters than any other alternative. It would thus win the plurality voting in this profile. Yet, A would be defeated by both other alternatives in pairwise comparison (both B and C would beat A with 5 votes to 4). Thus, the plurality voting system satisfies requirement (i) but not requirement (ii). In modern terminology requirement (ii) is called the Condorcet loser criterion, which dictates that whenever an alternative would be defeated by all other alternatives in pairwise contests with a majority of votes, then this alternative, called the *Condorcet loser*, should not be elected. The better-known criterion, the Condorcet winner, requires that when there is a Condorcet winner in a profile, it should be elected. The Borda count does not satisfy this criterion (see Table 7.10 for an example).

7.4.1   *Borda count: two ways out*

Of the two requirements, Borda regarded (ii) more compelling and proposed his own system, the Borda count, to avoid a conflict with it (DeGrazia 1953). This system can be implemented in two ways.

First way

Given the profile of Table 7.2 compute the Borda scores as follows.

A's score: $4 \times 2 + 5 \times 0 = 8$
B's score: $4 \times 1 + 3 \times 2 + 2 \times 1 = 12$
C's score: $4 \times 0 + 3 \times 1 + 2 \times 2 = 7$

The winner is the alternative with the largest score, here B. The Borda scores can also be used in defining the social preference ranking over the alternatives, here BAC.

Second way

The other way is based on pairwise comparisons of alternatives. The profile of Table 7.2 can be transformed into an *outranking matrix* of 3 rows and 3 columns with entry (i, j) indicating the number of voters preferring the alternative

Table 7.3 Outranking matrix

	A	B	C	Sum
A	–	4	4	8
B	5	–	7	12
C	5	2	–	7

represented by row *i* to the alternative represented by column *j*. Table 7.3 gives the outranking matrix of Borda's paradox. It can be observed that the row sums of this matrix are identical to the Borda scores of alternatives. This is, in fact, always the case. Thus, despite its 'positional' nature the Borda count can be implemented in a purely binary way, i.e. through paired comparisons.

7.4.2   *Problems of Borda count*

Although the Borda count avoids the most serious drawback of plurality voting, namely the election of the Condorcet loser, it has some undesirable features. Table 7.4 exhibits the most important of these.

The collective preference ranking produced by the Borda count is DABC. Let us now remove alternative D from the profile and recompute the Borda scores. The ensuing ranking now becomes: BCA, i.e. the ranking between A, B and C is reversed even though no voter has changed her mind.

7.4.3   *Condorcet's paradox*

Perhaps even better known than Borda's paradox is the phenomenon known as *Condorcet's paradox*. It is sometimes called simply the voting paradox or the phenomenon of *cyclic majorities*. An example is given in Table 7.5. A committee consisting of three groups of like-minded individuals is making a choice out of three candidates A, B and C. The sizes of the groups are such that any two of them constitute a majority of the committee.

Suppose that the choice is made using the widely used amendment procedure. In that system the alternatives are confronted with each other in pairs according to a pre-determined agenda. In each stage of voting, the alternative supported by a minority is eliminated and the winner continues to face the next alternative in

Table 7.4 Borda count at work

Voters 1–2	Voters 3–4	Voters 5–6	Voter 7
D	A	B	D
C	D	A	C
B	C	D	B
A	B	C	A

Table 7.5 Condorcet's paradox

Group I	Group II	Group III
A	B	C
B	C	A
C	A	B

the agenda. So, after $k - 1$ stages of voting only one alternative is left. It is the winner. Consider now the agenda: (1) A vs. B, and (2) the winner of the preceding vote vs. C. Clearly, A defeats B in the first pairwise comparison, but is defeated by C in the second. Thus, the winner is C. It is obvious, however, that C is not a robust winner. In fact, with any other agenda C would not win. In fact – and this is where the paradox lies – no matter which alternative one picks from the {A, B, C} set, there is always a majority that is frustrated in the sense of preferring some other alternative to the chosen one.

7.4.4   Condorcet's solutions

Like Borda, Condorcet also proposed to solve the encountered paradox. In fact, Condorcet proposed several non-equivalent solutions, three of which will be discussed in the following.[42]

Successive elimination

The successive elimination solution proceeds as follows. Given a preference profile, reverse the (pairwise) opinion with the smallest majority support and find out if the resulting set of opinions still contains cycles. If it does not, then we have found the collective preference relation. Otherwise, we consider the remaining majority opinions and reverse again the one with the smallest majority support, etc. By successively reversing the weakest relations, we eventually end up with a connected and transitive preference relation.

Consider the profile of Table 7.6. The corresponding outranking matrix is given in Table 7.7. The successive elimination method leads to the elimination of collective preference of C over A. Thus, ABC is the collective ranking.

Table 7.6 A modified Condorcet's paradox

4 voters	3 voters	2 voters
A	B	C
B	C	A
C	A	B

Table 7.7 Outranking matrix of preceding profile

	A	B	C
A	–	6	4
B	3	–	7
C	5	2	–

Maximal agreement

The other solution discussed by Condorcet can be called the maximal agreement solution. It works as follows. Given a preference profile and one of $k!$ possible collective preference rankings, determine, for each pair of alternatives, the number of agreements between the former and the latter. Choose that collective ranking with a maximum number of agreements with the given profile. This solution is nowadays known as Kemeny's rule (Kemeny 1959a) (see also Slater 1961).

The preceding profile has the following number of agreements with various collective rankings: ABC: 17, ACB: 12, BAC: 14, BCA: 15, CAB: 13, CBA: 10. Thus, ABC is the solution.

It is worth noting that the successive elimination and maximal agreement do not necessarily lead to the same outcome. Thus, these two solutions are not equivalent.

John Kemeny (1926–1992) was a Hungarian-born American mathematician and philosopher who made important contributions to a wide variety of subjects in logic, computer science and pure as well as applied mathematics. Of particular importance is his invention – with Thomas Kurtz – of the programming language BASIC. He also changed mathematics instruction by introducing what he called finite mathematics courses. These consist mainly of logic and algebra as well as some probability theory. Kemeny's main books are *Introduction to Finite Mathematics* (with Laurie Snell and Oskar Thompson) (1959), *A Philosopher Looks at Science* (1959), *Denumerable Markov Chains* (with Laurie Snell and Anthony Knapp) (1966) and *Mathematical Models in the Social Sciences* (with Laurie Snell) (1962). He received numerous honorary degrees and was elected to the American Academy of Arts and Sciences in 1967.

Condorcet's practical method

Condorcet also suggested a third procedure which is called Condorcet's practical method. It works as follows:

- Each voter votes for one alternative. If one alternative gets more than 50% of the votes, it is chosen.

Table 7.8 Condorcet's practical method at work

32 voters	38 voters	10 voters	10 voters	10 voters
B	C	B	C	A
A	A	C	B	B
C	B	A	A	C

- Otherwise, each voter votes for two alternatives. The alternative with the largest number of votes is chosen.

It is of particular interest to notice that Condorcet's practical method may end up with a Condorcet loser being elected. This is shown by Table 7.8. Here A, the Condorcet loser, is elected by Condorcet's practical method.

7.5   Problems of Condorcet's intuition

Condorcet's intuition about winning – captured in the Condorcet winner criterion – is still very much appreciated. In particular, there is a fairly wide-spread consensus concerning the desirability of an eventual Condorcet winner alternative being chosen. Yet, there are contexts in which the Condorcet winner does not seem to be the most plausible choice. Fishburn provides the following example (Table 7.9) (Fishburn 1973: 147).

In Table 7.9, D is the Condorcet winner, that is, it defeats all other alternatives in a pairwise vote by a majority. Yet, choosing the Borda winner E would seem pretty natural since E has as many first ranks (2) as D, more second and third ranks than D and no lower ranks than third. D, on the other hand, has one lowest and one next to lowest rank. So, there are contexts in which the choice of the Condorcet winner is not the most natural one.

Table 7.9 Fishburn's example

1 voter	1 voter	1 voter	1 voter	1 voter
D	E	C	D	E
E	A	D	E	B
A	C	E	B	A
B	B	A	C	D
C	D	B	A	C

Saari's (1995) work casts even more serious doubt on the plausibility of Condorcet winners. Saari shows that the Condorcet winner in a profile is sensitive to a transformation in the profile that intuitively should leave things unchanged. To wit, if there is a group of voters whose preference profile constitutes a completely symmetric Condorcet paradox, i.e. the groups in Table 7.5 are of

Donald G. Saari (born 1940) is a Finnish–American astronomer, economist, decision theorist and – above all – mathematician. Applying and developing geometric and topological methods to social choice problems he has profoundly influenced our understanding of voting systems, markets and mechanism design. Saari's ground-breaking book *Basic Geometry of Voting* (1995) was followed by two other booklength treatises on voting: *Chaotic Elections! A Mathematician Looks at Voting* (2001a) and *Decisions and Elections* (2001b), along with a large number of articles published in leading journals of the field. His most recent book, *Collisions, Rings and Other Newtonian N-Body Problems* (2005), analyzes some of the classic problems of physics and astronomy. Saari is *i.a.* a Fellow of the American Academy of Arts and Sciences, Fellow of the American Association for the Advancement of Science and a recipient of several doctoral degrees *honoris causa.*

equal size, then adding or subtracting such a sub-profile to or from any larger profile should leave everything unchanged as far as the collective preferences between alternatives are concerned. Yet, it can be shown that an alternative may be the Condorcet winner in a given profile, but cease to be that after an addition of a group of voters whose preferences are those of a symmetric Condorcet paradox. To illustrate, consider Table 7.10. Here we have a strong Condorcet winner, that is, an alternative ranked first by more than 50% of the voters. It is A.

Table 7.10 Borda count and strong Condorcet winner

7 voters	4 voters
A	B
B	C
C	A

Add now a group of 12 voters – four with preference ranking ACB, four with ranking CBA and four with ranking BAC – whose preferences, thus, constitute a Condorcet's paradox to the original group. The ensuing profile is shown in Table 7.11. We observe that the Condorcet winner in the new profile is B. Thus, adding a symmetric Condorcet's paradox profile undermines the Condorcet winner and brings about a new one.

Table 7.11 Added profile

7 voters	4 voters	4 voters	4 voters	4 voters
A	B	A	C	B
B	C	C	B	A
C	A	B	A	C

7.6   Voting procedures

Most real-word voting procedures have probably been adopted on intuitive grounds, i.e. without systematic experimentation or comparison with other possible procedures. Over the past decades scholarly work has, however, established a number of results on properties of various voting procedures. These results can, of course, be utilized in future debates concerning advantages and disadvantages of procedures.

7.6.1   Procedures

Existing voting systems can be classified in many ways, but perhaps from the practical point of view the following three-fold system is particularly useful (Nurmi 1983b). It classifies systems into binary, positional and multi-stage, non-binary ones.

In the first class we have systems which essentially resort to pairwise comparison of alternatives in determining the winners. The defining property of the systems in the second class is that the likelihood of an alternative being the winner depends on the position it occupies in the voters' preference rankings. In the third class the systems require several stages of computation before the winner can be determined. The following list gives examples of each class of procedures.

- binary: amendment, *Copeland, Dodgson, max–min*;
- positional: plurality, Borda count, approval voting;
- multi-stage: plurality runoff, *Nanson, Black, Hare, Coombs*.

Of these we have already discussed the amendment, plurality and approval voting as well as the Borda count and plurality runoff. Copeland's procedure is based on counting the number of victories of each alternative in pairwise comparisons with other alternatives. Typically, the victory is determined by simple majority, but one could envision other criteria of pairwise winning. In this book, however, the simple majority criterion will be used. The Copeland winner is an alternative that defeats more alternatives than any other alternative. Dodgson's procedure is also binary. It defines the winning alternative as one that can be rendered the Condorcet winner with the smallest number of preference changes in the given profile. The max–min winner is the alternative that has the largest minimum support in all pairwise comparisons.

Nanson's procedure is a Borda elimination one in the sense that it eliminates all alternatives with an average or smaller than average Borda score. After the elimination, new Borda scores are computed and again those with at most average score are eliminated. Eventually, no eliminations are possible and those alternatives one is left with are the winners.

Black's system is a hybrid one: it elects the Condorcet winner if one exists. Otherwise, it elects the Borda winner. Hare's system determines the winner as an alternative that has been ranked first by more than 50% of the voters. If no such alternative exists, one eliminates that alternative which has been ranked first by the smallest number of voters. After the elimination, one again checks if some alternative has been ranked first by more than 50% of voters. If such an alternative is found, it is elected. Otherwise, one proceeds with eliminating the next alternative, etc.[43] Coombs' procedure is identical with Hare's except that the alternatives that are ranked last by the largest number of voters are eliminated instead of those ranked first by the smallest number of voters.

All these systems have advantages and disadvantages. We now turn to some of these.

7.6.2   Criteria

The following criteria list is but a small subset of all those discussed in the literature (Fishburn 1977; Nurmi 1983b, 1987; Riker 1982; Straffin 1980). None the less, it provides a fairly rich picture of the criteria that are deemed relevant.

- *Condorcet criteria*: Condorcet winner, Condorcet loser. The former requires that the Condorcet winner should be elected whenever it exists in a profile. The latter, in turn, requires the exclusion of the Condorcet loser.
- *Monotonicity and no-show criteria*. The former amounts to requiring that an additional support should never be harmful for an alternative. The latter, in turn, rules out systems under which non-voting may result in an outcome that is preferable to that ensuing from voting.
- *Pareto*. This criterion requires that if all voters prefer x to y, then y is not chosen.
- *Choice set invariance*: consistency, property α. Consistency requires that if x is chosen by all subgroups of voters, then x should also be chosen by the group as a whole. Property α, in turn, is satisfied by systems that guarantee that any alternative x that is chosen from a set of alternatives, is also chosen from each such proper subset of alternatives that include x.

All the above requirements are plausible, but unfortunately no system satisfies all of them. In fact, each procedure in the preceding list has at least one serious shortcoming. We shall now briefly outline some of these.

7.6.3   Positional methods and Condorcet criteria

From the days of Borda it has been known that plurality voting fails on the Condorcet loser criterion. Since plurality voting can be regarded as a limiting case of the approval voting, it follows that the latter also fails on this criterion. Both systems also fail on the Condorcet winner criterion, which means that they may not always elect the Condorcet winner. Both of these failures are illustrated by Borda's paradox (Table 7.2). A, the Condorcet loser, is elected by the plurality voting and by approval voting if all voters vote for their top-ranked alternative. On the other hand, B, the Condorcet winner, is not elected.

Table 7.12 Borda count fails on Condorcet winning criterion

2 voters	2 voters	3 voters	2 voters
A	A	B	C
C	B	A	B
B	C	C	A

The Borda count satisfies the Condorcet loser criterion, but fails on the other Condorcet criterion. This is illustrated by Table 7.12 as well.

The weaknesses of positional procedures are related to Condorcet criteria. The binary procedures do naturally better on these. Yet, they have their drawbacks as well.

7.6.4   *Inconsistency of binary procedures*

The main shortcoming of the binary procedures is captured by the theorem of Young (1975): all consistent methods are incompatible with the Condorcet winning criterion.

> H. Peyton Young (born 1945) is an American economist and applied mathematician. He has made important contributions to the social choice theory, electoral systems studies and the evolutionary theory of social institutions. Young's books are *Fair Representation* (with Michel Balinski) (1982), *Equity in Theory and Practice* (1994), *Individual Strategy and Social Structure* (1998) and *Strategic Learning and Its Limits* (2004).

This is a very typical way of expressing results in social choice theory. One shows that two or more desiderata are incompatible. In the case of Young's theorem it is shown that if one wishes to have a procedure that always elects a Condorcet winner (as is done by typical binary procedures), one has to make do with systems that occasionally make inconsistent choices. The emphasis is on the word 'occasionally', since there are profiles in which a Condorcet winner in each subgroup is also the Condorcet winner in the overall group. For example, if a candidate is ranked first by more that 50% of the voters in each subgroup and if the Copeland's system is being resorted to, then this candidate is also elected in the group at large. Yet, Copeland's system is inconsistent, that is, there are profiles where it fails on consistency.

7.6.5   *Non-monotonicity of multi-stage procedures*

Perhaps the most dramatic shortcomings are failures on monotonicity and vulnerability to the no-show paradox. These are particularly dramatic since they

Table 7.13 The no-show paradox

35 voters	25 voters	15 voters	25 voters
A	B	B	C
B	C	C	A
C	A	A	B

show that it is possible that a system runs counter to the most obvious principle of democratic elections: increasing a candidate's support should improve her chances of being elected. A failure of monotonicity occurs when additional support for the winning candidate – other things being equal or *ceteris paribus* – makes it non-winning. The no-show paradox, in turn, refers to a situation where an individual or group of individuals is better off, *ceteris paribus*, by not voting at all than by voting according to her or its preferences. Consider the plurality runoff system and Table 7.13.

With all voters voting according to their preferences, there will be runoff between A and B, whereupon A wins. This is the last ranked alternative of the 40 voters whose rankings are listed in the two middle columns. Suppose now that 25 of those voters with preference ranking BCA abstain from voting. Under this scenario there will be a runoff A and C. This results in the victory of C. Clearly this is a preferable outcome to those who abstain since they prefer C to A.

Vulnerability to the non-show paradox is by no means the only weakness of the plurality runoff and Hare's system. The latter is equivalent to the plurality runoff in cases involving three alternatives as in the above example. Both of these systems are also non-monotonic as illustrated by Table 7.14.

This profile leads to A's victory. However, if the two right-most voters had improved A's position so that their preference had been ABC, then C would have won. Clearly, then, an increase in support may be detrimental for a candidate in plurality or Hare elections.

If one wishes to avoid the no-show paradox one should, of course, choose systems that are not vulnerable to it. For those who would still like to insist on the Condorcet winning criterion, the following theorem of Moulin (1988b) presents, however, a hard choice: all procedures that satisfy the Condorcet winning criterion are vulnerable to the no-show paradox.

Table 7.14 Non-monotonicity of plurality runoff (and Hare)

6 voters	5 voters	4 voters	2 voters
A	C	B	B
B	A	C	A
C	B	A	C

Hervé Moulin (born 1950) is a French–American mathematical economist and
social choice theorist. His works have focused *i.a.* on strategic voting and mechanism design. He has been the editor or associate editor of several leading scholarly
journals in his field. Moulin's most important books are *The Strategy of Social
Choice* (1983), *Axioms of Cooperative Decision-Making* (1988a) and *Fair Division
and Collective Welfare* (2003).

Note that this theorem says nothing about procedures that do not satisfy the
Condorcet winning criterion. In other words, those procedures may or may not
be vulnerable to the paradox. The plurality and Hare systems fail on both counts:
they do not necessarily elect a Condorcet winner and they are vulnerable to the
no-show paradox.

The results cited above are quite typical in the social choice literature. They
show that it is impossible to satisfy all reasonable-looking desiderata when choosing a voting procedure. While this is what these results strictly say, one should
keep in mind that to show an incompatibility between a system and a desideratum, say Condorcet winning criterion, all one has to do is to present an example,
i.e. a profile where the procedure does not elect the Condorcet winner. The result
itself says nothing about how common or likely these kinds of profiles are.

7.7   Choice procedures and performance criteria

The literature on voting systems and performance criteria is extensive. Table 7.15
gives a summary of 11 systems assessed in terms of 7 criteria (see Nurmi (1983b)
and (1987) for a fuller discussion).

The rows indicate the procedures and columns stand for the following criteria
of performance: a = Condorcet winner, b = Condorcet loser, c = majority

Table 7.15 A Comparison of voting procedures

Voting system	Criteria						
	a	b	c	d	e	f	g
Amendment	1	1	1	1	0	0	0
Copeland	1	1	1	1	1	0	0
Dodgson	1	0	1	0	1	0	0
Maximin	1	0	1	1	1	0	0
Plurality	0	0	1	1	1	1	0
Borda	0	1	0	1	1	1	0
Approval	0	0	0	1	0	1	1
Black	1	1	1	1	1	0	0
Plurality runoff	0	1	1	0	1	0	0
Nanson	1	1	1	0	1	0	0
Hare	0	1	1	0	1	0	0

winning, d = monotonicity, e = Pareto, f = consistency and g = property α. Most of the criteria have been defined above. The majority winning criterion is the requirement that whenever there is an alternative that is ranked first by more than 50% of the voters, then that alternative should be elected.

Entry '1' ('0', respectively) in the table indicates that the procedure represented by the row is compatible (incompatible) with the criterion indicated by the column. To demonstrate incompatibility one needs to present one profile in which the choice made by the procedure is not one allowed for by the criterion. To demonstrate compatibility one needs to show that in all profiles the choices made by the procedure are those allowed for by the criterion.

7.8   Two social choice theorems

Going through various procedures and lists of criteria is a straightforward way to proceed in finding satisfactory ways of making collective choices. A more general way is to work through criteria and their relationships. Thus, for example, one may ask whether property x is always satisfied by systems that satisfy property y. If the answer is no, then properties x and y are incompatible. The most celebrated results in the social choice literature are of this type. They demonstrate the incompatibility of properties or requirements imposed on choices. The more plausible the properties, the more dramatic are the results showing their incompatibility. In the following we shall mention just two well-known examples of this literature.

Theorem 1 *(Arrow 1963). No social welfare function satisfies the following conditions:*

1. *unrestricted domain*
2. *independence of irrelevant alternatives*
3. *Pareto*
4. *non-dictatorship*

This is by far the best-known theorem in social choice theory. Its main significance is to point out the incompatibility of a set of apparently plausible desiderata. Closer scrutiny reveals that the main culprit is the independence of irrelevant alternatives condition which – albeit at first blush plausible – is not satisfied by any of the 11 systems touched upon in the preceding (for an illuminating discussion on this condition, see Saari 1999).

The other example is the theorem of McKelvey (1976, 1979). It deals with spatial models of voting. In these models the voter ideal points and policy alternatives are represented as points in a multi-dimensional policy space (see section 6.5). In other words, the alternatives are characterized by their properties or values on various dimensions. Similarly, each voter is assumed to have an idea of the best possible property combination which is represented by a point in the space.

Kenneth J. Arrow (born 1921) is one of the best-known economists of our time. His works cover an extremely wide range of modern economics, but among the general public he is probably best-known for his work on social choice theory. The sheer volume of Arrow's contributions is enormous. *Collected Papers of Kenneth J. Arrow* (1983–1985) constitute six volumes. Of his booklength works, *Social Choice and Individual Values* (2nd edition 1963) is a classic. Also *Essays in the Theory of Risk Bearing* (1971) and *General Competitive Analysis* (with Frank Hahn) (1971) are well known within the economics profession. Arrow was awarded the John von Neumann Theory Prize in 1986 (Vane and Mulhearn 2005: 51–52). He became a Nobel Memorial Laureate in economics in 1972.

Moreover, each voter is assumed to have preferences that can be represented by means of a distance measure or norm defined in the space under consideration: the further a point is from a voter's ideal point (in terms of the distance measure), the less preferred is the corresponding alternative in the voter's mind.

Richard D. McKelvey (1944–2002) was an American political scientist and one of the pioneers in the laboratory experimentation of voting systems and other mechanisms. His contributions range from the mathematical theory of voting through game-theoretic solution concepts to computational economics. His theorems on the essential arbitrariness of the simple majority rule in spatial voting games are now classic in the social choice theory.

Let us assume that each voter has a *Euclidean utility function*:

$$xR_iy \text{ if and only if } D_E(x, I) \leq D_E(y, I)$$

where $D_E(x, I)$ denotes the Euclidean distance between policy proposal or alternative x and voter i's ideal point I. An alternative belongs to the core of the spatial voting game if and only if there is no other alternative that is preferred by majority to it. Now, *McKelvey's theorem* states the following.

Theorem 2 *(McKelvey 1976, 1979). Let R^k denote the k-dimensional Euclidean policy space. Suppose that the core is empty, i.e. for each alternative there is a majority preferred one. Then for any two points x and y in R^k, there is a sequence $z_1, \ldots, z_m$ of points (proposals) in R^k so that $z_1 = x$ and $z_m = y$ and z_{i+1} beats z_i by a simple majority for all $i = 1, \ldots, m - 1$.*

This theorem, thus, shows that if the voters always vote for the alternative closer to their ideal point – which is to say, for the alternative they prefer – then starting from an arbitrary point in the space one can end up with another arbitrary point 'democratically', i.e. using simple majority voting. Phrased somewhat differently, if the voters are myopic – that is, consider only two alternatives at a time – then the person who controls the agenda also controls the outcome of the sequential majority voting or amendment procedure.

7.9   Voting as a game

Thus far we have implicitly assumed that the voters express their true preferences in voting. In other words, voters choose their voting strategies so that these reveal their preferences over the outcomes. In political science literature this type of behavior is sometimes called *expressive* or *sincere voting*. It is, however, quite conceivable that the voters resort to other kinds of behavior. In particular, in certain circumstances it may be entirely plausible not to reveal one's preferences in choosing voting strategy if by so doing one achieves a more preferable outcome than by sincere voting. To illustrate, consider Borda's paradox again (Table 7.2). If the two voters with preference ranking CBA know the preference profile and assume that the other seven voters vote expressively, they also know that the outcome is bound to be A if they also vote expressively. If, on the other hand, they vote strategically – i.e. aiming at the best possible outcome, given other voters' strategy choices – they may bring about the victory of B by voting for B instead of C. Since these two voters prefer B to A, it makes sense to do so. Hence the two voters have an incentive not to vote 'sincerely', that is, according to their preference ranking.

What this illustration shows in game theoretic terms is that in the case of Borda's paradox the sincere voting strategies do not lead to a Nash equilibrium. Given the choice sincere strategies of the seven other players, the two players with ranking CBA are better off by not voting sincerely. Of course, Borda's paradox is just an example involving a specific profile and a specific voting rule, plurality voting. It suggests, however, an important general question: is the possibility of benefiting from strategic, in contradistinction to sincere, behavior common in voting situations? Furthermore, are there differences among voting systems in this regard, i.e. are some systems more likely to create incentives for strategic voting than others? Given that elections and referenda are primarily held in order to find out the voters' views of candidates or issues, these are, of course, fundamental questions.

Answers to them have been sought for several decades. The first groundbreaking work in this area is Farquharson's *Theory of Voting* (1969). This book suggested a distinction between sincere and *sophisticated voting strategies*. Given a preference profile and the assumption that its details are common knowledge among the voters, the sophisticated strategies for each voter are the ones that are left once all dominated voting strategies are eliminated. Farquharson focused on pairwise voting systems, that is, on systems where the decision alternatives are confronted with each other in pairs. Elimination of dominated strategies is, however, rather tedious when the number of alternatives is even moderately large (larger than 4).

Within 10 years from the publication of Farquharson's book, two important results where achieved. The first, methodological, one is due to McKelvey and Niemi (1978). It gives a general method for finding sophisticated voting outcomes in binary voting systems, that is, in systems where, at each stage of voting, the voters are faced with a choice between two options. These may be either alternatives or subsets of them. The other result is a theorem concerning the vulnerability of voting systems to strategic behavior. It is known as the *Gibbard–Satterthwaite theorem* (Gibbard 1973; Satterthwaite 1975). We shall discuss both of these in the following.

An example of binary systems is the amendment system, where the voters are voting for either one of two alternatives at each stage of voting. The successive procedure, on the other hand, is a typical representative of the other variant of binary systems, namely of those where the voters are comparing single alternatives with subsets of them. In successive voting the agenda consists of a specific sequence of alternatives, say, $a_1, \ldots, a_k$. In the first step the voters vote for either a_1 or for the subset consisting of all the other alternatives. If a_1 receives the majority of votes, it wins. Otherwise, a_1 is eliminated and the next vote taken between a_2 and the subset consisting of $a_3, \ldots, a_k$. If a_2 gets the majority, it wins. Otherwise one continues in similar way until the winner is found.

McKelvey and Niemi's method is an application of Zermelo's algorithm (discussed previously in section 5.2) to binary voting trees. These trees are representations of voting games emphasizing their strategic nature. Trees consist of nodes and edges. Each node in a binary voting tree represents a voting situation, that is, a choice between two options (alternatives or sets of alternatives). An edge emanating from a node represents a choice (again either alternative or set of alternatives) made in the node. To illustrate, consider the following three-voter profile (Table 7.16). This profile has a background in the real world. When considering applications to the vacant chair of an academic department X, the faculty council of the social sciences at university U invited three referees to assess the scholarly merits of the applicants. There were ten applicants. The referees were asked to provide a ranking of the candidates they regarded as most competent for the chair. The symbols A–G stand for those candidates ranked among the five top ones by the three referees. The table indicates these rankings (with a minor modification) reported by the referees.

Table 7.16 Profile illustrating the McKelvey–Niemi method

Referee 1	Referee 2	Referee 3
E	A	B
F	B	F
G	G	G
B	E	E
D	C	A

The ranking differs from the ones we have discussed above in one respect: not all candidates appear in all rankings. For example, candidates C and D appear in only one ranking.

According to the university statutes the faculty council makes its nomination partly on the basis of the referee reports and partly using other criteria, such as teaching skills. Suppose, however, that the referees are to make the nomination proposal themselves. Suppose, moreover, that the referees resort to the successive procedure with the following agenda:

1. B vs. the rest of candidates,
2. A vs. the remaining candidates,
3. C vs. the remaining candidates,
4. D vs. the remaining candidates,
5. E vs. the remaining candidates, and
6. F vs. G.

This agenda can be presented as the following tree (Figure 7.1).

The preference over a set of alternatives does not in general enable us to infer preferences over pairs that consist of a single alternative and a set of alternatives. Thus we cannot predict what will be the outcome of successive voting, given the above agenda, unless we make some further assumptions about voter preferences. Let us assume that the voter always votes for the subset (that consist of one or several alternatives) that contains her most preferred alternative of those that have not yet been eliminated. Under this assumption, we can predict that sincere voting

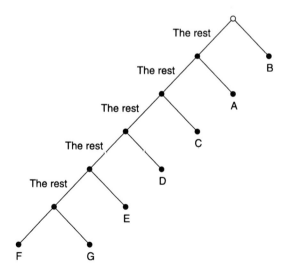

Figure 7.1 The successive agenda.

strategies lead to the victory of F. This shows that the successive procedure does not necessarily end up with the Condorcet winner (here B) under sincere voting.

To find out sophisticated voting outcomes McKelvey and Niemi suggest backward induction. First they define the *multi-stage sophisticated equivalent* (SE, for short) of a node in the game tree. It represents the rational outcome expectation under the assumption that this node will be reached. For terminal nodes, that is, those lowest in the tree (F and G in our example), these are simply identical with those very outcomes. For non-terminal nodes, i.e those higher than terminal ones in the game tree, the sophisticated equivalent is the majority preferred alternative among those emanating from the node. In our example, the SEs of the terminal nodes are F and G. The SE of the last nonterminal node, in turn, is F, since F is preferred to G by two referees out of three. The outcomes written in bold-faced letters in Figure 7.2 are the SEs of our example. The upper-most SE is the sophisticated voting outcome. Thus, in our example the sophisticated voting outcome is B.

B, it will be recalled, is the Condorcet winner in this example. McKelvey and Niemi show that this is the case in general, that is, the sophisticated voting outcome in successive voting always coincides with the Condorcet winner when the latter exists.

The same applies to the amendment procedure which differs from the successive one in resulting in an eventual Condorcet winner also under sincere voting. McKelvey and Niemi show that in monotonic binary voting systems, sophisticated voting leads to the Condorcet winner when one exists. In other words, the 'nice' behavior of sophisticated voting is not restricted to the best

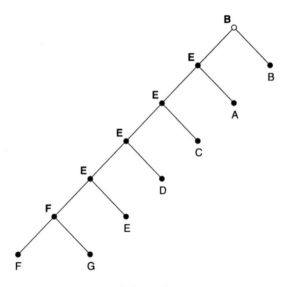

Figure 7.2 The SEs of department X chair agenda.

known binary procedures, amendment and successive one, but extends to any type of monotonic binary procedure.

Another major result of McKelvey and Niemi is related to the other theorem of McKelvey (1976, 1979) discussed above. According to it, the outcomes of sincere pairwise majority voting can be found anywhere in a multi-dimensional policy space, unless there exists a Condorcet winner or core alternative. The core alternative is one which beats or ties all other alternatives in sincere voting. In short, the amendment procedure with sincere voting can lead to an arbitrary outcome under fairly general conditions. The McKelvey and Niemi result states that this is no longer the case with sophisticated voting. Rather, the outcomes are restricted to a subset of the policy space, known as the *top cycle set*. Top cycle is the smallest subset A' of alternatives which satisfies the following condition: every alternative in A' defeats every alternative not in A' (Miller 1995: 63).[44]

Thus, sophisticated voting can be regarded as an antidote against *agenda manipulation*. The latter means constructing voting agenda so that the objectives of the agenda setter are satisfied, i.e. she gets what she wants as the outcome of the process. Sincere voting combined with the amendment procedure gives the agenda setter maximal control over the outcomes (provided that no core alternative exists). Sophisticated voting restricts this control to a subset of alternatives. Yet, this subset is in a sense too large to characterize outcomes ensuing from sophisticated voting. Indeed, Miller (1977, 1980) has shown that all sophisticated voting outcomes of the amendment procedure must be located in a subset of the top cycle set, that is, the *uncovered set*. This consists of alternatives that are not covered by any other alternative. An alternative x covers another alternative y if it defeats both y and all those alternatives that y defeats.

The plausibility of the uncovered set as a solution concept is fairly obvious: choosing a covered alternative means that one foregoes another alternative that not only beats the chosen one but also all the others that the latter beats. So, Miller's result amounts to showing that the amendment procedure results in one of these plausible alternatives if the voters are sophisticated.

The uncovered set is, however, in general 'too large'. It may contain outcomes that cannot result from sophisticated voting under any amendment agenda. Banks (1985) gives a full characterization of the sophisticated voting outcomes under amendment procedure. He shows that a subset of the uncovered set, now known as the *Banks set*, contains all possible outcomes of sophisticated voting and no other alternatives. To define the Banks set we need the concept of the Banks chain. Given any alternative x, the chain is formed as follows. We look for an alternative that defeats x. If such an alternative, say y, exists, we have a chain $x - y$. We now look for an alternative, say z, that defeats both x and y. If such a z is found, we now have the chain $x - y - z$ and we continue by looking for another alternative that defeats z and both its predecessors. Continuing in this manner, we shall eventually reach a point where no alternative beats all those in the chain. Let the last alternative in the chain be w. It defeats all the previous ones and no other alternative defeats it along with all the others in the chain. The end point w is then one element of the Banks set. There may be several chains beginning from x. The Banks set consists of endpoints of all Banks chains. In other words, it consists of all end points of the chains starting from all alternatives.

Jeffrey S. Banks (1958–2000) was an American political scientist and social choice theorist who during his brief career achieved several important results in the theory of voting, game theory and mechanism design. Apart from his numerous scholarly articles he published *Signaling Games in Political Science* (1991), *Positive Political Theory I: Collective Preference* (with David Austen-Smith) (1999) and (posthumously) *Positive Political Theory II: Strategy and Structure* (with David Austen-Smith) (2005).

The department X chair example demonstrates that sincere and sophisticated voting may result in different outcomes. The question now arises as to how general is this discrepancy. Does it extend to all binary voting procedures? It does. In fact the discrepancy covers a very wide class of voting systems, as shown by the Gibbard–Satterthwaite theorem. It states that all *non-discriminating* and resolute voting systems are either manipulable or dictatorial. Non-discrimination means in this context that the system does not treat alternatives or voters in a discriminating manner. An example of a discriminating system is a committee voting by plurality where ties are broken by the chairperson's vote.[45] Another example is the parliamentary amendment system which places the status quo alternative – which means keeping the existing legislation intact – always in the last pairwise comparison. In general, however, it is regarded plausible that a system not discriminate for or against alternatives or voters. Among non-discriminating systems the theorem, thus, confronts us with a choice between dictatorial systems or those vulnerable to preference manipulation. Both are negative properties. Dictatorial voting systems are those where there is a voter whose preference decides the choice regardless of the opinions of other voters. Manipulability, in turn, means that revealing one's true preferences does not always result in a Nash equilibrium. In other words, there are profiles where a voter gets a better outcome (from her own point of view) by not revealing her true preferences than by voting sincerely. So, the discrepancy between sincere and sophisticated voting is quite widespread.

The fact that a system is manipulable means that under some circumstances it makes it possible for a voter to benefit from misrepresenting her preferences. It is, however, easy to exaggerate the practical importance of the theorem. Firstly, it is basically an existence result in the sense that it states that there are profiles which make preference misrepresentation beneficial for some voters. It says nothing about the likelihood of those profiles in voting bodies. Secondly, even if such a profile were to materialize, it might not provide incentives for the voters to vote sophisticatedly as they do not necessarily know the voting strategies of the others. Knowing the preference profile is not the same as to know the voting strategies. Thirdly, the voters might be expressive voters, that is, they might wish to express their preferences even at the risk of ending up with worse outcomes than they would if they resorted to sophisticated voting.[46] None the less, it is natural to consider voting as a game where opinions are transformed into voting strategies and these, in turn, according to the procedure specific rules, into outcomes.

7.10 Suggested reading

Black (1958) is the classic treatise on voting in committees. The historical background of voting is extensively covered by McLean and Urken (1995). Arrow (1963) and Sen (1970) are also classic works, as is Pattanaik (1971). Peleg (1984) discusses the committee voting from the strategic perspective. In the 1990s, Saari introduced a new, geometric, approach to voting. Saari (1995) gives the basics of the approach which is further developed in Saari (2001a) and (2001b) as well as in numerous technical articles, e.g. Saari (2000a) and (2000b). Sophisticated voting and agenda institutions are analyzed extensively in Miller (1995). Widgrén (2002) presents a model of agenda-based voting in the European Union.

8 Designing for elections and public goods provision

We now turn from committee voting systems to a discussion of systems applied in large scale (nationwide, municipal) elections. The problems encountered in electoral systems design do not differ essentially from those discussed above in the context of committee voting, but often there is a new assignment to be dealt with, namely that of building a multi-member representative body. In other words, there is an additional consideration involved that pertains to how the elected representatives and their views are related to those of their electors. In his book *Principles of Electoral Reform*, Michael Dummett (1997) splits the question of the choice of electoral system into two parts. Firstly, which parties and/or individuals should represent the people at large? Secondly, which electoral system would best guarantee the desired distribution of elected candidates and parties? He then goes on to argue that the answer to the first question is, in fact, much more difficult than one would perhaps anticipate. Furthermore, once this question is answered, the answer to the second one is often relatively simple, although it may require devising new electoral systems.

Dummett's focus is on electoral reform and, more specifically, on the types of reforms that have been debated in the United Kingdom over the decades. From the more general constitutional design perspective, his analysis brings forth, however, an important preliminary insight: in order to come up with reasonably well-behaving institutions, one should pay careful attention to specifying one's desiderata. In particular, one should aim at specific criteria for the evaluation of proposed reforms. Once these have been set up and arranged in order of importance, the choice of the institutions is a relatively straightforward matter.

In the following we shall discuss on a fairly general level the issues related to setting up such criteria of performance of political institutions. Of particular interest are, of course, criteria pertaining to democratic and efficient institutions. Before going into the details of those criteria, a few remarks on the perspective from which we approach the institutions are in order.

Our approach is in certain respects similar to that adopted by the social philosophers of the social contract tradition. That is, we shall try to find out justifications for institutional arrangements stemming from a 'neutral' setting that precedes them in time. From the practical point of view, this approach is, of course, unrealistic since all institutional reforms take place in specific socio-political contexts. That is, the real-world situations involving institutional design or reform are necessarily preceded by a status quo situation which provides a natural basis for comparison. Thus, some actor groups (interest groups, parties, ethnic, religious or linguistic minorities) typically benefit from certain types of reforms, while some others may lose thereby. This makes the practical institutional design situations akin to games of strategy.

For example, in the United Kingdom the modification of the electoral system from the present first-past-the-post system to some version of proportional representation is likely to be accompanied with parliamentary seat losses to both the Labour and the Conservative parties. This conjecture is based on the assumption that the geographical distribution of support for all parties in Britain remains largely as it is. The fact that the consequences of the proposed systems can be compared to the status quo by the parties makes the reform more difficult than it would be behind the *veil of ignorance*, to use John Rawls's famous concept (Rawls 1971). Behind the veil of ignorance all actors involved in the institutional design are assumed to be ignorant about the issues to be decided upon in the future, their own positions in the new institutional framework, even their abilities, etc.

Yet, there are institutional issues that can be discussed *in abstracto*, that is, without any particular constitutional starting position in mind. These deal with the various desiderata of institutions, i.e. various properties one would wish the institutions to possess. These are the foci in the following.

8.1 The majority rule

One of the oft-cited hallmarks of democracy is the majority rule. It says that given two mutually exclusive propositions (e.g. joining or not joining an economic alliance), the one supported by a majority should be adopted. It makes perfect sense to argue that the majority rule is indeed the only reasonable way of deciding in this kind of situation. To choose otherwise (i.e. against the majority opinion) would seem discriminatory. Either one of the two alternatives is discriminated for (or against) or some voters' opinions are being discriminated for (or against).

In fact, K.O. May (1952) showed half a century ago that the majority rule is the only rule that satisfies non-discrimination and the following two requirements:

1. *duality*: if everyone changes their mind regarding the alternatives, the outcome should also change accordingly, and
2. *strict monotonicity*: if equally many voters support each of the two alternatives, then only one voter needs to change her mind to change the outcome from a tie to the victory of one of the alternatives.

That the simple majority rule has these properties is, upon a moment's reflection, pretty obvious, but the converse, i.e. the fact that any rule that satisfies the above requirements is equivalent to the majority rule, is perhaps less straightforward. None the less, this is what May proved. Clearly, these properties are quite plausible.

From another point of view the majority rule can also be justified by referring to the costs an individual incurs when acting in a group rather than on her own (Buchanan and Tullock 1962). Behind the veil of ignorance, the individual has no way of knowing which kinds of issues will appear on the agenda of the collective decision-making body. What she can anticipate, however, is that some of the collective decisions will be against her interests, while others are favorable to them. Obviously, the individual would like to minimize the probability of the former type of decisions and maximize the probability of the latter ones. The costs caused by the adverse decisions to the individual are called *external costs* by Buchanan and Tullock. These summarize, thus, the negative effects that the collective decisions have on the individual when they are against her interest. On the other hand, the individual is obviously keen on promoting collective decisions that are in accordance with her interests. In doing so, she incurs costs. These are called *decision-making costs*.

James M. Buchanan (born 1919) is one the founders of the public choice tradition. He is an economist by training. Many of his works touch upon foundational issues of societies, such as the proper role of the state. He has written extensively on constitutional economics, the rationale of rules, principles of taxation and constitutional contracts. Among his most important books are *The Calculus of Consent* (with Gordon Tullock) (1962), *The Limits of Liberty* (1975), *Power to Tax* (with Geoffrey Brennan) (1980) and *The Reason of Rules* (with Geoffrey Brennan) (1985). In 1986 Buchanan became the Nobel Memorial Laureate in economics.

The basic idea underlying the rational choice of the decision-making rule is that the external costs as well as the decision-making ones can be expressed as functions of the decision rule, i.e. the size of the majority required for proposals to pass. In particular, the external costs are monotone non-increasing functions of the size of the majority, while the decision-making costs are assumed to grow with the size of the majority (see Figure 8.1).[47] The precise form of the functions vary between individuals, but the above qualitative features make intuitive sense. That the external costs reach the minimum when a unanimous support is needed for a motion to pass is obvious since the individual may veto all proposals that are against her interests. Similarly these costs are maximal when the smallest possible group may dictate the collective decision. The decision-making costs, in turn, are minimal when the individual needs to persuade no others to support her proposal for it to be adopted. The maximum of those costs is reached when every member of the collectivity is required to support a motion.

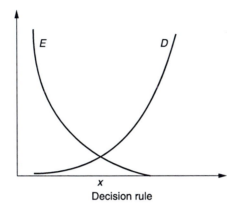

Figure 8.1 External and decision-making cost functions

Gordon Tullock (born 1922) is, with James Buchanan and Mancur Olson, one of the founders of the public choice school of thought. A lawyer by training Tullock introduced the concept of rent-seeking to the vocabulary of public choice theorists. He has also been a pioneer of law and economics research tradition. Tullock has written more than twenty books, *i.a. The Calculus of Consent* (with James Buchanan) (1962), *The Logic of the Law* (1971), *Autocracy* (1987) and *Rent Seeking* (1993). He is the founding editor of *Journal of Non-Market Decision Making* (later renamed *Public Choice*).

If the cost functions are symmetric, one would expect the curve representing the sum of the two cost types to reach its minimum in the middle of the line segment from 1 to *n*. Thus, the majority rule could be seen as a cost-minimizing rule for individuals choosing the decision rule behind the veil of ignorance. A somewhat more technical argument for the majority rule can be built using Douglas Rae's calculus of the probability of being on the winning side in collective decisions (Rae 1969). In dichotomous 'yes–no' decision situations assuming that the future agendas are unknown, an individual's probability of being on the winning side is maximal when the decision rule is the simple majority. In other words, any other decision rule results at most the same probability of being on the winning side (i.e. voting for 'yes' when 'yes' wins and for 'no' when 'no' wins) as the majority rule.

Given these basically plausible arguments for the majority rule, one may wonder why this rule is not universally adopted. At least two reasons can be cited:

1. many decision settings differ from the one that guarantees the nice performance of the majority rule, and

2. the wish to avoid *majority tyranny* whereby only slightly more numerous majority permanently subsumes the preference of the only slightly smaller minority (Guinier 1994; Miller 1983).

With regard to the first-mentioned reason, the most important difference is that, while the majority rule is defined for only two alternative decision settings, the real-world applications of collective decision making typically involve more, sometimes many more, than two alternatives. Of course, one may still act as if the decision setting were the same as the one defining the majority rule. So, for example, the amendment procedure used in many contemporary parliaments is based on pairwise comparisons of alternatives where the winner in each comparison is determined as in the definition of the majority rule. Condorcet's paradox shows, however, that the outcome of this procedure may be essentially arbitrary (see Table 7.5 in the preceding chapter). Furthermore, McKelvey's theorem shows that when the majority rule fails, it fails completely in the sense that one cannot be assured that the outcomes are anywhere near the voter ideal points.

8.2   Majority and plurality

The amendment procedure is one way of generalizing the majority rule into many-alternative settings. Perhaps a more widely known way, however, is the one-person-one-vote principle which is often held as the cornerstone of democracy. Given several alternatives, this principle calls for each voter to vote for one and only one alternative. Once the votes have been given, the winner is the alternative which has been voted for by more voters than any other alternative. This system is the plurality procedure which we have discussed above. With more than two alternatives, it may obviously happen that the plurality winner receives less than 50% of the votes.

This undoubtedly democratic procedure may, however, run into a head-on collision with the majority principle of the preceding section. It can happen that the plurality winner is by no means victorious in pairwise comparisons with other alternatives. In fact, as was shown by way of an example by Borda (see Table 7.2 in section 7.4), the plurality winner may fare extremely poorly in such comparisons (DeGrazia 1953).

The plurality procedure is used for example in the elections of the British parliament. Each constituency sends one member to the parliament. The fact that the elected member may have the support of less than 50% of the electorate provides motivation for the plurality runoff systems. These behave exactly as the plurality system in cases where one candidate has more than 50% of the total votes cast. In other cases, a runoff is arranged between the two largest vote-getters. Of these, one is bound to have a majority of votes. The runoff thus secures that the elected candidate has been supported by at least half of the active voters.

In the example of Table 7.2, B would be the likely runoff winner since it is ranked higher than its contestant A by 5 voters out of 9. Despite its 'majoritarian spirit', the runoff system may fail to elect a candidate that would defeat all others in pairwise contests. Modifying Table 7.2 so that the four voters on the left switch their preference between B and C, we end up with a situation where C would defeat both A and B with a simple majority. Yet, C would not make it to the second round. Thus, it would not be elected. This is obviously an unpleasant possibility for those who find the Condorcet winning criterion compelling.

Apart from the cyclic majority problems, the other main concern pertaining to the exclusive use of the simple majority rule is the majority tyranny. This concept refers to the possibility that a majority of voters forms a permanent coalition to the detriment of the minority (Miller 1983; Baharad and Nitzan 2002). Should a permanent coalition of 51% of voters form and the majority rule be applied, this coalition would in fact dictate each and every decision in the society. Surely, when thinking of the majority rule as an indicator of the rule by the people one would find this eventuality highly undesirable. Intuitively one tends to think that 51% of the voters should dictate roughly 51% of the decisions, not 100% of them. Under this intuition, then, democracy seems to contain an idea of proportionality.

It is well-known that the majoritarian systems do not guarantee proportionality. This fact was pointed out in the United States presidential election of the year 2000 where it turned out that the elected president, George W. Bush, had less popular votes than his opponent, Al Gore. Under the US constitution this kind of outcome is quite possible since the Electoral College which actually elects the president, albeit representing the states in somewhat proportional manner, works according to the 'winner-take-all' principle. Thus, all the electors of each state vote for the candidate which was supported by the majority of voters of that state.

As it happened, Bush won by 271 electors against Gore's 267. In terms of the popular vote numbers, Gore, however, received some 300,000 votes more than Bush. Thus, it could be (and was) argued that Bush had 'too few' votes to qualify as the real winner of the contest. This argument misses the essential nature of the majoritarian US system. Bush would have won even with a dramatically smaller number of votes. In fact, all the votes he received in those states where Gore won the majority of votes, were in a sense redundant for Bush since they did not increase the number of his electors. Similarly, in those states where Bush received the majority of votes, all those votes in excess of the majority were redundant since he would have received all the electors in those states without them.[48]

The peculiarities of the majoritarian systems become perhaps even more vivid by the observation that in the US presidential election a candidate may receive overall more votes than any other candidate without getting a single elector (Nurmi 2002: 22). The plurality rule may thus lead to extreme deviations from proportionality. Yet, single-member districts and plurality voting can be defended on the grounds that they typically result in clear majorities in legislatures. Combined with parliamentarianism these systems then have the advantage of producing stable and fairly enduring governments. The latter, in turn, enable the governments to pursue relatively long-term social goals. The disadvantages of these systems are equally well-known: the legislation may largely benefit the supporters of the ruling majority and thus alienate the opposition. Of particular interest in systems with more or less permanent cleavages is the representation of the minorities, be they of religious, linguistic or ethnic nature. Let us now take a look at a procedure which can be seen as an attempt to secure minority representation without jeopardizing the majority's right to call the shots.

8.3   Single transferable vote

In Ireland, Malta and many municipalities of New England, the system used in electing collective bodies is called the single transferable vote (STV). In the Irish parliamentary elections the members of parliament (MPs) are elected from multi-member constituencies, but the system lends itself to an application in single-member constituencies as well. In those circumstances it is usually called the alternative vote or Hare's system. This has already been discussed above. In Britain, STV is often regarded as the main rival of the first-past-the-post system, but it is obviously not the only alternative. One of the main advantages of STV is the relative high degree of minority protection it provides. In other words, it guarantees that even fairly small voter minorities, when acting in concert, can guarantee representation in the elected bodies. Just how small minorities can do this depends, however, on the number of MPs elected in the constituency: the larger the constituency (i.e. the larger the number of MPs elected from it), the better the chances of even small minorities to get representation.

STV operates as follows. Given a set of candidates, each voter is asked to express a ranking of the candidates. The set of these rankings is the preference profile used in computing the winners. Suppose that the constituency we focus on sends k MPs to the parliament. In determining the election result, we first define the *Droop quota*, D, which is the smallest integer strictly larger than $n/(k + 1)$ where n is the number of voters who voted in the constituency. Next, one finds out whether some of the candidates have been ranked first by at least D voters. If such candidates exist, they are declared elected. Because of the rounding up involved in the computation of D, at most k candidates can be declared winners. Often the number of winners found after the first count is strictly less than k.

Once the candidates who have been ranked first by at least D voters have been found, the candidate who has been ranked first by the smallest number of voters is eliminated. This means that the votes given to her are assigned to those candidates mentioned in the second place of those ballot slips. Also, the votes in excess of D are reassigned to other candidates in proportion of the number of voters who indicate those candidates next in their ballots. Table 8.1 and Table 8.2 illustrate the computation of winners in a two-member constituency with 100 voters and four candidates (Nurmi 1996/7).

The Droop quota in Table 8.1 is 34. Table 8.2 shows the phases of computation. The result is that A and D emerge as winners.

STV is often regarded as a method that guarantees some proportionality in the voting outcomes. Indeed, with the increase of the district size, the minority protection of STV increases since clearly any minority of $1/(k + 1)$th of the district

Table 8.1 Computing the STV winners

15 voters	15 voters	10 voters	20 voters	25 voters	15 voters
A	B	B	C	D	A
D	C	C	A	B	D
C	A	A	D	A	C
B	D	D	B	C	B

Table 8.2 Phases of computation

Candidate	First count	Second count	Third count
A	30	$+20 = 50$	$-16 = 34$
B	25	25	25
C	20	$-20 = 0$	0
D	25	25	$+16 = 41$

electorate may through concerted action guarantee representation (k denoting the number of representatives elected from the district). This is certainly an important feature in some contexts. Another advantageous feature in STV is that it is difficult to benefit from misrepresentation of one's true preferences. In order to successfully benefit from it, one has to know a great deal about the preference ranking distribution of the electorate. While it is possible to find circumstances in which strategic voting might work under STV, there seems to be a fairly widespread consensus among election system experts that misrepresentation efforts are likely to backfire.

To balance these advantages, STV has several serious drawbacks. One of them, non-monotonicity, has been pointed out by Doron and Kronick (1977). In other words, additional support could under some circumstances decrease rather than increase a candidate's likelihood of being elected. More specifically, when STV (or some other non-monotonic system) is used, a candidate may have incentives to ask some of her voters not to vote for her lest her chances of being elected be jeopardized. This is obviously not a desirable property of a voting system. It has been argued, though, that the circumstances under which STV creates such incentives are extremely rare (Allard 1995).

A more serious problem in STV pertains to incentives to vote. To wit, STV is one of those systems which may result in a no-show paradox. It will be recalled that this paradox occurs when a group of voters would be better off by not voting at all than by voting according to its preferences. This feature is intuitively related to monotonicity, but on closer inspection, turns out to be logically distinct from it (Campbell and Kelly 2002). From the viewpoint of encouraging voter participation, the possibility of a no-show paradox is, of course, unpleasant. An instance of the paradox under STV can be seen in Table 8.1. Suppose that the 10-voter group with preference ranking *BCAD* abstained. Now, the Droop quota would reduce to 31. The first alternative to be eliminated would be B after which C as well as A would emerge as winners. Surely, this outcome is preferable for the abstainers to the original victory of A and D.

Another feature that is often regarded as a weakness of STV is the possibility that a Condorcet winner alternative is not elected. On a moment's reflection this is a relatively straightforward consequence of the fact that the alternative that would defeat all others in pairwise contests with a majority of votes is not necessarily ranked first by a single voter. Thus, it is very 'often' eliminated in the early rounds of computing the STV winners. Of course, the strong Condorcet winner, i.e. an alternative ranked first by more than 50% of voters will necessarily be elected by STV. Hence, STV avoids the most blatant type of conflict with the majority principle.

As Doron (1979) has pointed out, STV is an inconsistent procedure. This means that rather counterintuitive surprises may surface when STV is applied in several districts. In particular, it may happen that an alternative, say A, wins in all districts by STV, but when all districts are considered simultaneously, some other alternative wins (see also Fishburn and Brams 1982).

As all procedures, STV is thus characterized by a mixture of desirable and undesirable properties. Baharad and Nitzan (2002) provide an illuminating general discussion on how systems that are based on individual preference rankings, like the Borda count, are effective in countering majority tyranny. Thus, even though in the English-speaking world STV is often regarded as the most important way of guaranteeing some degree of proportionality and of avoiding majority tyranny, it is by no means the only way. In continental Europe, however, various list-type proportional representation systems are far more common. We now turn to some of these systems.

8.4   Quota and divisor methods

The explicit aim of proportional representation (PR) systems is that the elected body of representatives is to a reasonable degree a miniature of the political opinions of the electorate at large. In the following we shall call the elected body the parliament, but it is, of course, possible and even common to resort to PR in municipal and other types of elections. Hence, what will be said of PR systems and parliamentary election applies to these other types of elections as well.

In most PR systems one can distinguish two phases:

1. the allocation of parliamentary seats to districts, and
2. the allocation of seats within a district to parties or candidates.

The former phase is often called *apportionment*. It precedes the election in time. There are PR systems in which the entire country (or municipality) is regarded as one district. Thus, the former phase is, in some cases, trivially solved.

Of the methods used in the apportionment stage, the *largest remainders* or *Hamilton's method* is very often used. This method is in a way 'natural' since it is based on the following intuitively plausible formula:

$$\frac{V_i}{V} = \frac{S_i}{S}.$$

Here V_i denotes the number of voters in district i, V the total number of voters, S_i the number of seats allocated to district i and S the house size, i.e. the total number of seats in the parliament. In the apportionment problem we are given the values of S, V_i and V. Thus, we can solve for S_i. This is the exact quota of district i. A new problem, however, emerges thereby. To wit, the value obtained is typically not an integer. How to deal with the fractional parts? One way is to simply ignore them and allocate seats to districts in accordance with the integer parts of S_i. This, however, would leave us with a few unallocated seats since the sum of the integer parts is typically smaller than S. The largest remainders method solves the problem by first allocating each district the number of seats corresponding to the integer part of its quota and then allocating the available additional seats to districts in the order of magnitude of the fractional parts of their quotas. Thus, the label 'largest remainders' gets its explanation (for an extensive and systematic treatment of various PR methods, see Balinski and Young 1982).

Although at first sight intuitively plausible, the largest remainders method may yield bizarre outcomes, one of which led to its abandonment as the apportionment method in the United States. This anomaly bears the name *Alabama paradox*, since it relates to the period during which the state of Alabama was to enter the union, i.e. in the early 1880s. During the process of new states entering, the constitution provided that they be allocated a share of seats in the House of Representatives that would correspond to the share of their population in the total US population. Up to the 1880s this had been interpreted as calling for the largest remainders allocation. In 1881, however, the chief clerk of the US Bureau of Census, C.W. Seton, reported an astonishing observation: on the basis of his calculations, Alabama would be entitled to 8 representatives if the House had 299 seats, but to only 7 if the House size were 300.

The requirement that the largest remainders method violated in the case of the Alabama paradox is nowadays known as *house monotonicity*: given a fixed distribution of seats over n districts in a house of size m, the amount of seats allocated to each district should be no less if the house size is increased to $m + 1$. It turns out that the method is vulnerable to other types of anomalies as well. Specifically, it may respond in a strange way to relative changes in the populations of states (see Balinski and Young 1982: 42–43). In 1901, the state of Virginia would have lost one seat to the state of Maine according to the census data and, yet, the ratio of the population of Virginia *vis-à-vis* that of Maine had increased (for similar observations in Finland, see Nurmi and Lagerspetz (1984) and Nurmi (1999: 114–115)).

To balance its unexpectedly poor performance when judged according to the criteria above, the largest remainders method has one clear advantage pointed out by Birkhoff (1976), that is, *binary fairness*. This most plausible requirement states that the allocation of seats should be optimal in the sense that any reallocation of seats between two districts would result in a larger deviation from strict proportionality with regard to these two districts.

Another virtue of the largest remainders method is that the resulting allocations always satisfy the quota, i.e. no district receives less than $s_i - 1$ or more than $s_i + 1$ seats. Yet, due to its failure on monotonicity, this method has been replaced by some divisor method in many countries. For example, in Finland the apportionment is conducted using the largest remainders method, but the allocation of seats to parties after the votes have been cast is done by *d'Hondt's method*, which is one of the divisor ones.

The *divisor methods* are characterized by a sequence of increasing divisor numbers $a(j)$ $(j = 1, \ldots, k)$ that are used in dividing the support given to each party list in elections. The seats available in a given district are then allocated to parties in the order of magnitude of the numbers obtained by dividing the party support in a district by consecutive numbers in the sequence. Thus, the first seats to each party are given in the order of the numbers obtained by dividing the party support by $a(1)$.

The divisor methods differ from each other with regard to the values of $a(i)$. d'Hondt's method is characterized by $a(i) = i$. The advantage of the divisor methods is that they are in general monotonic. But the most important source of disproportionality is the existence of multiple districts. Regardless of how one determines the candidates elected in districts, the country-wide distribution of parliamentary seats may grossly deviate from proportionality if there are no surplus or compensation seats to be allocated to parties on the basis of the overall support. Thus, the most straightforward way to achieve proportional distributions is to do away with districts, i.e. to consider the whole country as a single district. This method is used, for example, in the Netherlands and Israel. This has the disadvantage of playing down the local or area considerations in the composition of the parliament. Obviously, this is not entirely plausible in geographically large and heterogeneous systems. A more plausible way is to resort to allocation of a fixed share of parliamentary seats on the basis of country-wide support of parties, as has been done, e.g. in Germany.

8.5   Proportionality of what?

The intuitive concept of proportionality connects the views of members of the representative body with those of the electorate at large. According to this intuitive conception, the views of the electorate are reflected in the election results (see e.g. Baker 1996). But in typical elections, each voter can reveal very little of her opinions regarding candidates and/or parties. More often than not, she can only pick one alternative (party list or candidate) as her favorite. Sure, there are elections, notably of the STV variety, that allow for a richer expression

Table 8.3 Ambiguous proportionality

30% of voters	35% of voters	25% of voters	10% of voters
A	C	D	B
B	B	B	C
C	A	A	D
D	D	C	A

of opinions. The point, however, is that if we assume that the voters have opinions regarding all candidates or at least several of them, the notion of proportionality underlying current electoral systems becomes ambiguous. Consider an example (Table 8.3).

Here we have four candidates competing for three seats in a constituency. Systems based on plurality as well as STV would elect A, C and D. Yet, B is ranked first or second by all voters, while D is ranked last by 65% of them. The exclusion of B would seem unreasonable.

By a slight modification of the above table one may create a situation where plurality and STV systems end up with different outcomes. By assigning 35% of the voters to the left-most group, 40% to the next one, 15% to the next one and 10% to the right-most group, we get different results with plurality-based systems and STV. The former ends up with A, C and D, while STV results in A, B and C. It is not difficult to see that our notion of proportionality is crucially dependent on the voting system. This – along with voter preferences – determines what kind of seat distributions we consider proportional. Thus, it seems that the very meaning of proportionality hinges on an implicit assumption of the social choice procedure to be used. Consequently, it may well happen that, given a preference profile, we may have several proportional outcomes (e.g. allocations of parliamentary seats to parties) depending on the underlying choice procedures (e.g. STV, Borda count, plurality).

Suppose now that nearly perfect proportionality has been achieved in the sense that there is an agreement as to what voting procedure is used in defining proportionality and that, moreover, the seat distribution of parties corresponds closely to the distribution of support in the electorate. The voting body is then assumed to be a miniature model of the electorate at large in relevant respects (opinions on the main political issues). Surely our assumption is very strong, but nevertheless it can be easily seen that crucial problems remain open even if the proportionality of seat distribution were our sole desideratum. This is shown in the following.

Consider a voting body – say, a parliament – with 100 seats. Suppose, moreover, that on the basis of elections held, the perfectly proportional seat distribution would give party A 55 seats, party B 25 seats and party C 20 seats. Now, the main role of parliaments is to enact laws and other norms. In passing legislation, the parliaments resort to collective decision-making procedures. Very often the majority rule is being applied. In other words, one looks at decision alternatives in a binary fashion and, at any given stage of the procedure, chooses that alternative which is supported by a majority in a contest with another alternative (or set of alternatives). The amendment and successive procedures, discussed above, are of this variety. It is clear that when the number of seats of a party exceeds that of a majority, it determines the winners in every pairwise contest. Thus, the influence of such a party over the legislative outcomes is decisive. In our example, party A clearly determines the outcome of every pairwise vote. Hence its control over the legislation is complete. With 55% of the seats – and, by assumption, of the popular support – it controls 100% of the legislation.

On the basis of examples like this one could argue that what should be distributed proportionally is not seats but voting power, i.e. influence over legislative outcomes. This, however, begs the question of measuring the latter. What the above example suggests is that the seat distribution is at times a poor proxy of voting power distribution. In particular, under circumstances where one party is capable of dictating the voting outcomes, the distribution of seats to others is largely irrelevant. But is the negative conclusion valid in general, that is, are we in general entitled to the conclusion that the seat distribution gives a distorted picture of the voting power distribution?

The answer to this question depends on one's measure of voting power. Some of these have been discussed in the preceding. These measures equate voting power with the importance of a party when voting coalitions are assumed to form in specific ways. For example, the Banzhaf index makes the simplifying – and often empirically false – assumption that all winning coalitions are equally likely to form. Under this assumption and taking into account the seat distribution as well as the required number of votes to pass legislation, it counts the number of winning coalitions in which a party is non-redundant. These coalitions are the swings of the party. Dividing the number of swings of a party with the total number of swings of all parties gives the normalized Banzhaf index value of the party.

The Banzhaf index is but one of many measures of *a priori* voting power. Its advantages and disadvantages *vis-à-vis* other similar measures has been a subject of debate for some time.[49] Whatever its shortcomings, it is certainly a more informative and useful measure of voting power than the practice of distributing seats to parties in proportion to their popular support. What this practice ignores is the fact that decisions in collective bodies are always made in accordance with decision rules. Typically these state the vote thresholds that have to be exceeded in order to pass new legislation. That a measure which takes these thresholds into account is superior to the common practice seems pretty obvious. What remains an open question is whether one should include more institutional detail into power measures. One such detail, already discussed in the preceding, is the existence of a spatial continuum along which the parties occupy more or less fixed positions. The traditional left–right continuum is an obvious candidate for such a spatial dimension. Whether it still today constrains the parties in their coalition behavior is, however, somewhat questionable. In any event, the concept of proportionality is ambiguous and, thus, a rich source of issues for political debate.

8.6 The general design problem

Designing voting systems for committees and electorates at large is a special case of a more general problem, namely that of institutional design. What kind of institutions would bring about the desired socio-political outcomes? This is the general formulation of the institutional design problem. This formulation begs the question of what is meant by desired outcomes. It also leaves open the meaning of 'bring about'.[50] Depending on the context the concept of desired outcome may have a wide range of different meanings. For example, in the design of voting procedures, one might consider it desirable that the procedure always results in an outcome that is Pareto optimal. Or we might view the choice of an eventual Condorcet winner desirable.

Stated more precisely, a *mechanism* consists of two parts (Palfrey and Srivastava 1989; Thomson 1996; Jackson 2001). Firstly, it includes the set of strategies of each player, formally an *n*-tuple of sets, if there are *n* individuals. Secondly, it includes a rule that associates an outcome to each collection of strategies given by the individuals. These strategies – often called *messages* in the literature – may be votes, bids or any other acts. A mechanism simply determines the outcome once the individuals have chosen their strategies. A mechanism is, thus, 'almost' a game: it is a game form, that is, a game without utilities or preferences assigned to the outcomes. Consider now a social choice function that assigns an outcome to each preference profile of individuals.[51] It is said to be *implementable* by a mechanism if the latter – when augmented with individual preferences – always results in the same outcomes as the social choice function so that these outcomes are game theoretic solutions or equilibria in some specific sense, e.g. Nash or subgame perfect equilibria. The equilibrium concept is then used in the characterization of the implementation. Thus, some choice functions are Nash-implementable, subgame perfect implementable and so on. The theory of mechanism design, that is, of conditions under which choice rules are implementable by game forms, is nowadays fairly abstract. In the following we shall, however, assume a less abstract approach and focus on mechanism that are devised for the specific task of public goods provision.

There are several ways of showing why the standard supply and demand mechanism fails when public goods are considered. The classic *tragedy of commons* is a story in which there is a relatively large area of land that is suitable for cattle grazing (Hardin 1968). There are several cattle owners who make use of this land. Since the land is relatively large and each additional animal consumes only a minuscule quantity of the available vegetation, each cattle owner has the incentive to increase the size of her herd. However, there is an upper limit to the number of animals that the commons can sustain. Once this limit is exceeded, the yield of the commons in terms of meat production begins to deteriorate, thus decreasing the income of all cattle owners using the commons.

Yet, each cattle-owner faces the dilemma: refraining from bringing more animals to the commons contributes to the welfare of the cattle already grazing there, but only under the condition that other cattle-owners do not take advantage of this by bringing their new animals to the commons. Thus, the maintenance of the commons seems to require coordination and enforcement of contracts.

In the preceding we have already discussed some elementary game theoretical models of public goods provision. In those games – PD and Chicken – the setting is one where a 'lumpy' public good is focused upon (lighthouse, bridge). This is somewhat restrictive. We, therefore, now broaden the perspective by introducing public goods – like security – that can be provided in varying amounts. The model discussed in the following section is based on Feldman's (1980) text.

8.7   Optimizing the public goods provision

The problem of optimal amount of public good will be approached in the simplified context where there are only two goods in the economy, one public and one private. Let x denote the amount of the public good. To simplify the expressions below we assume that each unit of the public good costs one unit of currency, i.e. the price of an additional unit of the public good is 1. It follows then that x denotes both the amount and the cost of the public good.

Let y_i denote the amount of private good in the possession of individual i. To simplify things further, let us assume that the welfare level of each individual – her utility – is a sum of her utility of possessing a certain amount of private good and her utility of the available amount of the public good, i.e. her utility function with regard to the private and public good is *separable*. Thus, we can express i's utility as

$$u_i = v_i(x) + y_i$$

where v_i is a continuous function.

Let now $\Delta v_i/\Delta x$ be i's marginal utility of the public good at point P, that is, when the amount of public good already available is P. This is approximately the amount that her utility increases when the amount of public good increases by one unit while her consumption of the private good remains constant. $v_i'(x)$ denotes i's marginal utility when the amount of public good is x.

The amount of money to be allocated to the public and private goods comes from the individual original possessions denoted by w_i. In other words, in this highly simplified economy the individuals allocate all their original possessions to private and public goods. Furthermore, there is no borrowing.

Thus, the ensuing allocation has to satisfy the following feasibility condition:

$$x + \sum_i y_i = \sum_i w_i.$$

In other words, the entire original possessions – no more and no less – are allocated to public and private goods. Now, what is the optimal amount of public good?

To derive what is known as *Samuelson's optimality condition* we consider the following inequality:

$$v_1'(x) + v_2'(x) + \cdots + v_n'(x) > 1$$

In other words, the sum of the first derivatives of $v_i(x)$ with respect to x is set strictly larger than 1. This means that we are looking at those supply levels of x for which the sum of marginal utilities of individuals is larger than 1. Let us assume that for all individuals the amount of private good exceeds the marginal utility of the public good at x, that is, $y_i > v_i'(x)$. We show that the level of public goods provision at which the sum of marginal utilities exceeds unity is too small to be optimal.

To see this let us decrease the private goods consumption of each i by $v_i'(x)$. Hence, for each individual i the new private goods consumption is:

$$\bar{y}_i = y_i - v_i'(x).$$

Altogether we have decreased the private good consumption by:

$$v_1'(x) + v_2'(x) + \cdots + v_n'(x) = 1 + \Delta$$

with $\Delta > 0$, since the left hand side of the inequality is by assumption larger than unity.

Take now a part of this aggregated decrease, namely 1 unit, from the private good and allocate that to the provision of the public good. The new amount of public good is:

$$\bar{x} = x + 1.$$

With this new amount of public good each i's utility increases approximately by the amount of her marginal utility at x, that is, by $v_i'(x)$. Therefore, when the consumption is at the level $(\bar{x}, \bar{y}_1, \ldots, \bar{y}_n)$ each i is approximately equally well off as at $(x, y_1, \ldots, y_n)$. But we still have Δ of the decreased private goods left over. This can be distributed among the individuals so that at least some fare strictly better than they did at $(x, y_1, \ldots, y_n)$. Consequently, if

$$v_1'(x) + v_2'(x) + \cdots + v_n'(x) > 1$$

then the situation is not optimal in the Pareto sense since one can reallocate resources by diminishing the consumption of the private good and increasing that of the public good so that some individuals are strictly better off and no one is worse off after the reallocation.

In a similar way we can show that if

$$v_1'(x) + v_2'(x) + \cdots + v_n'(x) < 1$$

the level of public goods provision is not Pareto optimal. In this case it is by increasing the private goods consumption that one can improve at least some individuals' welfare without a loss to anyone.

Hence, we must conclude that a necessary condition for Pareto optimal allocation is

$$v_1'(x) + v_2'(x) + \cdots + v_n'(x) = 1$$

This is known as *Samuelson's optimality condition* for public goods. What it says, then, is that in optimal allocation the sum of individual marginal utilities of the public good sums to unity.

It turns out that this optimality condition coincides with the maximum of the aggregated net utility of the public good. To see this, consider the net aggregated utility of the public good, i.e. the utility sum minus the costs of buying the public good:

$$v_1(x) + v_2(x) + \cdots + v_n(x) - x = \sum_i v_i(x) - x.$$

To find the maximum of this expression we set its first derivative with respect to x equal to zero and solve for x. We get

$$\sum_i v_i'(x) = 1$$

which is identical with the Pareto optimality condition for public goods. Hence, the Samuelson condition is not only necessary but also sufficient for the optimal level of provision of the public good.

Can we expect the optimal level of public goods provision to be reached in practice? The answer is no. To see this, let us assume that each individual i purchases the public good in a rational fashion, i.e. each individual i tries to maximize

$$u_i = v_i(x) + y_i$$

so that the following budget constraint is satisfied:

$$x + y_i = w_i.$$

Substituting for y_i this amounts to maximizing

$$u_i = v_i(x) - x + w_i.$$

Now, w_i is constant which means that the function to be maximized is $v_i(x) \quad x$. Graphically this is the vertical distance between $v_i(x)$ and the line $y = x$. Since $v_i(x)$ is assumed to be concave upwards – i.e. the returns from additional units of public good are diminishing – the distance is maximized at the point where the slope of the tangent of $v_i(x)$ equals the slope of $y = x$. In other words, at the maximum

$$v_i'(x) = 1.$$

Let $\hat{x}_i$ be the amount of public good that would maximize i's utility and assume that i undertakes to purchase this amount. After all, this would seem to be the rational thing to do. It follows then that x can be consumed by others as well. Now, we may well find an individual j for whom $v_j'(\hat{x}_i) < 1$. For such a person giving up a unit of the private good in order to purchase an additional unit of the public one would decrease her overall utility. Hence this individual does not contribute to the public goods provision. Instead she takes the free ride offered by i.

There may, of course, be individuals k for whom $v_k'(\hat{x}_i) > 1$. These individuals would benefit from giving up a unit of the private good in order to purchase an additional unit of the public good. Indeed, one would expect those individuals to keep on purchasing additional public good units until $v_k'(x) = 1$. So, the process of buying additional public good units will stop once we have reached the level x which is characterized by:

- there is at least one individual i for whom $v_i(x) = 1$, and
- for all members j: $v_j'(x) \leq 1$.

However, the fact that $v_i(x) = 1$ for some individuals i and the fact that for all individuals j: $v_j'(x) > 0$ mean that

$$v_1'(x) + v_2'(x) + \cdots + v_n'(x) > 1$$

In other words, the sum of marginal utilities exceeds 1 which implies that the amount purchased is not optimal.

The above reasoning provides an explanation to Olson and Zeckhauser's (1966) finding that in public goods provision it is often the case that the 'big' members pay a disproportionately large share of the costs of public goods. This might well be a result of the fact that the optimal level of public goods is larger for those members than for small ones. Hence, once the big members have purchased their optimal level, purchasing additional units would actually decrease the welfare of the smaller ones.

Without coordination, then, the amount of public good provided is likely to be non-optimal. Mere coordination is, however, not enough to secure optimality. For example, arrangements whereby individuals would signal their utility functions regarding the public good to a coordinator who would then determine the level of public goods provision as well as allocate the costs among individuals are likely to fail because of the incentive problem. When asked, the individual has an incentive to play down her utility of the public good. If everyone acts on this incentive, the outcome is likely to be a substantially sub-optimal level of public goods. Is this unavoidable, i.e. is it impossible to connect individual true preferences for public goods with the amount they are charged? It turns out that this connection between payment shares and utility levels can be made in a fair manner. The solution is known as the *demand revealing mechanism* which makes use of the *Clarke tax* (Tideman and Tullock 1976; Clarke 1980; Hillman 2003: 110–125). It works as follows.

First, the mechanism calls for all the individuals to report their utility functions regarding various levels of supply of the public good. The reports may be truthful or distorted. Once the reports have been given, the benevolent tax authority differentiates them with respect to x and solves the following for x:

$$\sum_i u_i'(x) = 1.$$

It will be recalled that this is Samuelson's optimality condition for public goods which is also the amount of the good that maximizes the sum of individual net utilities of the public good x. Let us denote the value of x that satisfies this optimality condition by $\bar{x}$. So, if all messages used in determining $\bar{x}$ are truthful, then the aggregate net utility of the good is maximized at this point. Next the tax authority computes the Clarke taxes T_i of each individual i as follows:

$$T_i = \bar{x} - \sum_{j \neq i} m_j$$

where m_j denotes the value that individual j reports to the tax authority. The Clarke tax of i is thus a function of the messages of all other individuals, but does not depend on i's own message.

Suppose that a public project, say a street lamp, is to be set up and paid for by individuals $1, \ldots, 4$. The individuals know the mechanism and may suspect that they might be better off by reporting values that differ from their true valuations. Let the total cost of the project be 100 dollars. The individual messages regarding the value of the lamp expressed in dollars are: $u_1 = 50$, $u_2 = 10$, $u_3 = 20$, and $u_4 = 0$.

We thus get the following Clarke taxes: $T_1 = 70, T_2 = 30, T_3 = 40, T_4 = 20$. Intuitively this makes sense since the individuals with higher reported valuations of the public good get higher taxes. We observe, however, that the tax authority makes a huge profit by collecting 160 dollars for a 100 dollar project.

This problem of budget balance turns out to be endemic, but can to some extent be ameliorated by subtracting a report-independent amount from each individual's Clarke tax. That is, each individual's tax amount is diminished by an amount that does not depend on her report or on the level of public good.[52] More important, however, is the question of whether this mechanism induces truthful reporting.

It turns out it does (Feldman 1980: 122–129; Hillman 2003: 110–114). Instead of a proof, let us illustrate the fact by considering individual 1's strategies. Suppose that 50 dollars is, indeed, her true valuation of the street lamp, but instead of 50 she reports only 40 dollars as her valuation. Provided that the others give the same reports as above, 1's Clarke tax remains 70. However, the amount of public good provided, that is, the value of $\bar{x}$, changes. It is no more the optimal one in terms of i's true valuation. Hence, i pays the same tax as for the optimal amount of public good, but the level of the good is not optimal for her.

As we saw above, this mechanism does not in general balance the budget, that is, the collected taxes may amount to more or less than the cost of the public good provided. It turns out that there is no way in which the excess payments could be returned to the tax payers in proportion to their taxes without destroying the demand revealing nature of the mechanism. Therefore, it is necessary to augment the above description of the mechanism by requiring that the taxes not be used for the purpose of funding the provision of the public good in question (Hillman 2003: 112). Rather the taxes must be collected in the government budget from which all kinds of goods and services are funded. Another, somewhat more desperate way of dealing with the excess funds is to destroy them or donate them to another country (Feldman 1980: 128).

The incentive to *free riding* as well as the sub-optimal level of public goods provision may be regarded as important explanations for the emergence and prevalence of political decision-making mechanisms, e.g. in the form of governments. However, the elimination or reduction of negative externalities – i.e. negative external effects of activities – caused by individuals or groups to other individuals or groups are often results of government activities. For example, the government may step in to restrict production activities which bring about major negative externalities to the population in the form of environmental damage. Indeed, Pigou (1929) argued that because of the externalities accompanied with production, consumption and leisure activities, the interaction between individuals and groups often leads to suboptimal outcomes unless there is a government interference. On the other hand, government activity itself is often a major source of externalities (Tullock 2005).[53] But are these the only important reasons for the existence of governments? The next chapter will deal with this question. We shall also discuss the plausibility of the assumption of a benevolent government.

8.8   Suggested reading

A theoretical overview and analysis of the main proportional election systems is presented in Balinski and Young (1982), and also Taagepera and Shugart (1989) as well as Shugart and Carey (1992) introduce research methods and discuss findings on a variety of electoral systems. Another important source book on electoral systems is Colomer (2004). The properties of majority rule are discussed in Hillman (2003: section 3.1) and Mueller (2003: Chapters 5–6). The former as well as Feldman (1980: Chapters 6 and 9) also discuss majority rule in public goods provision. The mechanism design literature tends to be rather technical. Hurwicz (1972) and (1979) as well as Maskin (1985) are important works in this field. The theory of implementation is also developed in Jackson *et al.* (1994), Moore and Repullo (1988) and Moulin (1984).

9 What kind of government?

One of the fundamental roles of the state is to provide a specific kind of public good – security – for its citizens. This has likely been the most important consideration in establishing ancient states and certainly the most important criterion used in the assessment of their success. Reflecting this importance, the modern theory of state suggests that the emergence of states can be explained as a natural response to the security needs of the individuals in a hypothetical stateless 'original position'.

9.1 States as bandits

In *Anarchy, State and Utopia*, Nozick (1974) presents a theory of the emergence of state in a fictitious situation where individuals possess a set of natural rights, such as personal freedom, the right to the product of one's own labor or to the income that is voluntarily transferred from one individual to another.[54] Given this state of affairs, Nozick argues that the emergence of the state can be given an *invisible hand explanation*. In other words, the state can be seen to emerge as a by-product of the security demands of individuals. In the first stage groups of individuals, realizing their common need to protect their possessions from theft or robbery, arrange for common protection of the possessions of group members. Eventually, protective agencies form to respond to demand for security services. Thus, security service becomes marketable. Because of the relative nature of the service provided – i.e. the quality of the service depends on the resources of other agencies – a dominant protective agency emerges. In Nozick's terminology this is called the *ultra-minimal state*. It is the end result of a process whereby each actor tries to maximize her own utility. However, the result itself is no one's goal. Hence, invoking the process is called an invisible hand explanation: the process leads inevitably to an end state which no one has intended.[55]

Robert Nozick (1938–2002) was one of the most influential American philosophers of the 20th century. As his contemporary John Rawls, also Nozick represented analytic tradition of social philosophy. His best known work is *Anarchy, State and Utopia* (1974), where he proposed a theory of justice which in many ways contradicts Rawls's theory. Indeed, Nozick came to be seen as a champion of libertarianism and neo-conservatism. In contrast to Rawls, however, he was not keen on defending and further developing his work on social philosophy. Instead his attention focused on other philosophical topics. *Philosophical Explanations* appeared in 1981 and *The Nature of Rationality* in 1993. Also noteworthy is his last book *Invariances* (2001), which deals with the foundations of epistemology. Nozick received the National Book Award for *Anarchy, State and Utopia*.

In Nozick's view, the ultra-minimal state is, however, not a morally defensible end state. The reason is that the agency having the monopoly of the means of protection is providing its services to only those willing and capable of paying for them. Therefore, Nozick argues, one more step in the process of state formation is needed to make the end result morally defensible. This is one where all individuals get equal protection from the dominant protective agency regardless of their payments. Once this step is taken, we have reached the *minimal state*: a night-watchman state enforcing property rights and securing the personal freedoms of its citizens. Up to this point the process is morally defensible, but anything beyond it is not, says Nozick. In particular, all activities related to redistribution of values from individuals or groups to other individuals or groups are not morally defensible in this theory.

Nozick's theory is consistent with another, more economically motivated view, namely Olson's account of the process of 'rational monopolization of theft' (Olson 1991, 1993; McGuire and Olson 1996). Olson argues that in an anarchical original position it is to be expected that there are individuals who see it advantageous for themselves to rob other people's harvests and other products instead of – or in addition to – engaging in productive activities themselves. The social class of roving bandits is based on this utility calculus. However, given the ever-present risk of losing one's harvest or other output of production, the productive population is unlikely to produce a whole lot to steal. Thus, even banditry is unlikely to be a highly profitable source of income. Olson argues that in time some bandits realize that they can maximize their profits by not stealing their victims' entire livelihood, but leaving them enough resources to continue their productive activities so that the bandits, upon returning at some later point in time, may find some new products to steal. Of course, the returning bandits have to make sure that they are the only robbers visiting these victims. The best way to guarantee this is to become a stationary bandit. The crucial characteristic of these kinds of bandits is that they possess the monopoly over the means of violence in the area under their control. Thereby they become the dominant protective organization, in Nozick's terminology.

Olson emphasizes the economic motives behind the formation of the ultra-minimal state. The people who produce benefit from stationary as opposed to roving banditry, since the former leaves them enough resources to continue production – and, indeed, if rational, so much resources that the production capacity is maximized – while the latter would leave them empty-handed. But the bandits also benefit from becoming stationary since they now have a reasonably steady stream of income instead of an unpredictable one. The parallelism of interests between those with coercive power and their subjects does not end with stationary banditry. McGuire and Olson construct a model of an economy where the interests of those in power are largely consistent with the interests of the society and those subject to the power. The consistency is the larger the more encompassing are the interests of the power-holder. When these interests are sufficiently encompassing, McGuire and Olson (1996: 74) argue that the power-holder treats 'those subject to its power as well as it treats itself.' This is a result of utility maximization of the power-holder.

The key concept is that of encompassing interest. Whenever an individual or group has an encompassing interest in a society, it is *ipso facto* interested both in its share of the gross national product (GDP) of the society but also in the size of the GDP. Groups with limited interests, on the other hand, are typically maximizing their utility by maximizing their share of the GDP.[56]

This argument makes no distinction between autocracies and democracies, i.e. between systems governed essentially at the will of one person or a clique and those where all citizens have a role in determining the composition of the bodies enacting laws and enforcing the most important policy decisions. This means that in both types of systems the economic interests of the rulers are to a large extent consonant with those of the ruled. The end result is proportional taxation of incomes, that is, no income redistribution among citizens. This result is also largely the same – although mathematically more elaborated – than the upshot of Nozick's theory.

Nozick's and Olson's theories do not invoke any other normative elements except the economic one: utility maximization. There is no benevolence involved, but no sheer malevolence either. States that provide decent living conditions for everyone regardless of their productive capabilities seem to be at odds with the views of Nozick and Olson. Similarly at odds are kleptocracies or robber states which bear close resemblance to roving banditry. The latter exemplify rulers who do not have encompassing interests in the society. This may be due to general instability of the system, external threats or – God forbid – irrationality of the power-holders.

But there are distinctly normative theories of state as well. Indeed, many people would instinctively think that the states and/or governments exist in order to establish and maintain certain norms.

9.2   A just state

Undoubtedly best-known modern normative theory of the state precedes Nozick's theory in time. In fact, the latter was intended as a criticism and refutation of Rawls's (1971) normative theory. This theory belongs to the tradition of contract theories. The defining characteristic of contract theories is that they envision states emerging as a result of voluntary contract between the individuals in an original position which in the case of Rawls is 'Hobbesian', i.e. a war of all against all. Rather than looking for processes that might lead to the emergence of state in this situation, Rawls sets out to find the rules that rational individuals would voluntarily agree upon as guidelines for their cooperation.

Principles voluntarily agreed upon are, however, not necessarily just. To the extent that the original position immediately preceding the agreement is biased – e.g. in resource allocation – one cannot expect voluntary agreement to correct this bias. If, for example, two persons are about to make a contract about principles of compensation for labor and if in the original position one of them has a control over both actor's food supply, one can expect that the contract will likely be biased in the controlling actor's favor. Hence, Rawls introduces the concept of 'justice as fairness' by which he means that contracts voluntarily agreed upon by rational actors in unbiased original position must be viewed as just in virtue of being entered into under fair conditions. This leads to the question of what is a fair original position.

The crucial feature of the original position is the veil of ignorance which means that the actors do not know their future position in the society to be established. They do not know even their own characteristics as these might condition their preference regarding principles of justice. Indeed, the list of facts of themselves that the individual are not supposed to know is fairly extensive: tastes, wealth, generation to which they belong and so on (Mueller 2003: 599). Rawls argues that any principles of division of rights and duties voluntarily agreed upon under the veil of ignorance is fair because of the unbiasedness of the original position. By the same token, these agreements are just. This gives the theory the characterization: justice as fairness. It is not thereby claimed that the prevailing norms of justice were results of such a bargaining, but the construct of a fair original position has an important role to play in evaluating existing norms. Any observed norm that could conceivably have been a result of a contract agreed upon by rational actors behind the veil of ignorance, can be deemed justified. Thus, the theory provides us a benchmark for comparing existing norms.

The principles of justice that, according to Rawls (1971: 60–62), emerge in the fair original position under veil of ignorance are the following:

1. each individual is to have right to the most extensive basic liberty that is compatible with other individuals having similar liberty,
2. social and economic inequalities are to be such that:

   - one can reasonably expect them to benefit all, and
   - they are attached to positions that are open to all.

So, liberty and equality are the basic norms which according to Rawls will be chosen behind the veil of ignorance. Of these, the latter has received the most attention. In particular, the rendering that Rawls gives to the requirement that inequalities, if justified, should be to the benefit of all. This interpretation is known as the *difference* or *maximin principle*. It says that in order to be justified the inequalities should benefit the worst-off individuals of the society. This criterion allows for ordering of social states or political systems. Suppose that there are two systems, A and B, so that the welfare level of the worst-off individual in A is strictly higher than the welfare of the worst-off individual in B. The difference principle will then strictly prefer A to B regardless of the welfare levels of other individuals. Applying this principle consecutively leads to maximizing the welfare of the individual with the minimum income or possessions. Hence, the term 'maximin principle'.

The difference principle contains a *lexicographic ordering* (Mueller 2003: 600). One first looks at the welfare levels of the worst-off individuals. Should these be the same in A and B, one then focuses on the next to worst-off individuals. If their welfare is higher in B than in A, then B is to be preferred. If even these levels are identical in A and B, one then moves on to individuals whose welfare level is third-lowest and so on.

Rawls's principles of justice are listed in the order of their priority in the theory. In fact, the order of principles themselves is lexicographic. In other words, when comparing systems or states, one first considers principle 1 (maximal liberty to all) and only in those cases where the systems or states do not differ in terms of this criterion is the second principle invoked. This gives the theory a distinctively 'liberal' outlook (Barry 1973). Whenever a distinction can be made with regard to the amount of liberty between systems or states, the preference in terms of justice is thereby determined and in a sense the second principle is entirely redundant. Thus, no matter how high the level of welfare of the worst-off individual in system B, system A is more just in the sense of Rawls if the liberty it allows its citizens to enjoy is even infinitesimally larger than that of system B.

Brian Barry (born 1936) is a British political and moral philosopher. He has written extensively of justice, rights and politics. His best-known works are *Political Argument* (1965), *Sociologists, Economists and Democracy* (1970), *Justice as Impartiality* (1995) and *Culture and Equality* (2001). In 2001 he was awarded the Johan Skytte Prize in political science.

The difference principle may lead to somewhat bizarre conclusions. Consider, for example, the possibility that in system A all individuals have the same level of welfare, say $\bar{w}$ and that in system B one individual has the welfare level that is almost the same as $\bar{w}$, but just barely recognizably lower. All others in B enjoy levels of welfare much higher than $\bar{w}$. Now the difference principle would deem A preferable to B.

Examples like this make the *utilitarian principle* look more plausible. This principle determines the preference between A and B in terms of the sum or average of welfare levels of the individuals in these two systems. Whichever system has the larger sum or average is preferred to the other. In the preceding example this would make B more 'just' than A. The utilitarian principle can also lead to intuitively questionable results. Consider two systems, C and D, with populations of equal size. Suppose that in the former the population is partitioned into two homogeneous classes C_1 and C_2. C_1 consists of people who live in luxury, while those in C_2 have to endure extreme poverty. In system D, on the other hand, all people live under comfortable, if not luxurious, conditions. As long as the sum of utilities of the individuals in C exceeds the corresponding sum in D, the utilitarian principle ranks C higher than D. The difference principle, in contrast, prefers D to C.

9.3   Redistribution and rent seeking

The literature on social justice is extensive, but our focus on Nozick and Rawls can be defended on the grounds that these two represent in some ways two principal views on the nature of justice and government. In Nozick's view it makes no sense to discuss and evaluate social states in terms of justice. Justice, in his view, is not something that characterizes states. Looking merely at a distribution of possessions, rights and duties at a given point in time is simply not sufficient for an evaluation of their justice. One needs a historical record and, more specifically, an account of how these possessions, rights and duties have come about. In Nozick's theory a distribution is just if everyone is entitled to those possessions, rights and duties that she has in that distribution. Justice is about entitlements or principles of acquisition (production, exchange) and transfer.

Rawls's principles, on the other hand, are applicable to the evaluation of social states, that is, distributions as such. Provided we are able to spot the worst-off individual,[57] we are immediately able to compare the systems. The central difference between Rawls and Nozick is, however, the fact that the former presents a normative theory, while the latter sets out to outline the moral limits of government activity. Protection against theft and enforcement of contracts are within those limits, while redistribution is not. Rawls' theory, on the other hand, is all about redistribution.

Reducing externalities is one of the tasks of governments. The citizens may, however, disagree as to how one should go about it. Tullock (2005: 29–30) points out that it is an oversimplification to argue that governments carry out actions agreed upon by citizens. Very often there is no consensus regarding the action that should be taken in reducing externalities. Indeed, it may happen that there is no consensus even about the existence of an externality. For example, a person drinking alcohol while sitting on a bench in a public park next to the playground for children is likely to create a negative externality for the parents of those children, but the person herself may see no such externality. Governments are needed to carry out actions not agreed upon by everyone. Moreover, the externality reduction may result in redistribution of welfare. The person evicted by the police from the bench probably experiences her welfare being reduced, while the parents' level of welfare is improved by the government action.

By definition governments engage in coordinating economic and political activities through legislation and other norm setting actions. A vast network of norms guides economic activities in most countries of today. Typically these norms can be justified on public interest grounds. For example, the existence of legislation against fraud is likely to encourage people to conduct business transactions thereby invigorating economic activities which, in turn, create wealth and prosperity. Hence, the legislation is in public interest. However, there are also norms, even legislative ones, that are socially wasteful. Some of these relate to rents. These are defined as 'benefits that a person receives beyond what is necessary to provide incentives to perform particular tasks' (Hillman 2003: 447). A typical example of the benefits are monopolist's profits. These are very often in excess of those ensuing from competitive pricing. The behavior aiming at securing rents (such as achieving the status of monopolist or monopsonist) is called rent-seeking.[58] Basically all activities aiming at restriction of competition can be viewed as rent-seeking. For example, labor legislation, tariffs, standardization – all typical public sector activities – are of interest to those organizations that seek rents for their members. Governments in the wide sense of the word are important arenas for rent-seeking activities, as can be observed in the extensive networks of contacts established by lobbying organizations with cabinet ministers, MPs and government officials.

So, governments' role in reducing externalities may sometimes be accompanied with creating new ones. By solving problems of coordination, e.g. through legislation and thus reducing or removing externalities the state may give rise to new externalities in the form of rent-seeking. Governments also engage in public policy making. We shall now turn to evaluating these policies.

9.4   Suggested reading

Both Nozick's (1974) and Rawls's (1971) theories have provided inspiration to a wide range of scholarly publications. Before dwelling on this secondary literature, it is advisable to study the original texts in some detail. Barry (1973) and (1989) together with Daniels (1975) offer a variety of criticisms of Rawls's theory. Rawls has later on returned to his theory. Indeed, Rawls (2005) modifies and continues the themes of Rawls (1971) by taking into account and responding to the criticisms leveled against the latter. The libertarian view of the state is spelled out and elaborated in Buchanan (1975, 1991a and 1991b). Kolm (1996) gives a comparative overview of theories of justice. Morris *et al.* (2004, parts I–II) contains several relevant articles on the emergence and design of institutions.

10 Aspects of policy evaluation

Over the past decades public sector institutions have, to an unprecedented extent, been subjected to evaluations.[59] This has also been the case in institutions of higher learning, where evaluations have traditionally been restricted mainly to academic posts and scholarly publications. Although the methods discussed in this chapter apply to evaluation in any field of public policy, we shall illustrate them using universities as examples. Today it is common that not only individual scholars and publications but universities and schools as a whole are objects of evaluation. The typical method is still based on peer reviews. The evaluation process has several phases consisting of setting the goals of evaluation, gathering the review board, self-evaluation of the unit to be focused upon, etc.

Also in research funding organizations peer reviews are widely used both in project and candidate evaluations. When evaluations are repeated at regular intervals, it is customary to resort to explicit criteria to assure that the evaluation is made according to a reasonably stable set of characteristics of the applicants or projects. Peer reviews thus take on the form of multiple-criteria decision making augmented with group decision making, since the evaluators typically work in groups. In normal cases, the group strives at forming a common stand on the projects to be funded or applicants to be appointed to research posts. The process within review groups consists of two stages: one in which each group member forms an opinion on the alternatives (projects, candidates, etc.) and one in which the group, through voting or bargaining, forms a collective opinion of the alternatives.

This pattern is common in other evaluation contexts as well. In this chapter the focus is on the first stage of the process, i.e. the stage in which the alternatives are evaluated according to the criteria that are deemed relevant. We shall discuss some counterintuitive phenomena that can be encountered at this stage of policy evaluation. The main goal is to show that, despite their widespread use, certain methods of deriving policy recommendations on the basis of empirical data should be used – if at all – with caution.

10.1 Deciding the number of criteria

In the evaluation of institutions of higher learning there are certain 'obvious' criteria, such as the level of research and teaching, that have to be included in any meaningful evaluation. Similar obvious criteria can be found in nearly all institutional evaluations. The lists of criteria seem, however, to have a tendency to grow, sometimes for quite plausible reasons. Often new criteria are introduced in order to enhance the accuracy and descriptive power of the evaluations. For example, the research performance criteria of universities nowadays often include measures of networking of scholars in addition to the more traditional indices of academic research output. The introduction of new criteria is often justified by referring to the opportunities for giving a more nuanced picture of the units under consideration. Similarly, the evaluation boards are often augmented with new members in order to include more relevant aspects of units in the evaluations.[60]

This process is, however, accompanied with the problem of how to form an overall assessment of the units to be evaluated on the basis of a multiplicity of criteria. We are confronted here with the problem of information aggregation or, more specifically, with the problem of choice of the right aggregation method. When our task is to choose the best alternative, it is possible to utilize methods based on the majority rule or principle. With two alternatives this principle does, indeed, work without complications (May 1952; Plott 1976; Lagerspetz 2002). It is, after all, natural to choose the alternative ranked first by more criteria of performance than the competing alternative. The plausibility of this choice depends, however, on the assumption that each criterion is given the same weight in the evaluation.

10.2 Majorities, positions, weights

With more than two alternatives the majority principle loses its precise meaning. As an extension of this principle, one could think of the plurality rule, which considers best the alternative that is ranked first on more criteria than any other alternative. There is another way of extending the majority principle: one could require that the alternative that in pairwise contests with all other alternatives is ranked higher than its competitor on a majority of criteria should be considered best. These two extensions are not equivalent: the best alternative in the plurality sense may not be the best in the pairwise sense. A classic example is Borda's voting paradox (see Table 7.2 in chapter 7). We are thus led to ask whether the unit ranked first on more criteria than any other unit should be given priority, or whether priority should be given to a unit that in a pairwise contest with any other unit would be ranked higher by more than half of the criteria.

At first sight one could look for the answer in the weighting of criteria, but, alas, the problem remains. To take a hypothetical example from university evaluation, consider a case where three criteria have been invoked: the level of research, the quality of teaching and the external impact of the university. Let us assume that our evaluator has decided to give these criteria the weights 7, 5 and 4, respectively. Three units are under scrutiny: A, B and C. These are ranked on the three criteria as in Table 10.1.

In terms of the weights given to criteria, A is the best unit, followed by B, and C is the last. In pairwise contests A, however, is defeated by B with weight scores 7 to 9 and by C with identical scores. C, on the other hand, defeats B with

Table 10.1 University evaluation with weighted
criteria

Research	Teaching	External impact
A	B	C
C	C	B
B	A	A

weights 11 to 5. Thus, C defeats both A and B if the above weights are given
to the criteria. C is the Condorcet winner. We conclude that giving weights to
criteria does not solve the conflict between the plurality and pairwise principles.

The plurality principle pays attention to how the alternatives are positioned in
the rankings defined by each criterion. The principle, however, utilizes only a
very limited amount of this positional information, that is, only the first ranks
count. Still, the plurality principle is a positional one in the sense that the position
of each unit in the ranking that results from overall evaluation is determined solely
by the position of that unit in each criterion's ranking.

There are many other *positional rules*. Let there be k alternatives and let $w =
(w_1, \ldots, w_k)$ be a vector so that w_i is the score assigned to the alternative ranked
ith and $w_i \geq w_j$ whenever $i < j$. In other words, higher ranked alternatives are
given larger scores than lower ranked ones. Any such vector w defines a positional
rule in which the ranking of alternatives is determined by the total scores. The
latter are the sums of scores that each alternative obtains from its rank in each
criterion. Thus, the Borda count is the positional rule: $w_B = (k-1, k-2, \ldots, 1, 0)$.

In the hypothetical example above, the overall ranking on the basis of the
Borda count would be $C(AB)$, i.e. C is ranked first followed by A and B, which
obtain the same score. The antiplurality rule gives all positions except the last one
the same number of points, i.e. 1. More formally, the *antiplurality rule* is defined
as $w_{AP} = (1, 1, \ldots, 1, 0)$. In this example this rule results in the ranking CBA.
Thus, plurality, antiplurality and Borda rules result in different overall rankings.
The outcome of the evaluation may thus crucially depend on the choice rule
rather than on the merits of the units under investigation.

10.3 Changes in alternative sets

In academic evaluations as well as in public policy, the set of alternatives
may undergo changes during the evaluation process. Funding applications may
be cancelled, the evaluation may involve stages where some alternatives are
eliminated, etc. It would, of course, be desirable that the aggregation rule behave
in a reasonably consistent way during these stages.

Unfortunately this may be too much to ask, at least insofar as the positional
rules are concerned. Saari (1989) shows that nearly anything can follow from
the elimination of one or several alternatives in the course of applying positional aggregation rules. More precisely, the positional rules do not satisfy *binary*

consistency. This requirement pertains to preferences in subsets of alternatives. It states that for any subset of alternatives the aggregated preference ranking has to coincide with the ranking obtained by considering the aggregated ranking for the set of all alternatives and ignoring all but those alternatives in the subset under study. Thus, for example, the aggregated preference ranking between A and B has to be the same when the subset $\{A, B\}$ is considered as the ranking of A relative to B in the set $\{A, B, C\}$.

The example introduced in the preceding section illustrates binary consistency. Considering the entire set of three alternatives and assigning each criterion the weight specified above, the aggregated ranking using the plurality rule is ABC. Assuming that C is not a legitimate alternative (e.g. the proposal C is withdrawn from the contest), the plurality ranking between A and B becomes BA. If B is withdrawn, the aggregated preference between A and C is reversed into CA. If A is withdrawn, the ranking between B and C becomes CB. Thus, all binary preference rankings contradict the one obtained when considering the 'global' ranking ABC. This shows that the plurality rule does not satisfy binary consistency.

Saari's result is a generalization of Fishburn's (1981). Fishburn considers a situation involving four alternatives and several criteria. Upon eliminating an alternative and holding the relative positions of the other alternatives fixed, he observes that, when the Borda count is used, the preference ranking between the remaining three alternatives may be completely reversed. Saari's result extends this possibility to all positional procedures.

Positional rules, thus, seem sensitive to changes in alternative sets. Arrow's (1963) independence of irrelevant alternatives as well as Chernoff's (1954) condition can be viewed as attempts to avoid this kind of sensitivity (see Aizerman and Aleskerov 1995; Plott 1976). Chernoff's condition requires that if something wins in a set of alternatives, it should also win in each subset it belongs to. Positional procedures have, however, properties that come pretty far in compensating for the lack of binary consistency. It is also worth pointing out that both independence of irrelevant alternatives and Chernoff's condition are extremely rare among aggregation procedures. In particular, the binary procedures that are used in practice fail on these conditions.

10.4   Close and yet so far

Most straightforward to conduct are evaluations where the units end up in identical preference rankings on each criterion. In these cases the overall ranking naturally coincides with the one appearing on each criterion. Also in those situations where a given unit is placed first on each criterion, it would seem plausible to rank this unit first in the overall evaluation. This plausible requirement is known as the *respect for unanimity* (Baigent 1987). It requires that a unit or project ranked first on every criterion should also be first in the overall evaluation. It is difficult to envision an aggregation rule that does not satisfy this requirement. Equally natural are requirements that amount to excluding discrimination for or against certain alternatives or criteria. Let us impose yet another requirement on aggregation rules, namely that small changes in criterion-wise evaluations are accompanied by no more than small changes in overall evaluations. This requirement is known as *preference proximity* (Baigent 1987). It amounts to insisting that if small mistakes are made in measurements on one criterion, this does not result in dramatic changes in the overall assessment.

The preference proximity requirement is quite a desirable property since it guarantees a degree of stability in the choice process. Baigent (1987) shows, however, that no aggregation rule that respects unanimity and is non-discriminating can satisfy preference proximity. In other words, in all unanimity respecting and non-discriminating procedures, it may happen that small measurement errors in criterion rankings lead to large changes in overall assessments. The following example illustrates this (Nurmi 2002: 76–78).

Two universities, A and B, are being evaluated. Two criteria are invoked: the level of research and the level of teaching. Assume that the true rankings are those presented in Table 10.2.

Suppose that in measuring the performances of units on the first criterion, we make a minor error in reporting so that Table 10.3 ensues.

Had we made a mistake in measuring both criteria, we would have had Table 10.4.

Clearly, Table 10.4 results from a large mistake since basically all true values are reported in an erroneous manner. We show now that the distance of the true

Table 10.2 University evaluation: true rankings

Level of research	Level of teaching
A	B
B	A

Table 10.3 University evaluation: small mistake

Level of research	Level of teaching
B	B
A	A

Table 10.4 University evaluation: large mistake

Level of research	Level of teaching
B	A
A	B

evaluation result from overall evaluation outcome involving a small mistake is in fact larger than the distance from the former to the overall evaluation involving a large mistake. In other words, a small mistake brings about large consequences in overall assessments.

We denote the distance between two rankings i and j by $d(i,j)$. With the aid of this, we define the distance between two measurement profiles (tables) I and J, denoted by $D(I,J)$, so that it equals the sum of criterion-wise distances. Thus, the distance between Tables 10.2 and 10.3 above is the sum of the distance between Tables 10.2 and 10.3 on level of research criterion and of the distance between these profiles on the level of teaching criterion. We notice that

$$D(10.2, 10.3) = d(AB, BA) + d(BA, BA).$$

Since $d(BA, BA) = 0$, we have $D(10.2, 10.3) = d(AB, BA)$.
   Similarly,

$$D(10.2, 10.4) = d(AB, BA) + d(BA, AB).$$

We now focus on the distances between evaluation outcomes in these displays. Let $g(i)$ be the overall evaluation outcome in profile i, that is, a ranking of units resulting from the evaluation. Assuming that the aggregation rule is non-discriminating, we see that $g(10.2) = g(10.4)$ since these two profiles differ only in terms of the labels of criteria, i.e. interchanging columns in Table 10.2 leads to Table 10.4 and vice versa. From the assumption of respect of unanimity, it follows that $g(10.3) = BA$.

Consider now $d(g(10.2), g(10.3))$ *vis-à-vis* $d(g(10.2), g(10.4))$. The former denotes the distance between the evaluation resulting from true values and the evaluation in which a small measurement error has been made, while the latter is the distance between the true evaluation and the one resulting from a large error. Now the latter distance is obviously 0, while the former must be larger than that, since one of the criterion rankings has been inverted. In other words, the distance between the overall evaluations in Tables 10.2 and 10.3 is larger than the corresponding distance between Tables 10.2 and 10.4. This shows that aggregation rules satisfying non-discrimination and respect for unanimity may lead to assessments where small errors lead to larger errors in overall evaluations than large errors.

In the preceding we have considered a very large class of aggregation rules, namely those that are non-discriminating and respect unanimity. To take a closer look at the significance of measurement errors, we shall now focus on a subset of this class, non-monotonic rules. This subset consists of many multi-stage voting procedures, e.g. plurality runoff. From the viewpoint of policy evaluation, the interest of non-monotonic rules is in their unexpected reaction to certain types of measurement errors. An error that is favorable to an alternative in the sense of giving it a higher rank, *ceteris paribus*, on certain criteria than it would rightly deserve, may exclude it from the set of winners where it would belong without

Table 10.5 Plurality runoff rule in evaluation: true rankings

Criteria 1–6	Criteria 7–12	Criteria 13–17
A	B	C
C	C	B
B	A	A

the error. Let us illustrate this possibility with an example involving 17 criteria and 3 units: A, B and C (Table 10.5).[61]

When the plurality runoff system is applied, one first finds out whether one of the alternatives has been ranked first by more than 50% of the criteria, i.e. on at least 9 criteria. Obviously this is not the case in our example. One then proceeds by eliminating the alternative that is ranked first by the smallest number of criteria. This is C. On those criteria where C is ranked first, the second ranked alternative is lifted to the top rank. One then checks whether some alternative has now more than half of the first ranks. Clearly B has. It is, thus, the winner.

Assume now that in evaluating the units A, B and C one has made a small mistake in B's favor: on two first criteria B has been accidentally ranked ahead of A and C. Thus, the above 'real' situation has been falsely reported as in Table 10.6.

In this perturbed setting A is first eliminated, whereupon C wins. Thus, the measurement error that was in B's favor turned out to be fatal for it: had the error not occurred, B would have won, with the error it does not.

Non-monotonicity is a quite common flaw in multi-stage aggregation rules. Positional rules are, however, basically immune to it.

10.5   One more criterion cannot do any harm, can it?

The criterion sets tend to grow with time. The reasons for this vary, but usually one justifies new criteria by the need to give a more nuanced picture of the units at hand. Obviously strategic considerations also play a role: representatives of units tend to introduce criteria that they believe will favor their units.

Table 10.6 Plurality runoff rule in evaluation: false rankings

Criteria 1–2	Criteria 3–6	Criteria 7–12	Criteria 13–17
B	A	B	C
A	C	C	B
C	B	A	A

When rules of forming overall assessments are based on pairwise unit comparisons, the introduction of new criteria may lead to counterintuitive consequences in assessments. Thus, it is possible that the introduction of a criterion on which unit A would be first ranked might lead to an outcome that ranks A lower than if the criterion had not been invoked. It may even happen that A would become first ranked in the overall assessment if this criterion were not used, but lower ranked if it were present. An example illustrates this (Table 10.7).

Table 10.7 Introducing new favorable criteria may backfire

Criteria 1–2	Criteria 3–5	Criteria 6–7	Criteria 8–9
A	B	C	C
B	C	A	B
C	A	B	A

Let us assume that we form an overall assessment on the basis of pairwise unit comparisons so that the winner in each comparison is determined by the number of criteria favoring each of the alternatives: the alternative with more criteria in its favor wins. We assume that the agenda of comparisons is such that first A is confronted with B and then the winner of that comparison faces C. The winner of the latter comparison is the overall winner.

With this method B first defeats A and then C, becoming thus the overall winner. Let us assume that criteria 8 and 9 turn out to be defective so that they are abandoned. Applying now only criteria 1–7 we observe that A defeats B in the first comparison, but is defeated by C on the second one. Thus, C becomes the winner. The counterintuitive fact is that C is ranked first by those very criteria whose absence guarantees C's victory.

It is thus possible that adding criteria that are in a most obvious way favorable to an alternative may, in fact, decrease the likelihood of that alternative being chosen. The connection between criterion success and choice probability becomes perverted. Unfortunately, this phenomenon is not a nuisance of just a few aggregation rules, but it has been shown by Pérez (2001) that we may encounter it when using almost any Condorcet extension, i.e. any rule that ends up with the Condorcet winner when it exists. Positional rules, in contrast, are immune to it.

There is another problem that relates to pairwise rules. This problem is analogous to the one that may be encountered in positional rules with varying number of alternatives. In pairwise rules, the problem emerges when the number of criteria is varied. To illustrate, consider the following setting (Table 10.8).

If we look at the subset of criteria 4–6, 7–9 and 12–14, we observe that the rankings on those criteria form a Condorcet cycle: A defeats C, C defeats B and B defeats A, each with six criteria against three. In this subset of criteria, the situation is entirely symmetric: no grounds exist of preferring one alternative to the rest. There seems to be a perfect tie in this subset.

Table 10.8 Introducing new criteria that exhibit a tie

Criteria 1–3	Criteria 4–6	Criteria 7–9	Criteria 10–11	Criteria 12–14
A	A	C	B	B
B	C	B	C	A
C	B	A	A	C

Table 10.9 Introducing new tied
criteria: the reduced profile

Criteria 1–3	Criteria 10–11
A	B
B	C
C	A

As a perfect tie does obviously not help us in making a choice, we can omit these nine criteria in the overall assessment. The remaining part of the setting is given by Table 10.9.

In this subset the choice is easy: A, since it is first ranked on more than 50% of the criteria. It is not only the Condorcet but also the plurality winner. In the original 14-criterion setting, there was also a Condorcet winner, but it was B. Thus, the removal of the intuitively unhelpful Condorcet cycle leads to a change in the Condorcet winner. In contradistinction, both the Borda and plurality winners remain the same in each setting. The pairwise rules seem to react in an implausible way to a removal of intuitively meaningless criteria from the criterion set. The analogy with the removal of alternatives in positional rules is obvious.

10.6   Forest and the trees

In the preceding we have focused on settings where a decision maker ranks the units under scrutiny on various criteria. The way in which the ranking is arrived at may vary a great deal. It may be based on a purely subjective and qualitative assessment, but its background might as well be a property that is quantitative and objectively measurable. In either case one may encounter problems that are variants of *Simpson's paradox*.[62] The following example, based on Saari and Sieberg (2001), illustrates the problem in a policy evaluation context.

Two universities, say A and B, experiment with a new incentive system to encourage the faculty members to publish in top-tier scholarly outlets. In both universities there is an experimental population consisting of those departments where the new system is being applied and a control population of those departments where the system has not been introduced. It turns out that 1/3 of experimental faculty members in A and 2/3 of experimental faculty members in B managed to have their research published in the intended outlets within a given observation period. In the control populations the ratio was 1/4 in A and 1/2 in B. So, the relative publication frequency was higher in the experimental than in the control populations in both universities. However, when looking at the faculty population as a whole (i.e. adding up the faculty members of A and B), it turns out that the relative publication frequency is higher in the control than in the experimental population. Thus, considering the two universities together, the incentive system seems to fail to produce the intended results. Yet, in both universities the incentive system seems to work, i.e. to increase publication frequency. How is this possible?

Let $K(A)$ and $K(B)$ denote the experimental populations in A and B, respectively. Similarly, $L(A)$ and $L(B)$ denote the control populations in A and B. The ratios mentioned above imply that

$$\frac{\frac{2}{3}K(B) + \frac{1}{3}K(A)}{K(A) + K(B)} \tag{10.6}$$

is smaller than

$$\frac{\frac{1}{2}L(B) + \frac{1}{4}L(A)}{L(A) + L(B)} \tag{10.7}$$

What we have here is an instance of Simpson's paradox. It is not the only possible one, but there is a very large set of values of the variables $K(A)$, $K(B)$, $L(A)$ and $L(B)$ that satisfy the above inequality (i.e. that expression (10.2) is larger than (10.1)). One example can be constructed by choosing a number between 1/3 and 2/3, i.e. between the publication ratios in the experimental populations in A and B. Let us take 2/5. We now set (10.1) equal to the selected value 2/5 and solve for $K(B)$ in terms of $K(A)$ to obtain $K(B) = \frac{1}{4}K(A)$. Thus, for example, values $K(A) = 40$ and $K(B) = 10$ will satisfy the inequality.

We next choose a number between 1/2 and 1/4, i.e. between the publication ratios in the control populations of A and B, so that the number is larger than 2/5, the value we chose above. Let us choose 5/11. We now set (10.2) equal to 5/11 and solve $L(B)$ in terms of $L(A)$. We obtain $L(B) = 4.5L(A)$. Thus we can choose values $L(A) = 10$ and $L(B) = 45$. Thus, even if the incentive system were efficient, we might well obtain the impression that it is not, if our experimental and control populations are composed as in Table 10.10.

The composition reveals that the control group consists predominantly of university B faculty, while the experimental one has mostly A's members. This, together with the observation that the university B faculty seems to be much more productive on the whole than its colleagues in A, explains why the aggregated control population–experimental population comparison leads one to infer that the incentive system does not work. The faculty population is not homogeneous as far as its publication propensity is concerned and this is reflected in the contingency tables.

Table 10.10 Experimental and control populations in two universities

University	Experimental	Control
A	40	10
B	10	45
Total	50	55

A paradox of more recent origin is related to converting *cardinal scale* measurements into ordinal scale ones and using the latter in evaluating the overall performance of units. Let us assume that three units A, B and C are evaluated in terms of a cardinal measurable criterion.[63] For concreteness, let the cardinal measurable property be the average number of publications in scholarly journals per faculty member in a calendar year. Units B and C resort to traditional uniform standard faculty compensation, while A adopts a production-based compensation. Average productivity measurements are made at two time points x and $x + 3$. Separate productivity measurements are made for international and domestic journals.

Let the average productivity measures for international journals be:

	Unit A	Unit B	Unit C
Year x	2.69	2.63	2.62
Year $x + 3$	2.74	2.71	3.00

For domestic journals we assume the following scores:

	Unit A	Unit B	Unit C
Year x	2.89	2.81	2.80
Year $x + 3$	2.98	2.90	5.99

Expressed in ordinal numbers both of these tables take the form:

	Unit A	Unit B	Unit C
Year x	4	5	6
Year $x + 3$	2	3	1
Sum	6	8	7

In words, both in the light of international and domestic journal publications, the ranking of the units is the same: C's performance in year $x+3$ is best followed by A's record in the same year, etc.

Let us sum up the performance scores to obtain an overall measure of publication success. In terms of these sums of ordinal numbers the units can be ranked in terms of productivity as ACB. This applies to both international and domestic publications. Thus the new production-based compensation seems to have some effect over both time periods.

However, had we tabulated the measurements simultaneously for all – i.e. domestic and international – journals, we would have the following table of ordinal numbers:

Unit A	Unit B	Unit C
3	4	1
5	6	2
8	9	7
10	11	12

Now the ordinal number sums translate into the productivity ranking: CAB. Thus, the production-based compensation scheme appears not to affect productivity. Obviously our procedure of aggregating ordinal ranks is not consistent. The policy recommendation seems to depend on the way the measurements are aggregated: A does better than C both in domestic and international journals and, yet, it does worse than C when both classes of outlets are considered simultaneously.

More precisely the procedure is not consistent under replication as defined by Haunsperger (2003): a procedure is consistent under replication if the aggregate of any k sets of data, all of which correspond to the given matrix of ranks, gives rise to the same ordering of the candidates as does the matrix of ranks for any positive integer k. Clearly in terms of productivity both in international and in domestic outlets, we obtain the same matrices of ordinal numbers, but when the data are looked at simultaneously for all journals, we have different overall ranking.

The straightforward summing up of the rank numbers seems, thus, to ignore information that would be essential to preserve consistency. But there are clearly circumstances where the procedure does not lead to inconsistent outcomes. The most obvious case is one where all data matrices are identical in cardinal numbers. In such cases our procedure works without problems. But this is, of course, a very special case. It is therefore worth asking if there are other circumstances that guarantee consistency under replication. There are, but again the environments are very restrictive. Haunsperger (2003) proves the following: a data matrix is consistent under replication if and only if it is row-ordered. A word of explanation is in order. A data matrix is simply a tabular organization of data in a given number of rows and columns. In the example above, we have seen 2×3 matrices, since we had three units each characterized by two measurements of average productivity. Now, a matrix of this type is row-ordered if the observations of each unit or alternative can be arranged in an order so that every row of the matrix gives rise to the same ranking of the units or alternatives.

The next matrix is an example of a row-ordered matrix. It is thus consistent under replication.

Unit 1	Unit 2	Unit 3
4	5	6
1	2	3
10	11	12
7	8	9

We see that the order of magnitude of numbers in each row is the same: unit 1 smallest, then unit 2 and finally unit 3. The next one, in contrast, is not row-ordered.

Unit 1	Unit 2	Unit 3
1	2	3
4	6	5
7	8	9
10	11	12

Here the order is the same in each row except for the second one where unit 1 is followed by unit 3, while it is followed by unit 2 in other rows.

The conditions for consistency are, thus, highly restrictive: at each time point the measurements have to yield an identical order of the cardinal values. This means that the performance of the units in terms of the cardinally measurable property has to define an identical order of priority at each time point.[64]

10.7   Voters are much the same as criteria

The problems discussed above are mainly extensions of voting paradoxes to multi-criteria choice contexts. They show the basic similarity of social choice and multi-criteria decision making. Since this chapter has primarily dealt with a setting where a single decision maker is in charge of evaluating a set of units or policy alternatives, this means that the problems in fact reappear in the 'natural' setting of voting theory, i.e. at the stage where several decision makers have to come up with an evaluation. What we have seen is that the social choice paradoxes do not go away if collective decisions are replaced by those of a benevolent dictator.

Although many facts reported above are of the notorious incompatibility nature – i.e. one cannot have procedures with all nice properties – the main message is constructive. Although serious problems exist, some of them can be avoided or at least rendered less serious. Even in cases where little can be done, the awareness of the problems may cast a shadow of healthy doubt on outcomes that may, in fact, be arbitrary. To start from the number of criteria used in the evaluations, it is often argued that the more criteria used, the richer the picture one has of the entities being evaluated. At first blush, this makes sense, but overlooks the new difficulty arising out of multiplicity of criteria, namely how to weigh them? Obviously no general answer can be given, but it makes sense to experiment with slightly different weights to see how much difference they make in the ensuing overall evaluation outcomes.

The issue of positional versus pairwise procedures touches the very foundation of preference aggregation theory and has been debated for more than two hundred years. One upshot of the debate is the observation that while the positional procedures are sensitive to changes in the policy alternative set, the pairwise systems are similarly sensitive to changes in the criterion set. Obviously, in group decision settings, both of these facts can be strategically utilized, but in individual policy evaluations their significance is in calling attention to the essential importance of focusing on all realistic alternatives and all important criteria (with proper weights) and only them. Again experimentation with slightly enlarged or trimmed alternative or criterion sets may help in estimating the robustness of one's overall evaluations.

Simpson's paradox is explained by the inhomogeneity of various sub-populations. As such, it casts doubt on any association observed in a large population with possibly inhomogeneous parts. This paradox can also take the form of suggesting – on the basis of an association found in all sub-populations that a connection between policy variables exists, when in fact this is not the case. Simpson's (1951) example is particularly instructive in this regard. The paradox is particularly puzzling in areas where randomization and experimentation are ruled out. The so-called 'small-N' methodology is obviously particularly vulnerable to Simpson's paradox.[65] Again experimentation with varying subpopulations may, whenever feasible, give hints about the reliability of the conclusions.

10.8 Suggested reading

The paradoxes that appear in inferring properties of a system from those of its parts are illustrated by Ostrogorski's and Anscombe's paradoxes. These along with some other similar paradoxes are discussed in Bezembinder and Van Acker (1985), Daudt and Rae (1978), Lagerspetz (1995) as well as Nurmi (1997, 1999). Saari and Sieberg (2001, 2004) provide a thorough analysis of the underlying reasons. The connection between aggregation paradoxes and multiple-criteria decision making is discussed in Nurmi and Meskanen (2000).

11 *Homo œconomicus*: should we let him go?

The journey through the basic models of political economy reveals that the bulk of these models is built on the assumptions that individuals have connected and transitive preferences over alternatives and that all the action in political economy is about making choices. Taken together, these assumptions imply that essential to political economy is maximizing behavior. As we saw in chapter 4, *homo œconomicus* has been under attack for quite some time, but survived in remarkably good shape. Much of the success of this model is due to the lack of credible alternatives. If one abandons the assumption of rationality in the thin sense, then the floodgates are open for nearly arbitrary explanatory accounts of human behavior. If the systematic violations of rationality axioms are taken as the point of departure – as e.g. in prospect theory – the simple elegance of the axiomatic choice theory is lost and we are left with a bewildering variety of theoretical systems which account for some particular types of violations of the standard theory.

Homo œconomicus as a concept fits nicely in the tradition of thinking that Smith (2005) – using Hayek's (1973) term – calls constructivist rationality. The basic tenet of this tradition is that social institutions are to be seen as results of conscious human reasoning. Whenever an institution appears, there is also an agent who has consciously designed it. This tradition has its roots in the rationalist philosophy. Smith contrasts this tradition with what he calls ecological rationality which allows for – and is particularly interested in – those institutions which have rational characteristics and, yet, have not been designed by anyone. The ecological rationality tradition investigates the preconditions and processes of evolution or emergence of social systems out of interaction of individuals and groups following their behavioral norms and strategies. These individuals and groups may not have any idea of the order or system emerging out of this interaction.

As characterized by Hayek and Smith the constructivist rationality seems implausibly narrow. Admittedly there are institutions that have been designed with certain desiderata in mind and which turn out to achieve those very desiderata. However, there are also institutional designs which bring about unintended changes in other institutions. For example, the abandonment of trade barriers in Europe over the past decades is changing the organization of the labor markets.

Similarly, the establishment of the European Parliament and the growth of its importance in the Union legislation will undoubtedly be reflected in the national parliaments. So, the constructivist rationality represents an unduely narrow view of institutions: very few of them – probably none – have been designed to their last detail anticipating all effects on other institutions.

Accepting the ecological view of rationality presents new challenges to *homo œconomicus* as a descriptive model. These are illustrated with the PD tournament strategies discussed in section 5.4. The dominant strategy in a one-shot PD leads to very low aggregated payoff in sequential PD tournaments. A population of TFT players reaches a higher level of aggregated payoff than a population of players resorting to the dominant strategy in each game. Obviously, TFT as a general norm has a better survival capability than the dominant strategy.

The ecological rationality plays a central role in what is known as evolutionary economics. As the term suggests this approach traces the over-time variation of economic behavior, structures and – most importantly – institutions. It differs from neoclassical economics not only in terms of rationality concept, but also in the importance attached to equilibria (Young 1998: 3–6). Its focus is in processes whereby standards, customs, norms and behavior patterns emerge over time out of interactions between individuals going about their business not necessarily realizing that what they are involved in is an institution building process. Nevertheless, this approach does not do away with rationality as the primary predictor of individual activity. Instead of looking at one-shot or repeated games with invariant rules, it focuses on adjustments of individuals and rules to external shocks. So, the difference between neoclassical and evolutionary economics is not in the former's concentration on equilibria and short-term behavior, but in the latter's focus on out-of-equilibrium adjustments and learning processes that eventually may lead to an equilibrium. Thus, even in evolutionary economics *homo œconomicus* has a role to play.

Even the most ardent advocate of rationality in the axiomatic sense is likely to admit that predictions based on player rationality are sometimes counterintuitive and burdened with a large body of contrary experimental evidence (see Colman 2003). The best-known examples are one-shot and sequential PD games, but also in Rosenthal's (1981) centipede game and in several other settings the game-theoretic solution methods, like backward induction, lead to implausible outcomes.[66] This has motivated the development of behavioral game theory (Camerer 1997, 2003). It has some similarities with the ecological rationality concept, but is not exclusively concerned with institutions. Instead, it looks for principles of reasoning that would make the observed deviations from the game theoretic predictions intelligible. The behavioral game theory is very much akin to prospect theory and other similar attempts to account for the observed deviations from the EU theory. Colman argues that the weakness of game theory is that its concept of rationality as expected utility maximization defined in individual decision settings does not readily apply to interactive decisions, i.e. those dealt with by game theory proper. Yet, he is ready to admit that 'game theory has vastly increased our understanding of interactive decision making, and no alternative theory even comes close to challenging its power' (Colman 2003: 152). Indeed, the main value of game theory and its underlying concept of rationality is in its relative simplicity and simultaneously in its explanatory and predictive power. The latter is by no means universal, but provides a good benchmark for experimental and, more generally empirical work. So, *homo œconomicus* continues to be an important construct in the research on political economy. It is, after all, primarily a model, and as such a useful approximation or idealization of politico-economic agents of the real world. Experimental and other empirical observations have occasionally cast a shadow on its usefulness in certain areas, but due to its conceptual simplicity and intuitive plausibility it remains a useful research tool in many other domains. Eventually, it is likely to be replaced by at least as general and predictively more successful model, but at present no such model is in sight.

Notes

1 Many a scholar pursues her research primarily in order to earn a living. This is also a quite personal objective, but falls rather in the realm of labor economics than of political economy.
2 There is a vast literature on the adequacy of Hempel's views. See e.g. Achinstein (1971), Collins (1966), and Scriven (1962). Treatises discussing the role of explanation in philosophy of science include Achinstein (1983), Braithwaite (1953), Nagel (1961), and Scheffler (1963).
3 Much has been written about the applicability of Hempel's account to human sciences, especially to historiography. See for example Dray (1957, 1968), Winch (1958), and von Wright (1971).
4 Lest there be any confusion about the term, it should be mentioned that 'F' comes from 'Friedman'.
5 For example, the invasion of the allied forces in Normandy in June of 1944 was preceded by deception landings along the western coast of continental Europe to mislead the German forces as for the location of the imminent invasion.
6 To keep the example simple, we assume, perhaps unrealistically, that the inspectors have no mercy, i.e. all passengers caught without a ticket will be charged 100 euros.
7 To keep the example reasonably transparent we overlook a number of considerations that undoubtedly play a role in real life, such as, the embarrassment of the passenger if caught without a valid ticket, the possibility of an increased fine in cases of repeated rides without ticket, etc. Introducing these considerations to the passenger decision-making calculus presents no major conceptual problems, but is unnecessary in an illustrative example.
8 This condition is needed only in cases where the number of alternatives is infinite.
9 The proof of this as well as of the other representation theorem can be found in Harsanyi (1977: 22–47).
10 We shall dwell on this point at some length in the next chapter.
11 For a more extensive discussion of the axioms as well as for the proof of the representation theorem, see Harsanyi (1977. 32–43). These axioms were originally presented by Herstein and Milnor (1953).
12 More precisely, the second axiom imposes the following constraint on any three certain outcomes A, B and C. Let $I(B; A, C)$ denote the inferior probability set of B which means that it consists of all those probability values p for which $B \succeq (A, p; C, 1 - p)$. Similarly, $S(B; A, C)$ is the set of those values of q for which $(A, q; C, 1 - q) \succeq B$. Assume that a sequence of values $p_1, p_2, \ldots$ converges to the value p_0 and assume also that $B \succeq (A, p_i; C, 1 - p_i)$ for all the values p_i in the sequence. The requirement that $I(B; A, C)$ is closed amounts to that $B \succeq (A, p_0; C, 1 - p_0)$. The requirement that $S(B; A, C)$ be closed is formulated in an analogous manner.

13 This axiom should not be confused with the independence of irrelevant alternatives axiom which appears in social choice theory (Arrow 1963). Nor is it equivalent with the independence axiom of Nash's (1950) bargaining solution. We shall discuss both of these concepts later on.

14 The paradox is, according to Daniel Bernoulli, last of the five problems his cousin Nicolas Bernoulli submitted to mathematician Pierre Rémond de Montmort for solution (see Bernoulli 1968: 23). The term 'St. Petersburg paradox' is undoubtedly due to Bernoulli's affiliation with the Academy of Sciences of Imperial Russia in those times located in St. Petersburg.

15 The paradox obviously does not depends on the currency. Ducat is the currency of the original example.

16 One could argue that r_1 is not a risky prospect since it can result in only one outcome. It is definitely a very particular, indeed trivial, type of risky prospect. At the same time it shows that all certain prospects can be represented as trivial risky ones.

17 It can be verified that an identical contradiction ensues if one chooses r_2 rather than r_1, and r_4 rather than r_3.

18 We can assume that the ball picked in the first draw is returned to the jar so that the number of balls remains the same in the two choice situations.

19 Similar examples can easily be invented. For example, assume that you would like to buy mushrooms for cooking, but you do not know much about mushroom types. Three persons X, Y and Z volunteer to supply you with the required amount of mushrooms. The vertical dimension in Figures 4.3 and 4.4 represents the persons' collecting efficiency (reflected in price) and the horizontal one their expertise in recognizing edible and poisonous types. Given that certain mushroom types are known to be lethal, it would seem that the efficiency dimension is pretty irrelevant. Thus, hiring 'the compromise person' or the one that dominates one of the others does not seem rational at all.

20 An additional practical requirement is that the number of choices and stages of the game are both small.

21 The last conclusion is, however, redundant since the fact that even one player is better off by deviating from an outcome excludes it from the set of Nash equilibria.

22 These types of games are discussed by many authors. For example, Hamburger (1979: 72) and Tsebelis (1989) use the same model in discussing the interaction between speeding motorists and traffic controllers. Dutta's (1999: 114–115) random drug testing game for sports is also of the same strategic type. So is the classic matching pennies game (Hamburger 1979: 12) as well as the best-known two-person zero-sum game, i.e. the one that aims at modeling the crucial strategies of Admirals Imamura and Kenney in a major Second World War naval battle that took place in the Pacific war theater (see e.g. Nurmi 1998: 62–64).

23 In his article Selten calls this equilibrium perfect, but the term subgame perfect is more informative and, therefore, more often used in the literature. See Binmore (1987: 191).

24 We see that (*cooperative, stay out*) gives the chain store exactly the same payoff as the latter outcome, but that does not disqualify (*aggressive, stay out*) from the set of equilibria.

25 There are many similar examples in the literature. A relatively recent one is given by Filippov *et al.* (2001: 215). Earlier variations of the same theme can be found in Riker and Ordeshook (1973: 250–251), Hardin (1971, 1982) as well as Taylor and Ward (1982).

26 In the analytic theory of the state this explanation is very common. See e.g. Birnbaum *et al.* (1978). We shall return to this in later chapters.

27 In two-person games 'the other players', of course, reduces to one player.

28 In addition to effectiveness and credibility, also rationality of the threat is an important, albeit often trivial, requirement. It states that a successful threat improves the threatener's payoff from what it had been without compliance (Brams 1983: 131). Issues related to threats in game theory are discussed extensively by Brams and his co-workers; see e.g. Brams (1983); Brams and Hessel (1984); Brams (1990); Brams (1994).

29 See e.g. Salonen and Wiberg (1987) for game classifications using various factors affecting the rational behavior.

30 For a comprehensive discussion on games of incomplete information, see Aumann and Heifetz (2002).

31 The Bismark Sea Battle game is a 2 × 2 zero-sum game with no Nash equilibria in pure strategies. Its real world setting is a WWII naval battle involving Japanese naval convoy and the US air force squadrons. The Japanese had to pass a large island using either the northern or southern route. Using effective hours of bombing as the unit of payoffs, it is natural to think of this battle as a zero-sum one. For more detailed accounts, see Luce and Raiffa (1957: 64–65), and Brams (1975).

32 The axioms have been widely discussed. See for example Luce and Raiffa (1957), Roth (1979), and Salonen (1985).

33 The line AC can be expressed as equality $x + y = c$ where c is a constant. Thus all quadrangles delineated by the horizontal and vertical axes as well as a point (x, y) in the AC line have the area $x \times (c - x)$. Maximizing this gives the Nash solution. The maximum value for the area is reached at $x = c/2$, that is, at the midpoint of AC.

34 Other interpretations have been given to the characteristic function. Sometimes it is viewed as the value that S receives if its complement coalition $N \setminus S$ forms. See Riker and Ordeshook (1973: 121–123).

35 A more stringent condition than cohesiveness is often imposed on characteristic functions, namely that they be super-additive. This amounts to requiring that whenever two disjoint coalitions join to form one coalition, the value of the new coalition is never smaller than the sum of its constituent coalitions. Cohesiveness imposes this requirement on just the grand coalition with respect to its sub-coalitions (Osborne and Rubinstein 1994: 258).

36 The *magnum opus* on Banzhaf and Shapley values and their applications is Felsenthal and Machover (1998).

37 The voting weight distribution is the one that took force on 1 November 2004.

38 The index values have been computed using a program written by Tommi Meskanen. The program can be accessed at http://powerslave.utu.fi/ and is maintained by Antti Pajala. The vote distribution is from the Treaty of Nice.

39 Several other attempts to include player preference in the definition of voting power have been made, see e.g. Napel and Widgrén (2002, 2004). For a critique of these models, see Braham and Holler (2005).

40 This chapter is based on Nurmi (2003).

41 An important source book on the history of theory of voting is McLean and Urken (1995), where the central texts of the Enlightenment era can be found in English translation.

42 These solutions have been discussed by Nanson (1882). Nanson's article is reprinted in McLean and Urken (1995).

43 Hare's system is a special case of the single transferable vote system (STV) used, for example, in the Irish parliamentary elections. Hare's system is in fact nothing but the application of STV to single-member constituencies.

44 This definition assumes that the majority preference relation is complete and asymmetric, that is, there is a unique winner in every pairwise comparison of alternatives. In other words, there are no ties in voting outcomes. Allowing ties leads to somewhat more complicated solution concepts (see Schwartz 1986).

45 Despite the apparent edge this system gives to the chair, there are circumstances under which she is disadvantaged with respect to the ordinary committee members. These circumstances are known as the chairman's paradoxes. See Farquharson (1969), Brams *et al.* (1986) and Niemi *et al.* (1983).

46 The theorem has, furthermore, a technical restriction: it deals with singleton-valued choice functions. Since most voting systems used in practice may result in a tie, it can be argued that they do not fall into the domain of the theorem. It turns out, however, that all commonly used voting systems are in fact manipulable (Nurmi 1984).

47 A function is monotone non-increasing if increasing the value of the argument is never accompanied with an increase in the value of the function, i.e. the latter may either decrease or remain the same.

48 It may happen that no candidate gets the majority of Electoral College votes. Rehnquist (2004: 4) reports that this has occurred twice in the history of the US: in 1800 and 1824. The constitution provides that in these situations, the election be thrown to the House of Representatives. And so it happened that in the former case Thomas Jefferson and in the latter John Quincy Adams were elected.

49 See Felsenthal and Machover (1998) and Turnovec (2004) for arguments in support of the Banzhaf and Shapley–Shubik indices, respectively.

50 The notion of socio-political outcomes could also be questioned, but we shall bypass it simply by assuming that they are what the individual and collective opinions, preferences and decisions are aimed at.

51 In the modern literature it is common to use the term social choice correspondence instead of social choice function. Hereby one emphasizes that the mapping from preference profiles to the alternative set may be one to many, that is, several alternatives may be chosen for a given profile. Since we have defined social choice functions as mappings from profiles into the set of subsets of alternatives, the concept of choice function and choice correspondence amount to the same thing.

52 It is also possible that the Clarke taxes do not sum up the required amount. In these cases, the way to proceed is to add to each individual tax an amount that is independent on the reported values.

53 An extreme case is, of course, a war which typically is a government-organized activity and inevitably leads to serious negative externalities in the form of loss of life and property.

54 This original position differs from the 'war of all against all' situation, also known as the Hobbesian jungle. The latter refers to the situation described in Hobbes's ([1651]1982) *Leviathan.*

55 The terminology is obviously borrowed from Adam Smith who used analogous reasoning in explaining the formation of the market equilibrium.

56 Olson (1982) applies this argument to Western economies after the Second World War concluding *i.a.* that economies where the interest groups have encompassing interests tend to have higher growth rates than those economies where more traditional and narrowly defined interests are being pursued.

57 Not necessarily an easy task in practice (Harsanyi 1975).

58 According to Mueller (2003: 333) rents were first systematically discussed by Tullock (1967), but the concept of rent-seeking was coined by Krueger (1974) somewhat later. See also Buchanan (1980).

59 This chapter is based on Nurmi (2005).

60 It is becoming increasingly common to include people with business, especially marketing, skills in the evaluation bodies in order to bring the entire life span of a scientific finding, from the initial idea to the finished and marketable product, to the focus of evaluation. Of course, the idea of a marketable product as a goal of scholarly work is quite irrelevant in many fields of research work.

61 The number of criteria may seem unrealistically large, but it is not larger than for example the one used by the Commission of the European Union in assessment of national research and innovation systems.

62 The paradox has been named after Simpson's (1951) example, but earlier instances have been found in the literature, see e.g. Cohen and Nagel (1934: 449). In Cohen and Nagel's example the paradox consists of the finding that in 1910 the death rate from tuberculosis in two cities, New York City and Richmond, Virginia, was higher in the latter than in the former, yet at the same time the corresponding death rates in white and non-white sub-populations exhibited higher rates in New York. Simpson's example, in turn, shows that there are partitions of cards in a fair deck so that in both subsets of cards there is an association between redness and plainness of cards. Yet we know that in a fair deck no association exists in the deck as a whole.

63 This example is derived with minor modifications from Haunsperger and Saari (1991). It can also be found in Haunsperger (2003).

64 The concept of consistency discussed here has a well-known analogue in the theory of voting, see section 7.6 above and Young (1974). Many procedures are consistent, e.g. plurality voting and the Borda count, but quite a few are not, e.g. plurality runoff and the single transferable vote system.

65 Small-N refers to research settings where the number of units under investigation is too small to allow for statistical techniques to be resorted to. See Lijphart (1971).

66 In the centipede game two players take turns in stopping or continuing the game. The rules of the game specify a payoff for each player if the game is stopped at any stage. In the beginning player 1 may stop the game whereupon both players get a zero payoff. If she decides to continue, player 2 is in turn and can stop the game or continue it. If she does the former, player 1 loses one unit, while player 2 gets 10 units. Provided that player 2 continues, player 1 is now in turn and can either stop or continue the game in the third stage. If she stops, both get 9 units. If the game continues player 2 can stop in the fourth stage whereupon she gets 19 and player 1 18 units. The game continues so that at each stage one player may stop the game and if she does this, she gets 10 units more than she would have received had the other player stopped the game at the preceding stage. The player not stopping the game receives at each stage 1 unit less than her payoff would have been if she have stopped the game one stage earlier. Obviously, the payoffs increase rather rapidly. So, if the player anticipates that the other player does not stop the game, she is advised to continue the game herself. However, if the other is expected to stop the game, then she is better off stopping. Backward induction leads to the bizarre outcome that the first player stops the game right at the outset.

Bibliography

Achinstein, P. (1968) *Concepts of Science*, Baltimore and London: The Johns Hopkins Press.

Achinstein, P. (1971) *Law and Explanation: An Essay in the Philosophy of Science*, Oxford: Oxford University Press.

Achinstein, P. (1983) *The Nature of Explanation*, Oxford: Oxford University Press.

Aizerman, M. and Aleskerov, F. (1995) *Theory of Choice*, Amsterdam: North-Holland.

Aleskerov, F. and Monjardet, B. (2002) *Utility Maximization, Choice and Preference*, Berlin and Heidelberg: Springer-Verlag.

Allais, M. (1943) *A la Recherche d'une discipline économique, première partie: l'Economie pure*, Paris: Ateliers Industria.

Allais, M. (1947) *Économie et intérêt*, Paris: Impremerie Nationale.

Allais, M. (1953) Le comportement de l'homme rationel devant le risque. Critique des postulates et axiomes de l'ecole Americaine, *Econometrica* **21**, 503–546. Translated as: 'The foundations of a positive theory of choice involving risk and a criticism of the postulates and axioms of the American school', in M. Allais and O. Hagen (Eds) The *Expected Utility Hypothesis and the Allais Paradox*, Dordrecht: D. Reidel.

Allais, M. (1979) The foundations of a positive theory of choice involving risk and a criticism of the postulates and axioms of the American school, in M. Allais and O. Hagen (Eds) *The Expected Utility Hypothesis and the Allais Paradox*, Dordrecht: D. Reidel.

Allais, M. and Hagen, O. (Eds) (1979) *The Expected Utility Hypothesis and the Allais Paradox*, Dordrecht: D. Reidel.

Allard, C. (1995) Lack of monotonicity – revisited, *Representation* **33**, 48–50.

Anscombe, F. and Aumann, R. (1963) A definition of subjective probability, *Annals of Mathematical Statistics* **34**, 199–205.

Apel, K.-O. (1967) *Analytic Philosophy of Language and the Geisteswissenschaften*, Dordrecht: D. Reidel.

Arrow, K. (1963) *Social Choice and Individual Values*, 2nd edn., New York: Wiley.

Arrow, K. (1971) *Essays in the Theory of Risk Bearing*, Amsterdam: North-Holland.

Arrow, K. (1983–1985) *Collected Papers of Kenneth J. Arrow*, vols 1–6, Cambridge, MA: Harvard University Press.

Arrow, K. and Hahn, F. (1971) *General Competitive Analysis*, San Francisco: Holden-Day.

Aumann, R.J. (1989) *Lectures on Game Theory*, Boulder: Westview Press.

Aumann, R.J. (2000) *Collected Papers*, Cambridge, MA: MIT Press.

Aumann, R.J. and Heifetz, A. (2002) Incomplete information, in: R.J. Aumann and S. Hart (Eds) *Handbook of Game Theory with Economic Applications*, vol. 3, Amsterdam: Elsevier.

Aumann, R.J. and Maschler, M. (1964) The bargaining set for cooperative games, in: M. Dresher, L.S. Shapley and A.W. Tucker (Eds) *Advances in Game Theory*, Princeton: Princeton University Press.

Aumann, R.J. and Maschler, M. (1995) *Repeated Games with Incomplete Information*, Cambridge, MA: MIT Press.

Aumann, R.J. and Shapley, L.S. (1974) *Values of Non-Atomic Games*, Princeton: Princeton University Press.

Austen-Smith, D. and Banks, J. (1999) *Positive Political Theory I: Collective Preference*, Ann Arbor: University of Michigan Press.

Austen-Smith, D. and Banks, J. (2005) *Positive Political Theory II: Strategy and Structure*, Ann Arbor: University of Michigan Press.

Axelrod, R. (1980a) Effective choice in the prisoner's dilemma, *Journal of Conflict Resolution* **24**, 3–25.

Axelrod, R. (1980b) More effective choice in the prisoner's dilemma, *Journal of Conflict Resolution* **24**, 379–403.

Axelrod, R. (1981) The emergence of cooperation among egoists, *American Political Science Review* **75**, 306–318.

Axelrod, R. (1984) *The Evolution of Cooperation*, New York: Basic Books.

Axelrod, R. and Dion, D. (1988) A further evolution of cooperation, *Science* **242**, 1385–1390.

Baharad, E. and Nitzan, S. (2002) Ameliorating majority decisiveness through expression of preference intensity, *American Political Science Review* **96**, 745–754.

Baigent, N. (1987) Preference proximity and anonymous social choice, *The Quarterly Journal of Economics* **102**, 161–169.

Baker, J. (1996) Fair representation and the concept of proportionality, *Political Studies* **44**, 733–737.

Balinski, M. and Young, H.P. (1982) *Fair Representation. Meeting the Ideal of One Man, One Vote*, New Haven: Yale University Press.

Banks, J. (1985) Sophisticated voting outcomes and agenda control, *Social Choice and Welfare* **1**, 295–306.

Banks, J. (1989) Agency budgets, cost information, and auditing, *American Journal of Political Science* **33**, 670–699.

Banks, J. (1991) *Signaling Games in Political Science*, Chur: Harwood Academic Publishers.

Banzhaf, J. (1965) Weighted voting doesn't work: a mathematical analysis, *Rutgers Law Review* **19**, 317–343.

Banzhaf, J. (1966) Multi-member electoral districts – do they violate the 'One man, one vote' principle? *Yale Law Review* **75**, 1309–1338.

Barry, B. (1965) *Political Argument*, London: Routledge.

Barry, B. (1970) *Sociologists, Economists and Democracy*, London: Collier-Macmillan.

Barry, B. (1973) *The Liberal Theory of Justice*, Oxford: Oxford University Press.

Barry, B. (1989) *Theories of Justice*, Berkeley: University of California Press.

Barry, B. (1995) *Justice as Impartiality*, Oxford: Clarendon Press.

Barry, B. (2001) *Culture and Equality*, Cambridge: Polity Press.

Bernoulli, D. (1738) Specimen theoriae novae de mensura sortis, *Commentarii Academiae Scientiarum Imperialis Petropolitanae*, Tomus V, 175–192.

Bernoulli, D. (1954) Exposition of a new theory of risk evaluation (transl. L. Sommers), *Econometrica* **22**, 23–36. Reprinted 1968 in Baumol, W.J. and Goldfeld, S.M. (Eds) *Precursors in Mathematical Economics: An Anthology*, London: London School of Economics and Political Science.

Bezembinder, Th. and Van Acker, P. (1985) The Ostrogorski paradox and its relation to nontransitive choice, *Journal of Mathematical Psychology* **11**, 131–158.

Binmore, K. (1987) Modeling rational players. Part I, *Economics and Philosophy* **3**, 179–214.

Binmore, K. (1988) Modeling rational players. Part II, *Economics and Philosophy* **4**, 9–55.

Binmore, K. (1992) *Fun and Games. A Text on Game Theory*, Lexington, MA: D.C. Heath and Company.

Birkhoff, G. (1976) House monotone apportionment schemes, *Proceedings of the National Academy of Sciences, U.S.A.* **73**, 684–686.

Birnbaum, P., Lively, J. and Parry, G. (Eds) (1978) *Democracy, Consensus & Social Contract*, London and Beverly Hills: Sage Publications.

Black, D. (1958) *Theory of Committees and Elections*, Cambridge: Cambridge University Press.

Blais, A. (2000) *To Vote or Not to Vote*, Pittsburgh: University of Pittsburgh Press.

Braham, M. and Holler, M. (2005) The impossibility of a preference-based power index, *Journal of Theoretical Politics* **17**, 137–157.

Braithwaite, R.B. (1953) *Scientific Explanation*, Cambridge: Cambridge University Press.

Brams, S. (1975) *Game Theory and Politics*, New York: Free Press.

Brams, S. (1980) *Biblical Games*, Cambridge: MIT Press.

Brams, S. (1983) *Superior Beings: If They Exist, How Would We Know?* New York: Springer-Verlag.

Brams, S. (1990) *Negotitation Games*, New York: Routledge.

Brams, S. (1994) *Theory of Moves*, Cambridge: Cambridge University Press.

Brams, S. and Affuso. P. (1985) New paradoxes of voting power in the EC Council of Ministers, *Electoral Studies* 4, 135–139.

Brams, S., Felsenthal, D. and Maoz, Z. (1986) New chairman paradoxes, in: A. Diekman and P. Mitter (Eds) *Paradoxical Effects of Social Behavior: Essays in Honor of Anatol Rapoport*, Heidelberg: Physica Verlag.

Brams, S. and Fishburn, P. (1983) *Approval Voting*, Boston: Birkhäuser Verlag.

Brams, S. and Hessel. M (1984) Threat power in sequential games, *International Studies Quarterly* 28, 15–36.

Brams, S. and Taylor, A. (1999) *The Win–Win Solution*, New York: W.W. Norton.

Brams, S. and Wittman, D. (1981) Non-myopic equilibria in 2×2 games, *Conflict Management and Peace Science* 6, 39–62.

Brennan, G. and Buchanan, J. (1980) *Power to Tax*, Cambridge: Cambridge University Press.

Brennan, G. and Buchanan, J. (1985) *The Reason of Rules*, Cambridge: Cambridge University Press.

Bryce, R. (2002) *Pipe Dreams: Greed, Ego and the Death of Enron*, New York: Public Affairs.

Buchanan, J. (1975) *The Limits of Liberty*, Chicago: The University of Chicago Press.

Buchanan, J. (1980) Rent seeking and profit seeking, in: J. Buchanan, R. Tollison and G. Tullock (Eds) *Toward a Theory of the Rent-Seeking Society*, College Station: Texas A & M Press.

Buchanan, J. (1991a) *Constitutional Economics*, Oxford: Blackwell.

Buchanan, J. (1991b) *The Economics and Ethics of Constitutional Order*, Ann Arbor: University of Michigan Press.

Buchanan, J. and Tullock, G. (1962) *The Calculus of Consent: Logical Foundations of Constitutional Democracy*, Ann Arbor: University of Michigan Press.

Calvert, R. (1986) *Models of Imperfect Information in Politics*, Chur: Harwood Academic Publishers.

Camerer, C. (1997) Progress in behavioral game theory, *Journal of Economic Perspectives* 11, 167–188.

Camerer, C. (2003) *Behavioral Game Theory: Experiments on Strategic Interaction*, Princeton: Princeton University Press.

Campbell, D. and Kelly, J. (2002) Non-monotonicity does not imply the no-show paradox, *Social Choice and Welfare* 19, 513–515.

Caporaso, J. and Levine, D. (1992) *Theories of Political Economy*, Cambridge: Cambridge University Press.

Carnap, R. (1962) *Logical Foundations of Probability*, Chicago: University of Chicago Press.

Chernoff, H. (1954) Rational selection of decision functions, *Econometrica* **22**, 422–443.

Chernoff, H. and Moses, L. (1959) *Elementary Decision Theory*, New York: Wiley.

Clarke, E. (1980) *Demand Revelation and the Provision of Public Goods*, Cambridge: Ballinger.

Cohen, M. and Nagel, E. (1934) *An Introduction to Logic and Scientific Method*, London: Routledge and Kegan Paul.

Collins, A. (1966) The use of statistics in explanation, *British Journal of Philosophy of Science* **17**, 127–140.

Colman, A. (2003) Cooperation, psychological game theory, and limitations of rationality in social interaction, *Behavioral and Brain Sciences* **26**, 139–153.

Colomer, J. (Ed.) (2004) *Handbook of Electoral System Choice*, Basingstoke, UK: Palgrave Macmillan.

Dahl, R. and Lindblom, Ch. (1976) *Politics, Economics and Welfare*, Chicago: University of Chicago Press.

Daniels, N. (Ed.) (1975) *Reading Rawls*, Oxford: Basil Blackwell.

Daudt, H. and Rae, D. (1978) Social contract and the limits of majority rule, in: P. Birnbaum and G. Parry (Eds) *Democracy, Consensus & Social Contract*, London: Sage.

Davidson, D. (1980) Agency, in: D. Davidson (Ed.) *Essays on Actions and Events*, Oxford: Clarendon Press.

Deegan, J. and Packel, E. (1978) A new index for voting games, *International Journal of Game Theory* **7**, 113–123.

DeGrazia, A. (1953) Mathematical derivation of an election system, *Isis* **44**, 42–51.

Dilthey, W. (1914–1927) *Gesammelte Schriften I–VII*, Leipzig: B.G. Teubner.

Doron, G. (1979) The Hare voting system is inconsistent, *Political Studies* **27**, 283–286.

Doron, G. and Kronick, R. (1977) Single transferable vote: an example of perverse social choice function, *American Journal of Political Science* **21**, 303–311.

Dowding, K. (1995) Interpreting formal coalition theory, in: K. Dowding and D. King (Eds) *Preferences, Institutions, and Rational Choice*, Oxford: Clarendon Press.

Dray, W. (1957) *Laws and Explanation in History*, Oxford: Oxford University Press.

Dray, W.H. (1968) On explaining how-possibly, *Monist* **52**, 390–407.

Dummett, M. (1997) *Principles of Electoral Reform*, Oxford: Oxford University Press.

Dutta, P. (1999) *Strategies and Games: Theory and Practice*, Cambridge, MA: MIT Press.

Easton, D. (1965) *A Framework for Political Analysis*, Englewood Cliffs: Prentice-Hall.

Edwards, W., Lindman, H. and Savage, L. (1963) Bayesian statistical inference in psychological research, *Psychological Review* **70**, 193–242.

Ellsberg, D. (1961) Risk, ambiguity, and the Savage axioms, *Quarterly Journal of Economics* **75**, 643–669.

Ellsberg, D. (2001) *Risk, Ambiguity and Decision*, London: Routledge.

Elster, J. (1979) *Ulysses and the Sirens*, Cambridge: Cambridge University Press.

Elster, J. (1983) *Sour Grapes*, Cambridge: Cambridge University Press.

Elster, J. (1985) *Making Sense of Marx*, Cambridge: Cambridge University Press.

Elster, J. (1986) Introduction, in: J. Elster (Ed.) *Rational Choice*, Oxford: Basil Blackwell.

Elster, J. (1992) *Local Justice*, New York: Russell Sage Foundation.

Elster, J. (1999) *Alchemies of the Mind*, Cambridge: Cambridge University Press.

Elster, J. (2000) *Ulysses Unbound*, Cambridge: Cambridge University Press.

Enelow, J. and Hinich, M. (1984) *The Spatial Theory of Voting: An Introduction*, Cambridge: Cambridge University Press.

Farquharson, R. (1969) *Theory of Voting*, New Haven: Yale University Press.

Fedrizzi, M., Kacprzyk, J. and Nurmi, H. (1993) Consensus degrees under fuzzy majorities and fuzzy preferences using OWA operators, *Control and Cybernetics* **22**, 71–80.

Feldman, A. (1980) *Welfare Economics and Social Choice Theory*, Boston: Martinus Nijhoff.

Felsenthal, D. and Machover, M. (1998) *The Measurement of Voting Power*, Cheltenham: Edward Elgar.

Filippov, M., Ordeshook, P. and Shvetsova, O. (2001) Ensuring a stable federal state: economics or political institutional design, in: R. Mudambi, P. Navarra and G. Sobbrio (Eds) *Rules and Reason: Perspectives on Constitutional Political Economy*, Cambridge: Cambridge University Press.

Fishburn, P. (1970) *Utility Theory for Decision Making*, New York: Wiley.

Fishburn, P. (1973) *The Theory of Social Choice*, Princeton: Princeton University Press.

Fishburn, P. (1977) Condorcet social choice functions, *SIAM Journal of Applied Mathematics* **33**, 469–489.

Fishburn, P. (1981) Inverted orders for monotone scoring rules, *Discrete Applied Mathematics* **3**, 27–36.

Fishburn, P. (1985) *Interval Orders and Graphs*, New York: Wiley.

Fishburn, P. (1988) *Nonlinear Preference and Utility Theory*, Baltimore: The Johns Hopkins University Press.

Fishburn, P. and Brams, S.J. (1982) Paradoxes of preferential voting, *Mathematics Magazine* **56**, 207–214.

Freeman, J. (1989) *Democracy and Market: The Politics of Mixed Economies*, Ithaca: Cornell University Press.

French, S. and Xie, Zh. (1994) A perspective on recent developments in utility theory, in: S. Ríos (Ed.) *Decision Theory and Decision Analysis: Trends and Challenges*, Dordrecht: Kluwer.

Friedman, M. (1953) The methodology of positive economics, in: M. Friedman (Ed.) *Essays in Positive Economics*, Chicago: University of Chicago Press.

Friedman, M. and Friedman, R. (1980) *Free to Choose*, New York: Hartcourt Brace Jovanovich.

Friedman, M. and Schwartz, A. (1963) *A Monetary History of the United States, 1867–1960*, Princeton: Princeton University Press.

Fudenberg, D. and Tirole, J. (1991) *Game Theory*, Cambridge, MA: MIT Press.

Garrett, G. and Tsebelis, G. (1996) An institutional critique of intergovernmentalism, *International Organization* **50**, 269–299.

Gibbard, A. (1973) Manipulation of voting schemes: a general result, *Econometrica* **41**, 587–601.

Giere, R. (1979) *Understanding Scientific Reasoning*, New York: Holt, Rinehart and Winston.

Grether, D., Isaac, M. and Plott, Ch. (1989) *The Allocation of Scarce Resources*, Boulder: Westview Press.

Grether, D. and Plott, Ch. (1979) Economic theory of choice and the preference reversal phenomenon, *The American Economic Review* **69**, 623–638.

Guinier, L. (1994) *The Tyranny of the Majority*, New York: The Free Press.

Habermas, J. (1972) *Knowledge and Human Interest*, London: Heinemann.

Habermas, J. (1988) *On the Logic of the Social Sciences*, Cambridge, MA: MIT Press.

Hamburger, H. (1979) *Games as Models of Social Phenomena*, San Francisco: W.H. Freeman.

Hammond, J., Keeney, R. and Raiffa, H. (2002) *Smart Decisions*, New York: Broadway Books.

Hardin, G. (1968) The tragedy of the commons, *Science* **162**, 1243–1248.

Hardin, R. (1971) Collective action as an agreeable *n*-prisoners' dilemma, *Behavioral Science* **16**, 436–441.

Hardin, R. (1982) *Collective Action*. Baltimore: The Johns Hopkins University Press.

Hardin, R. (1995) *One for All: The Logic of Group Conflict*, Princeton: Princeton University Press.

Harsanyi, J. (1967) Games with incomplete information played by 'Bayesian' players, I–III, Part I. The basic model, *Management Science* **14**, 159–182.

Harsanyi, J. (1968a) Games with incomplete information played by 'Bayesian' players, I–III, Part II. Bayesian equilibrium points, *Management Science* **14**, 320–334.

Harsanyi, J. (1968b) Games with incomplete information played by 'Bayesian' players, I–III, Part III. The basic probability distribution of the game, *Management Science* **14**, 486–502.

Harsanyi, J. (1975) Can maximin principle serve as a basis of morality? A critique of John Rawls' theory, *American Political Science Review* **69**, 594–606.

Harsanyi, J. (1976) *Essays on Ethics, Social Behavior and Scientific Explanation*, Dordrecht: D. Reidel.

Harsanyi, J. (1977) *Rational Behavior and Bargaining Equilibrium in Games and Social Situations*, Cambridge: Cambridge University Press.

Harsanyi, J. (1982) *Papers in Game Theory*, Dordrecht: D. Reidel.

Harsanyi, J. (1986) Advances in understanding rational behavior, in: J. Elster (Ed.) *Rational Choice*, Oxford: Basil Blackwell.

Harsanyi, J. and Selten, R. (1988) *A General Theory of Equilibrium Selection in Games*, Cambridge, MA: MIT Press.

Haunsperger, D. (2003) Aggregated statistical rankings are arbitrary, *Social Choice and Welfare* **20**, 261–272.

Haunsperger, D. and Saari, D. (1991) The lack of consistency for statistical decision procedures, *The American Statistician* **45**, 252–255.

Hayek, F. (1973) *Law, Legislation and Liberty. Vol. I*, Chicago: University of Chicago Press.

Hempel, C. (1965) *Aspects of Scientific Explanation and Other Essays in the Philosophy of Science*, New York: The Free Press.

Hempel, C. and Oppenheim, P. (1948) The logic of explanation, *Philosophy of Science* **15**, 135–175.

Herne, K. and Setälä, M. (2004) A response to the critique of rational choice theory: Lakatos's and Laudan's conceptions applied, *Inquiry* **47**, 67–85.

Herstein, I. and Milnor, J. (1953) An axiomatic approach to measurable utility, *Econometrica* **21**, 291–297.

Heywood, A. (1997) *Politics*, Basingstoke, UK: Macmillan.

Hillas, J. and Kohlberg, E. (2002) Foundations of strategic equilibrium, in: R. Aumann and S. Hart (Eds) *Handbook of Game Theory with Economic Applications, Vol. 3*, Amsterdam: Elsevier.

Hillman, A.L. (2003) *Public Finance and Public Policy. Responsibilities and Limitations of Government*, Cambridge: Cambridge University Press.

Hobbes, Th. ([1651]1982) *Leviathan*, Harmondsworth: Penguin Books.

Holler, M. (1982) Forming coalitions and measuring voting power, *Political Studies* **30**, 262–271.

Holler, M. and Illing, G. (2003) *Einführung in die Spieltheorie*, 5. Aufl., Berlin, Heidelberg and New York: Springer-Verlag.

Hosli, M., van Deemen, A. and Widgrén, M. (Eds) (2002) *Institutional Challenges in the European Union*, London: Routledge.

Howard, N. (1971) *Paradoxes of Rationality*, Cambridge, MA: MIT Press.

Huber, J., Payne, J. and Puto, C. (1982) Adding asymmetrically dominated alternatives: violations of regularity and similarity hypothesis, *Journal of Consumer Research* **9**, 90–98.

Hurwicz, L. (1951) Optimality criteria for decision making under ignorance, *Cowles Commission Discussion Paper no. 370*.

Hurwicz, L. (1972) On informationally decentralized systems, in: R. Radner and C.B. McGuire (Eds) *Decision and Organization: A Volume in Honor of Jacob Marschak*, Amsterdam: North-Holland.

Hurwicz, L. (1979) On allocations attainable through Nash equilibria, *Journal of Economic Theory* **21**, 140–165.

Jackson, M. (2001) A crash course in implementation theory, *Social Choice and Welfare* **18**, 655–798.

Jackson, M., Palfrey, T. and Srivastava, S. (1994) Undominated Nash implementation in bounded mechanisms, *Games and Economic Behavior*, **6**, 474–501.

Kacprzyk, J., Fedrizzi, M. and Nurmi, H. (1992) Group decision making and consensus under fuzzy preferences and fuzzy majority, *Fuzzy Sets and Systems* **49**, 21–31.

Kahneman, D. and Tversky, A. (1979) Prospect theory: an analysis of decision under risk, *Econometrica* **47**, 263–291.

Kahneman, D. and Tversky, A. (Eds) (2000) *Choices, Values and Frames*, Cambridge: Cambridge University Press.

Kahneman, D., Tversky, A. and Slovic, P. (1982) *Judgment under Uncertainty: Heuristics and Biases*, Cambridge: Cambridge University Press.

Kalai, E. and Smorodinsky, M. (1975) Other solutions to Nash's bargaining problem, *Econometrica* **43**, 513–518.

Kelly, J. (1978) *Arrow Impossibility Theorems*, New York: Academic Press.

Kelly, J. (1991) Social choice bibliography, *Social Choice and Welfare* **8**, 97–169.

Kemeny, J. (1959a) Mathematics without numbers, *Daedalus* **88**, 571–591.

Kemeny, J. (1959b) *A Philosopher Looks at Science*, Princeton: Van Nostrand.

Kemeny, J. and Snell, L. (1962) *Mathematical Models in the Social Sciences*, New York: Blaisdell.

Kemeny, J., Snell, L. and Knapp, A. (1966) *Denumerable Markov Chains*, Princeton: Van Nostrand.

Kemeny, J., Snell, L. and Thompson, O. (1959) *Introduction to Finite Mathematics*, Englewood Cliffs: Prentice-Hall.

Kirman, A. and Widgrén, M. (1995) European economic decision making policy: progress or paralysis? *Economic Policy* **21**, 423–460.

Kolm, S. (1996) *Modern Theories of Justice*, Cambridge, MA: MIT Press.

Kramer, G. (1977) A dynamical model of political equilibrium, *Journal of Economic Theory* **16**, 310–334.

Krantz, D.H., Luce, R.D., Suppes, P. and Tversky, A. (1971) *Foundations of Measurement, Vol. I: Additive and Polynomial Representations*, New York: Academic Press.

Kreps, D.M. and Wilson, R. (1982a) Sequential equilibria, *Econometrica* **50**, 863–894.

Kreps, D.M. and Wilson, R. (1982b) Reputation and imperfect information, *Journal of Economic Theory* **27**, 253–279.

Krueger, A. (1974) The political economy of the rent-seeking society, *American Economic Review* **64**, 291–303.

Kuhn, H. and Nasar, S. (Eds) (2002) *The Essential John Nash*, Princeton: Princeton University Press.

Lagerspetz, E. (1995) Paradoxes and representation, *Electoral Studies* **15**, 83–92.

Lagerspetz, E. (2002) The legitimacy of majority rule, *Associations* **6**, 261–291.

Lane, J.-E. and Stenlund, H. (1989) *Politisk teori*, Lund: Studentlitteratur.

Laruelle, A. (2002) The EU decision-making procedures: some insights from non-cooperative game theory, in M. Hosli, A. van Deemen and M. Widgrén (Eds) *Institutional Challenges in the European Union*, London: Routledge.

Laver, M. and Schofield, N. (1990) *Multiparty Government*, Oxford: Oxford University Press.

Leininger, W. (1993) The fatal vote: Berlin versus Bonn, *Finanzarchiv* **50**, 1–20.

Lichtenstein, S. and Slovic, P. (1971) Reversal of preferences between bids and choices in gambling decisions, *Journal of Experimental Psychology* **89**, 46–55.

Lijphart, A. (1971) Comparative politics and comparative method, *American Political Science Review* **65**, 682–693.

Lindblom, Ch. (1977) *Politics and Markets: The World's Political Economic Systems*, New York: Basic Books.

Luce, R.D. (1959) *Individual Choice Behavior*, New York: Wiley.

Luce, R.D. (1967) Sufficient conditions for the existence of finitely additive probability measure, *Annals of Mathematical Statistics* **38**, 780–786.

Luce, R.D. (1986) *Response Times*, Oxford: Oxford University Press.

Luce, R.D. and Raiffa, H. (1957) *Games and Decisions*, New York: Wiley.

MacDonald, P. (2003) Useful fiction or miracle maker: the competing epistemological foundations of rational choice theory, *American Political Science Review* **97**, 551–565.

Machina, M.J. (1982) Expected utility analysis without the independence axiom, *Econometrica* **50**, 277–323.

Machina, M.J. (1987) Choice under uncertainty: problems solved and unsolved, *The Journal of Economic Perspectives* **1**, 121–154.

Marx, K. ([1939]1973) *Grundrisse. Foundations of the Critique of Political Economy* (transl. M. Nicolaus), Harmondsworth: Penguin Books.

Maskin, E. (1985) The theory of implementation in Nash equilibrium, in: L. Hurwicz, D. Schmeidler and H. Sonnenschein (Eds) *Social Goals and Social Organization: Essays in Memory of Elisha Pazner*, Cambridge: Cambridge University Press.

May, K.O. (1952) A set of independent, necessary and sufficient conditions for simple majority decision, *Econometrica* **20**, 680–684.

McGuire, M. and Olson, M. (1996) The economics of autocracy and majority rule: the invisible hand and the use of force, *Journal of Economic Literature* **34**, 72–96.

McKelvey, R.D. (1976) Intransitivities in multidimensional voting models and some implications for agenda control, *Journal of Economic Theory* **12**, 472–482.

McKelvey, R.D. (1979) General conditions for global intransitivities in formal voting models, *Econometrica* **47**, 1085–1112.

McKelvey, R. and Niemi, R. (1978) A multistage game representation of sophisticated voting for binary procedures, *Journal of Economic Theory* **18**, 1–22.

McLean, I. and Urken, A. (Eds) (1995) *Classics of Social Choice*, Ann Arbor: The University of Michigan Press.

Mill, J. ([1844]1995) *Elements of Political Economy*, London: Routledge.

Miller, N. (1977) Graph-theoritical approaches to the theory of voting, *American Journal of Political Science* **21**, 769–803.

Miller, N. (1980) A new solution set for tournaments and majority voting, *American Journal of Political Science* **24**, 68–96.

Miller, N. (1983) Pluralism and social choice, *American Political Science Review* **77**, 737–747.

Miller, N. (1995) *Committees, Agendas, and Voting*, Chur: Harwood Academic Publishers.

Milnor, J. (1954) Games against nature, in: R. Thrall, C. Coombs and R. Davis (Eds) *Decision Processes*, New York: Wiley.

Molander, P. (1985) The optimal level of generosity in a selfish, uncertain environment, *Journal of Conflict Resolution* **29**, 611–618.

Moore, J. and Repullo, R. (1988) Subgame perfect implementation, *Econometrica* **56**, 1191–1220.

Morris, I., Oppenheimer, J. and Soltan, K. (Eds) (2004) *Politics from Anarchy to Democracy: Rational Choice in Political Science*, Stanford: Stanford University Press.

Moulin, H. (1983) *The Strategy of Social Choice*, Amsterdam: North-Holland.

Moulin, H. (1984) Implementing the Kalai–Smorodinsky bargaining solution, *Journal of Economic Theory* **33**, 32–45.

Moulin, H. (1988a) *Axioms of Cooperative Decision Making*, Cambridge: Cambridge University Press.

Moulin, H. (1988b) Condorcet's principle implies the no show paradox, *Journal of Economic Theory* **45**, 53–64.

Moulin, H. (2003) *Fair Division and Collective Welfare*, Cambridge, MA: MIT Press.

Mueller, D.C. (2003) *Public Choice III*, Cambridge: Cambridge University Press.

Munier, B. (Ed.) (1988) *Risk, Decision and Rationality*, Dordrecht: D. Reidel.

Munier, B. and Shakun, M. (Eds) (1988) *Compromise, Negotiation and Group Decision*, Dordrecht: D. Reidel.

Murzi, M. (2001) Carl Gustav Hempel, *The Internet Encyclopedia of Philosophy*. Online. Available at http://www.iep.utm.edu/h/hempel.htm (accessed 22 June 2005).

Musgrave, A. (1981) 'Unreal assumptions' in economic theory: the F-twist untwisted, *Kyklos* **34**, 377–387.

Myerson, R. (1991) *Game Theory: Analysis of Conflict*, Cambridge: Harvard University Press.

Nagel, E. (1961) *The Structure of Science*, New York: Hartcourt, Brace and World.

Nagel, E. (1979) Assumptions in economic theory, in: A. Ryan (Ed.) *The Philosophy of Social Explanation*, Oxford: Oxford University Press.

Nanson, E.J. (1882) Methods of election, *Transactions and Proceedings of the Royal Society of Victoria* **XIX**, 197–240. (Reprinted in I. McLean and A. Urken (Eds) (1995) *Classics of Social Choice*, Ann Arbor: University of Michigan Press.)

Napel, S. and Widgrén, M. (2002) The power of a spatially inferior player, *Homo Oeconomicus* **19**, 327–343.

Napel, S. and Widgrén, M. (2004) Power measurement as sensitivity analysis, *Journal of Theoretical Politics* **16**, 517–538.

Nasar, S. (1998) *A Beautiful Mind. A Biography of John Foster Nash Jr.*, New York: Simon and Schuster.

Nash, J.F. (1950) The bargaining problem, *Econometrica* **28**, 155–162.

Nash, J.F. (1951) Non-cooperative games, *Annals of Mathematics* **54**, 286–295.

Nash, J.F. (1996) *Essays in Game Theory*, Cheltenham: Edward Elgar.

Niemi, R., Bjurulf, B. and Blewis, G. (1983) The power of the chairman, *Public Choice* **40**, 293–305.

Niskanen, W. (1971) *Bureaucracy and Representative Government*, Chicago: Aldine-Atherton.

Nitzan, S. (1981) Some measures of closeness to unanimity and their implications, *Theory and Decision* **13**, 129–138.

Nozick, R. (1974) *Anarchy, State and Utopia*, Oxford: Basil Blackwell.

Nozick, R. (1981) *Philosophical Explanations*, Oxford: Clarendon Press.

Nozick, R. (1993) *The Nature of Rationality*, Princeton: Princeton University Press.

Nozick, R. (2001) *Invariances*, Cambridge: Harvard University Press.

Nurmi, H. (1983a) The F-twist and the evaluation of political institutions, *Zeitschrift für Wirtschafts- und Sozialwissenschaften* **103**, 143–159.

Nurmi, H. (1983b) Voting procedures: a summary analysis, *British Journal of Political Science* **13**, 181–208.

Nurmi, H. (1984) On taking preferences seriously, in: D. Anckar and E. Berndtson (Eds) *Essays on Democratic Theory*, Tampere: Finnpublishers.

Nurmi, H. (1985) On apportionment and proportional representation, *Political Studies* **33**, 113–121.

Nurmi, H. (1987) *Comparing Voting Systems*, Dordrecht: D. Reidel.

Nurmi, H. (1996/7) It's not just the lack of monotonicity, *Representation* **34**, 48–52.

Nurmi, H. (1997) Compound majority paradoxes and proportional representation, *European Journal of Political Economy* **13**, 443–454.

Nurmi, H. (1998) *Rational Behaviour and the Design of Institutions*, Cheltenham: Edward Elgar.

Nurmi, H. (1999) *Voting Paradoxes and How to Deal with Them*, Berlin, Heidelberg and New York: Springer-Verlag.

Nurmi, H. (2002) *Voting Procedures under Uncertainty*, Berlin, Heidelberg and New York: Springer-Verlag.

Nurmi, H. (2003) Decision making in committees: an introductory overview, in: J. Kacprzyk and D. Wagner (Eds) *Group Decisions and Voting*, Warszawa: EXIT.

Nurmi, H. (2005) Aggregation problems in policy evaluation: an overview, *European Journal of Political Economy* **21**, 287–300.

Nurmi, H. and Kacprzyk, J. (2000) Social choice under fuzziness: a perspective, in: J. Fodor, B. De Baets and P. Perny (Eds) *Preferences and Decisions Under Incomplete Knowledge*, Heidelberg and New York: Physica-Verlag.

Nurmi, H. and Lagerspetz, E. (1984) Observations on the Finnish electoral system, in: D. Anckar and E. Berndtson (Eds) *Essays on Democratic Theory*, Helsinki: The Finnish Political Science Association.

Nurmi, H. and Meskanen, T. (1999) *A priori* power measures and the institutions of the European Union, *European Journal of Political Reaserch* **35**, 161–179.

Nurmi, H. and Meskanen, T. (2000) Voting paradoxes and MCDM, *Group Decision and Negotiation* **9**, 297–313.

Olson, M., Jr. ([1965] 1971) *The Logic of Collective Action. Public Goods and the Theory of Groups*, revised edition, New York: Schocken Books.

Olson, M. (1982) *The Rise and Decline of Nations*, New Haven: Yale University Press.

Olson, M. (1991) Autocracy, democracy, and prosperity, in: R. Zeckhauser (Ed.) *Strategy and Choice*, Cambridge, MA: MIT Press.

Olson, M. (1993) Dictatorship, democracy, and development, *American Political Science Review* **87**, 567–576.

Olson, M. (2000) *Power and Prosperity*, New York: Basic Books.

Olson, M. and Zeckhauser, R. (1966) An economic theory of alliances, *Review of Economics and Statistics* **48**, 266–279.

Osborne, M. (2004) *An Introduction to Game Theory*, Oxford: Oxford University Press.

Osborne, M. and Rubinstein, A. (1994) *A Course in Game Theory*, Cambridge, MA: MIT Press.

Owen, G. (2001) *Game Theory*, 3rd edn, New York: Academic Press.

Palfrey, Th. and Srivastava, S. (1989) Mechanism design with incomplete information: a solution to the implementation problem, *Journal of Political Economy* **97**, 668–691.

Pattanaik, P. (1971) *Voting and Collective Choice*, Cambridge: Cambridge University Press.

Peleg, B. (1984) *Game Theoretic Analysis of Voting in Committees*, Cambridge: Cambridge University Press.

Pérez, J. (2001) The strong no show paradoxes are common flaw in Condorcet voting correspondences, *Social Choice and Welfare* **18**, 601–616.

Persson, T. and Tabellini, G. (2000) *Political Economics. Explaining Economic Policy*, Cambridge, MA: MIT Press.

Pigou, A. (1929) *The Economics of Welfare*, London: Macmillan.

Plott, Ch. (1976) Axiomatic social choice theory: an overview and interpretation, *American Journal of Political Science* **20**, 511–596.

Plott, Ch. (2001) *Collected Papers on the Experimental Foundations of Economics and Political Science*, vols 1–3, Cheltenham: Edward Elgar.

Przeworski, A. (2003) *States and Markets. A Primer in Political Economy*, Cambridge: Cambridge University Press.

Rae, D. (1969) Decision rules and individual values in constitutional choice, *American Political Science Review* **63**, 40–56.

Raiffa, H. (1968) *Decision Analysis*, Reading, MA: Addison-Wesley.

Raiffa, H. (1982) *The Art and Science of Negotiation*, Cambridge: Harvard University Press.

Raiffa, H. (1994) The prescriptive orientation of decision making: a synthesis of decision analysis, behavioral decision making, and game theory, in: S. Ríos (Ed.) *Decision Theory and Decision Analysis: Trends and Challenges*, Dordrecht: Kluwer.

Raiffa, H. (with J. Richardson and D. Metcalfe) (2002) *Negotiation Analysis*, Cambridge: Belknap Press of Harvard University Press.

Rapoport, A. and Guyer, M. (1966) A taxonomy of 2 × 2 games, in *General Systems: Yearbook of the Society for General Systems Reaserch* **11**, 203–214.

Rasmusen, E. (1989) *Games and Information. An Introduction to Game Theory*, Oxford: Blackwell.

Rawls, J. (1971) *A Theory of Justice*, Oxford: Oxford University Press.

Rawls, J. (1993) *Political Liberalism*, New York: Columbia University Press.

Rawls, J. (1999) *The Law of Peoples*, Cambridge: Harvard University Press.

Rawls, J. (2001) *Justice as Fairness*, Cambridge: Harvard University Press.

Rawls, J. (2005) *Political Liberalism*, expanded edition (first edition 1993), New York: Columbia University Press.

Rehnquist, W. (2004) *Centential Crisis. The Disputed Election of 1876*, New York: Vintage Books.

Reichenbach, H. (1949) *The Theory of Probability*, Berkeley and Los Angeles: University of California Press.

Riker, W. (1962) *The Theory of Political Coalitions*, New Haven: Yale University Press.

Riker, W. (1964) *Federalism*, Boston: Little-Brown.

Riker, W. (1982) *Liberalism against Populism: A Confrontation between the Theory of Democracy and the Theory of Social Choice*, San Francisco: W.H. Freeman.

Riker, W. (1986) *The Art of Political Manipulation*, New Haven: Yale University Press.

Riker, W. and Ordeshook, P. (1973) *An Introduction to Positive Political Theory*, Englewood Cliffs: Prentice-Hall.

Ríos, S. (Ed.) (1994) *Decision Theory and Decision Analysis: Trends and Challenges*, Dordrecht: Kluwer.

Roberts, F. (1979) *Measurement Theory with Applications to Decision Making, Utility and Social Sciences*, Reading, MA: Addison-Wesley.

Rosenthal, R. (1981) Games of perfect information, predatory pricing and the chain-store paradox, *Journal of Economic Theory* **25**, 92–100.

Roth, A. (1979) *Axiomatic Models of Bargaining*, Berlin, Heidelberg and New York: Springer-Verlag.

Rubinstein, A. (1982) Perfect equilibrium in a bargaining model, *Econometrica* **50**, 657–664.

Saari, D. (1989) A dictionary for voting paradoxes, *Journal of Economic Theory* **48**, 443–475.

Saari, D. (1995) *Basic Geometry of Voting*, Berlin, Heidelberg and New York: Springer-Verlag.

Saari, D. (1999) Explaining all three-alternative voting outcomes, *Journal of Economic Theory* **87**, 313–355.

Saari, D. (2000a) Mathematical structure of voting paradoxes I. Pairwise vote, *Economic Theory* **15**, 1–53.

Saari, D. (2000b) Mathematical structure of voting paradoxes II. Positional voting, *Economic Theory* **15**, 55–101.

Saari, D. (2001a) *Chaotic Elections! A Mathematician Looks at Voting*, Providence, RI: American Mathematical Society.

Saari, D. (2001b) *Decisions and Elections: Explaining the Unexpected*, Cambridge: Cambridge University Press.

Saari, D. (2005) *Collisions, Rings and Other Newtonian N-Body Problems*, Providence, RI: American Mathematical Society.

Saari, D. and Sieberg, K. (2001) The sum of the parts can violate the whole, *American Political Science Review* **95**, 415–433.

Saari, D. and Sieberg, K. (2004) Are partwise comparisons reliable? *Research in Engineering Design* **15**, 62–71.

Salmon, W.C. (1967) *The Foundations of Scientific Inference*, Pittsburgh: University of Pittsburgh Press.

Salmon, W.C. (1971) Statistical explanation, in: W. Salmon (Ed.) *Statistical Explanation and Statistical Relevance*, Pittsburgh: University of Pittsburgh Press.

Salonen, H. (1985) A solution for two-person bargaining problems, *Social Choice and Welfare* **2**, 139–146.

Salonen, H. (1987) Partially monotonic bargaining solutions, *Social Choice and Welfare* **4**, 1–8.

Salonen, H. and Wiberg, M. (1987) Reputation pays: game theory as a tool for analyzing political profit from credibility, *Scandinavian Political Studies* **10**, 151–170.

Samuelson, P.A. (1947) *Foundations of Economic Analysis*, Cambridge: Harvard University Press.

Samuelson, P.A. (1948) *Economics: An Introductory Analysis*, New York: McGraw-Hill.

Samuelson, P.A. (1954) The pure theory of public expenditure, *Review of Economics and Statistics* **36**, 387–390.

Samuelson, P.A. (1955) A diagrammatic exposition of a theory of public expenditure, *Review of Economics and Statistics* **37**, 350–356.

Sandler, T. (1992) *Collective Action: Theory and Applications*, Ann Arbor: University of Michigan Press.

Sandler, T. (2004) *Global Collective Action*, Cambridge: Cambridge University Press.

Satterthwaite, M. (1975) Srategy-proofness and Arrow's conditions, *Journal of Economic Theory* **10**, 187–217.

Savage, L. (1954) *Foundations of Statistics*, New York: Wiley.

Scheffler, I. (1963) *The Anatomy of Inquiry*, New York: Knopf.

Schoemaker, P. and Russo, J.E. (1994) A pyramid of decision approaches, in: S. Ríos (Ed.) *Decision Theory and Decision Analysis: Trends and Challenges*, Dordrecht: Kluwer.

Schofield, N. (1978) Generalised bargaining sets for cooperative games, *International Journal of Game Theory* **7**, 183–199.

Schofield, N. and Laver, M. (1985) Bargaining theory and portfolio payoffs in European coalition governments 1945–83, *British Journal of Political Science* **15**, 143–164.

Schwartz, Th. (1986) *The Logic of Collective Choice*, New York: Columbia University Press.

Scriven, M. (1962) Explanations, predictions, and laws, in: H. Feigl and G. Maxwell (Eds) *Minnesota Studies in the Philosophy of Science*, Minneapolis: University of Minnesota Press.

Searle, J. (1980) *Speech Act Theory and Pragmatics*, Dordrecht: D. Reidel.

Searle, J. (1996) *Construction of Social Reality*, London: Penguin.

Searle, J. (2002) *Consciousness and Language*, Cambridge: Cambridge University Press.

Selten, R. (1975) Re-examination of the perfectness concept for equilibrium points in extensive games, *International Journal of Game Theory* **4**, 22–55.

Selten, R. (1978) The chain store paradox, *Theory and Decision* **9**, 127–159.

Selten, R. (1988) *Models of Strategic Rationality*, Dordrecht: Kluwer.

Selten, R. (1999) *Game Theory and Economic Behaviour: Selected Essays*, 2 vols, Cheltenham: Edward Elgar.

Sen, A. (1970) *Collective Choice and Social Welfare*, San Francisco: Holden-Day.

Shafir, E.B., Osherson, D. and Smith, E. (1989) An advantage model of choice, *Journal of Behavioral Decision Making* **2**, 1–23.

Shafir, E.B., Osherson, D. and Smith, E. (1990) Comparative choice and the advantage model, in: K. Borcherding, O. Larichev and D. Messick (Eds) *Contemporary Issues in Decision Making*, Amsterdam: North-Holland.

Shafir, E.B., Simonson, I. and Tversky, A. (2000) Reason-based choice, in: D. Kahneman and A. Tversky (Eds) *Choices, Values, and Frames*, Cambridge: Cambridge University Press.

Shapley, L.S. (1953) A value for *n*-person games, in: H. Kuhn and A. Tucker (Eds) *Contributions to the Theory of Games, Vol. II. Annals of Mathematical Studies, No. 28*, Princeton: Princeton University Press.

Shapley, L. and Shubik, M. (1954) A method for evaluating the distribution of power in a committee system, *American Political Science Review* **48**, 787–792.

Shugart, M. and Carey, J. (1992) *Presidents and Assemblies*, Cambridge: Cambridge University Press.

Siebe, W. (1992) Game theory, in: V. Kremenyuk (Ed.) *International Negotiation: Analysis, Approaches, Issues*, San Francisco: Jossey-Bass.

Simon, H. (1972) Theories of bounded rationality, in: Ch. McGuire and R. Radner (Eds) *Decision and Organization*, Amsterdam: North-Holland.

Simonson, I. (1989) Choice based on reasons: the case of attraction and compromise effects, *Journal of Consumer Research* **16**, 158–174.

Simpson, E. (1951) The interpretation of interaction in contingency tables, *Journal of the Royal Statistical Society B* **13**, 238–241.

Skinner, Q. (1978) *Foundations of Modern Political Thought, I–II*, Cambridge: Cambridge University Press.

Slater, P. (1961) Inconsistencies in a schedule of paired comparisons, *Biometrica* **48**, 303–312.

Smith, A. ([1776]1961) *The Wealth of Nations*, London: J.M. Dent.

Smith, V.L. (Ed.) (1979) *Research in Experimental Economics*, vol. 1, Greenwich: JAI Press.

Smith, V.L. (Ed.) (1982) *Research in Experimental Economics*, vol. 2, Greenwich: JAI Press.

Smith, V.L. (Ed.) (1985) *Research in Experimental Economics*, vol. 3, Greenwich: JAI Press.

Smith, V.L. (2005) Behavioral economics research and the foundations of economics, *The Journal of Socio-Economics* **34**, 135–150.

Steunenberg, B., Schmidtchen, D. and Koboldt, C. (1999) Strategic power in the European Union, *Journal of Theoretical Politics* **11**, 339–366.

Straffin, Ph. (1980) *Topics in the Theory of Voting*, Boston: Birkhäuser.

Taagepera, R. and Shugart, M. (1989) *Seats and Votes: The Effects and Determinants of Electoral Systems*, New Haven: Yale University Press.

Taylor, M. and Ward, H. (1982) Chickens, whales and lumpy goods, *Political Studies* **30**, 350–370.

Thomson, W. (1981) A class of solutions to bargaining problems, *Journal of Economic Theory* **25**, 431–441.

Thomson, W. (1996) Concepts of implementation, *Japanese Economic Review* **47**, 133–43.

Thomson, W. and Lensberg, T. (1989) *Axiomatic Theory of Bargaining with a Variable Number of Agents*, Cambridge: Cambridge University Press.

Tideman, N. and Tullock, G. (1976) A new and superior process for making social choices, *Journal of Political Economy* **84**, 1145–1159.

Tietzel, M. (1981) 'Annahmen' in der Wirtschaftstheorie, *Zeitschrift für Wirtschafts- und Sozialwissenschaften* **101**, 237–265.

Tsebelis, G. (1989) The abuse of probability in political analysis, *American Political Science Review*. **83**, 77–91.

Tsebelis, G. and Garrett, G. (1996) Agenda setting power, power indices, and decision making in the European Union, *International Review of Law and Economics* **16**, 345–361.

Tullock, G. (1967) The welfare costs of tariffs, monopolies, and theft, *Western Economic Journal* 5, 224–232.

Tullock, G. (1971) *The Logic of the Law*, New York: Basic Books.

Tullock, G. (1987) *Autocracy*, Dordrecht: Kluwer.

Tullock, G. (1993) *Rent Seeking*, Cheltenham: Edward Elgar.

Tullock, G. (2005) *Public Goods, Redistribution and Rent Seeking*, Cheltenham: Edward Elgar.

Turnovec, F. (2004) Power indices: swings or pivots? in: M. Wiberg (Ed.) *Reasoned Choices*, Helsinki: The Finnish Political Science Association.

Tversky, A. (1969) Intransitivity of preferences, *Psychological Review* 76, 31–48.

Ullman-Margalit, E. (1977) *The Emergence of Norms*, Oxford: Oxford University Press.

Van Damme, E. (1987) *Stability and Perfection of Nash Equilibria*, Berlin: Springer-Verlag.

Van Damme, E. (2002) Strategic equilibrium, in: R. Aumann and S. Hart (Eds) *Handbook of Game Theory with Economic Applications, Vol. 3*, Amsterdam: Elsevier.

Vane, H. and Mulhearn, Ch. (2005) *The Nobel Memorial Laureates in Economics*, Cheltenham: Edward Elgar.

von Neumann, J. and Morgenstern, O. (1944) *Theory of Games and Economic Behavior*, Princeton: Princeton University Press.

von Wright, G. (1971) *Explanation and Understanding*, Ithaca: Cornell University Press.

Widgrén, M. (1994) Voting power in the EC and the consequences of two different enlargements, *European Economic Review* 38, 1153–1170.

Widgrén, M. (2002) Agenda-setting, amendments, information and optimal level of integration, in: M. Hosli, A. van Deemen and M. Widgrén (Eds) *Institutional Challenges in the European Union*, London: Routledge.

Winch, P. (1958) *The Idea of a Social Science and Its Relation to Philosophy*, London: Routledge and Kegan Paul.

Young, H.P. (1974) An axiomatization of Borda's rule, *Journal of Economic Theory* 9, 43–52.

Young, H.P. (1975) Social choice scoring functions, *SIAM Journal on Applied Mathematics* 28, 824–838.

Young, H.P. (1994) *Equity in Theory and Practice*, Princeton: Princeton University Press.

Young, H.P. (1998) *Individual Strategy and Social Structure. An Evolutionary Theory of Institutions*, Princeton: Princeton University Press.

Young, H.P. (2004) *Strategic Learning and Its Limits*, Oxford: Oxford University Press.

Zermelo, E. (1913) Über eine Anwendung der Mengenlehre auf der Theorie des Schachspiels, in: *Proceedings of the Fifth International Congress of Mathematicians* 2, 501–504.

Name Index

Subject Index

Lightning Source UK Ltd.
Milton Keynes UK
31 July 2010

157555UK00004B/79/A